ATHEISM

D0372618

ATHEISM

A
Reader

Edited by

S. T. JOSHI

 **Prometheus Books**

59 John Glenn Drive
Amherst, New York 14228-2197

Published 2000 by Prometheus Books

Inquiries should be addressed to
Prometheus Books
59 John Glenn Drive
Amherst, New York 14228-2197
VOICE: 716-691-0133, ext. 207
FAX: 716-564-2711
WWW.PROMETHEUSBOOKS.COM

Library of Congress Cataloging-in-Publication Data

Atheism : a reader / edited by S. T. Joshi.
    p. cm.
    Includes bibliographical references.
    ISBN 1-57392-855-0 (pbk. : alk. paper)
    1. Atheism—History. I. Joshi, S. T., 1958–

BL2751 .A88 2000
211'.8—dc21   00-058879

Printed in the United States of America on acid-free paper

CONTENTS

INTRODUCTION

A VOLUME LIKE THIS SHOULD not be necessary. After at least twenty-five hundred years in which some of the keenest human minds have established the extreme unlikelihood of the major religious tenets—that God exists; that human beings are made in the image of God; that the "soul" is immaterial and immortal; that God is guiding the human race in some particular direction—the great majority of the human populace continues to embrace these views with blind and unthinking tenacity, and even those who claim a more reasoned "faith" are unwilling to abandon them in spite of overwhelming evidence to the contrary. Of course, religions have always used the inability of science definitively to disprove the existence of God as an excuse for continued belief, forgetting both that it is just as impossible to prove God's existence. In fact, however, the probable truth or falsity of religious beliefs seems nowadays to matter so little to the pious—or, rather, the truth of religion is regarded as something so incapable of challenge—that it is deemed rather offensive and disreputable even to make the attempt. But in the interests of truth and sanity, the attempt must continually be made.

Let us not be deceived. The overwhelming majority of people on this earth—including most of those 97 percent of the American population who profess belief in God in some form or other—are beyond persuasion on this matter. They are, quite literally, incapable of comprehending the issues at stake. It is not merely that they are unable to conduct a course of logical reasoning on this (or any other) matter; it is that, even if the scientific and philosophical evidence were presented to them in a form they could understand, they would rebel at the evidence, because their religious belief is so essential to their psychological well-being that they could not abandon it. In an issue so emotionally charged as this, they cannot think rationally and objectively. To them this book is not directed. They would scoff, they would be offended (as if that reaction in itself were some disproof of its arguments), they would condemn it as heresy, impiety, immorality, and all the other obscurantist smokescreens used by religion from the dawn of time to deflect criticism from itself.

This book, then, is intended only for those who profess an open mind on the subject of the validity of religion and religious belief. My primary concerns are not the social or political effects of religion, although they are indeed treated here, but a much more fundamental issue: *Is religion true?* That is to say, are the doctrines espoused by any given religion—most broadly, the very existence of an entity called God—true to the facts of Nature as we now know them? All other questions, including that of life after death or of the incursion of religion into social and political life, are secondary.

Religion of course occupied the playing field first: its existence from the dawn of recorded time is well attested. What religions, past and present, have done is to provide simple—and, for a time, satisfying—answers to the questions that most perplex us as we gradually awaken to our position in the world and the universe. How did we get here? What is our purpose in being here? Where will we be after we die? Of course, primitive peoples—and many not so primitive—are unaware that these questions are perhaps faulty in the very manner of their formulation. It is inconceivable to such people that we very likely "got" here by natural rather than supernatural means; that there is no "purpose" to our existence beyond the goals we envision for ourselves; that life ends utterly upon our deaths. When the advance of human knowledge presents answers such as these, many individuals rebel against them—not because they are not true (they are indeed overwhelmingly likely to be true), but because they are not the answers they hope for. The conclusions are rejected not because they are false, but because they are unpalatable.

Recent objections to scientific criticisms of religion rest largely on the undoubted fact that science itself is not quite as "certain" as it used to be. This uncertainty has provided the religious with convenient excuses to continue belief; but what is ignored in this clever ploy is that, if the "truth" is now only a matter of statistical probabilities, the probabilities remain overwhelmingly against the likelihood of the truth of the religious world-view. Even if scientific truth is not quite as definitive as it was thought to be in the nineteenth century, some things are still far more likely to be true than others; religion is not one of them.

Human knowledge—not merely the sciences but all avenues of intellectual inquiry—has made remarkable strides in the last five hundred years. In many ways the most important developments, as far as the overthrow of religion is concerned, have occurred in the sciences of anthropology, history, and psychology, which have accounted in an entirely satisfying manner for the origin and continued existence of religious belief. The very notion that such a continuance of belief argues for some kernel of truth to religion is a version of what I call the democratic fallacy: the notion that truth can be determined by a vote of the majority. If that were the case, then we would be forced to acknowledge that, at various times in human history (and in some instances even today), such beliefs as the flatness of the earth, the revolution of the sun around the earth, and the biological inferiority of African Americans to Caucasians were or are "true." One would hope there are not many who think so.

What anthropology—beginning with the work of David Hume in *The Natural History of Religion* (1757)—has done is to show how religious belief was naturally instilled in human beings at the very earliest stage of their development, a result of their ignorance of natural phenomena, their fears of death, and their puzzlement over the nature and source of dreams; how that belief was perpetuated through the ages by relentless indoctrination of religious dogma into young and old, supported by governments and the society at large and usually involving the suppression of opposing views; and how the findings of science, even though they have now destroyed many of the underpinnings of religious orthodoxy, have relatively little effect upon the average citizen, who in this regard is not much better than his ancestor of the caves. In particular, this anthropological argument (united with advances in psychology) has done away entirely with the validity of the "internal" argument for religion: that the *intensity* of one's religious sentiments is some indication of their metaphysical *truth*. We now know that all kinds of fantasies, hallucinations, and delusions can be induced by a variety of natural means; the "evidence of the heart" is no evidence at all. A given individual may feel very deeply that he is the reincarnation of Julius Caesar, but the likelihood of his actually being the reincarnation of Julius Caesar is probably not great.

In our own time, religion retains its dominance not merely by its immensely powerful network of churches, but by utilizing all the technological innovations available to it: advertising, entire networks on cable television, and the Internet. The remarkable thing is that, in the face of this imposing hierarchy, social influence, and political power, secularism has managed to triumph among a very large segment of the intelligent population. It would be comforting to believe that truth is always victorious, but a quick glance at human history establishes, at the very least, the naïveté of such a view.

It does not seem necessary to waste much time on the religious conception of the "immortality of the soul." Let us bypass the initial difficulty of determining exactly what the "soul" is—where it is in the body, or whether it is anything more than a kind of makeshift shorthand term for a variety of mental and psychological functions of the physical body. The notion that the "soul" can survive the body is so obviously a holdover from primitive superstition that many theologians of the nineteenth and twentieth centuries seem to have all but abandoned it. The belief is founded strictly on fear—fear of death, or, more particularly, fear of the oblivion that we all know in our hearts will follow death. Believers overlook that what the great majority of people want is not immortality of the soul, but immorality of the body: they want to continue living in their current bodies indefinitely—with, of course, mental and physical health magically preserved. But since even the most naive and self-deluded of us realize that this is hopeless, they conveniently transfer their wishes to some airy substance that will magically revive after the dissolution of our bodies and allow us to continue sensation and consciousness. Exactly how this is to be effected without a physical body, and exactly what we are really to *do* aside from playing harps, floating about our loved ones in a probably vain effort to gain their attention, or sit at the right hand of God, has never been clarified.

It has become fashionable to declare that there is, in fact, no conflict between science and religion. If that is so, it is only because most people fail to recognize the degree to which the advance of knowledge has completely overthrown the central tenets of religion—in other words, the degree to which this conflict has become a rout. In this sense, contemporary fundamentalists are actually more sensible than their "liberal" theological counterparts in regarding science as a direct threat to their beliefs.

In our day religious criticism has centered upon the theory of evolution and the big bang theory. We need take little notice of those devout fundamentalists who assert that, *because* these theories are contrary to the Bible, *therefore* they must be false: all we can do against such backwoods anti-intellectualism is chuckle in our sleeves and move on. For those of the pious who actually try to deal with the issues at hand, not much more attention is needed. Many of them focus on the notion that these scientific conceptions are mere "theories"—that they are "unproven," especially since "no one was around" to witness the big bang or the progress of evolution by natural selection. Aside from the awkward fact that "no one was around" for most of the early creation of the universe as recorded in Genesis, this attitude would invalidate a great part of our scientific and historical knowledge; indeed, pressed to the limit, it would invalidate *all* knowledge except that which a given individual secures for himself or herself. Even if "someone was around" to witness such events, how are we to know that that person is not lying? On this principle, what evidence do the people of today have that the American Revolution or the Civil War took place? Once again, the real solution is the cardinal principle of *probabilities*: evolution and the big bang are infinitely more probable, given our current state of knowledge, than Genesis. At this point some clever theists assert that perhaps evolution and the big bang were themselves produced by God! Such a theory can neither be proven nor disproven, but there is simply no evidence to support it. And it also falls into that philosophical error enunciated by Shelley: "We can only infer from effects causes exactly adequate to those effects." The notion that God produced evolution or the big bang (an unwitting reversion to the "clockmaker" analogy of eighteenth-century Deism) is supernumerary: since evolution and the big bang are themselves sufficient to explain the phenomena at hand, the addition of God becomes, logically, otiose.

Some pious folk now feel that they have come up with an alternative to evolution by propounding the notion of an "intelligent creator" who designed everything in the world to "fit" in perfect accord. This is really nothing more than a minimally refashioned version of the old argument from design, which was already systematically destroyed by David Hume two and a half centuries ago. (The poet Shelley's "Refutation of Deism," included here, founds many of its arguments upon those of Hume.) To my mind, it was refuted most pungently by a half-line in Lucretius: *tanta stat praedita culpa* ("there is so much wrong with the world"; *De Rerum Natura* 5.199). If this "creator" was so "intelligent," he neglected to inform us of the intelligibility of earthquakes, cancer, and other phenomena that appear to show that the various parts of his world do not in fact "fit" very well. And if the design of this world is "intelligent," it must necessarily have a purpose, but no one can possibly tell what that purpose is. Surely it cannot be the proliferation of the human race, since we have proliferated only by overcoming the numerous obstacles in our path: the frigidity of the poles, the heat of deserts, and the overriding fact that water covers three-fourths of the globe. Indeed, one could easily argue that God cares more for fishes than for human beings, since he gave them three times as much space to flourish than he gave us.

The relation of religion and ethics is a subject of great concern to fundamentalists and conservatives generally. The secularist of course denies that there is any such relation. One can point to classical antiquity, where ethics was strictly the province of the philosopher, and religion a matter of ritual with no ethical implications. What the atheist wishes to assert is that (a) religion is not necessary for moral behavior, and (b) religious ethics are themselves faulty and corrupt.

In regard to the first point, the existence of even a single morally upright individual who is an atheist, agnostic, or secularist[1] would invalidate the *necessity* of religion as a basis for morality; the best one could do is to assert that religion is somehow *helpful* to good morals. Even this, as numerous contributors in this volume maintain, is dubious; as Bertrand Russell states, "It is ... very doubtful whether belief in God has all the beneficial moral effects that are attributed to it. Many of the best men known to history have been unbelievers. . . . And many of the worst men known to history have been believers."

Religionists do not apparently wish to acknowledge the secularist's claim that moral (i.e., socially approved) behavior is, or can be, a product of the individual's rational decision as to what is honorable and conducive to the smooth running of society, or even of long-term advantage to oneself. They instead fear that the average person will "run amok" and be completely amoral without the impetus of religion—without, in other words, the heavy emotional burden of realizing that his or her actions are constantly being monitored by a supernatural scorekeeper who, upon the individual's death, will make a tally and determine the person's ultimate destination, either above or below. If religionists really wish to assert that people, if left to themselves, are so inherently evil and corrupt, that is their choice.

Some religionists express concern that science itself as amoral and that a morality founded upon it will be unwelcome—illiberal, regimented, with human beings being used in scientific experiments, or some such thing. They point to the baneful new weapons of mass destruction produced by science (forgetting that the atomic bomb was developed in this country not by scientists as such, but by scientists working under orders from the U.S. military), the possibility that we will all be cloned, and on and on. They appear unaware that scientists have always been in the forefront of such ethical concerns as nuclear disarmament, protection of the environment, and overpopulation. The picture of the ruthless scientist forcing individuals to undergo bizarre operations, heedless of the moral or social consequences of his actions, is a reality only in cheap horror films.

As for the second point, there need be no belaboring of the obvious fact that the history of religion is itself full of appalling cruelty, folly, hypocrisy, and actual evil. We can only be grateful that advancing knowledge has caused such things as the divine right of kings, witchcraft persecution, forced conversion of "heathens" by missionaries, and enforcement of religious orthodoxy to pass utterly into the dustbin of history—not, however, without exacting a horrific cost in shattered lives and minds. By comparison, the threats posed by today's fundamentalists, whether Christian or Islamic or some other sect, seem tame indeed, although they are eminently worth combating. And whenever such relics of barbarism as trials for heresy, religious schisms, or a fatwa against a novelist occur, we are alternately amused and repulsed at this recrudescence of medieval ignorance. Many people now conveniently forget that the three principal religions of the West—Christianity, Judaism, and Islam—all once claimed (and, by the logic of their tenets, were obliged to claim) *exclusive* knowledge of the truth: that their views were right and all others' were wrong, impious, heretical, and deserving of everlasting damnation. The very evolution of religious toleration is a product of what Charles Bradlaugh termed the "indifference of scepticism." Most religions have now concluded that it is, at the very least, rather tactless to maintain the mortal error of other beliefs than their own; perhaps they recognize secularism as their common enemy, so they band together like a circle of covered wagons in order to present a unified front to the infidel.

The role of religion in politics and society is manifold and complex, and I can offer only a few hints here. Secularists are much concerned over the increasing political activity of religious fundamentalists, and it is indeed a genuine concern. And yet, governments—even our U.S. government, a government purportedly based on the separation of church and state—have always found religion a useful means for controlling its citizens. History makes clear, as A. J. Ayer notes, "the tendency of religious hierarchies to side with the oppressors rather than the oppressed." There is not much hope that this state of affairs will change significantly in the near future. Certainly, our current crop of politicians, whatever their actual religious beliefs, are not about to do anything but toe a safe party line in the matter: they have no doubt read polls showing that a full two-thirds of our populace would refuse to vote for any politician who declared himself or herself an atheist or agnostic, regardless of his or her other views. And so the placating of the great religious masses will continue, with minimal differences of emphasis.

To my mind, the inculcation of religious belief into the young—a process that can scarcely be termed anything but brainwashing—is religion's great crime against humanity. Billions have been prejudiced in favor of one religion or another by this kind of indoctrination, and it requires a tremendous strength of mind and will to overcome it in later years. It need hardly be added that communists' indoctrination of atheism is equally to be deprecated. One would suppose that religionists would wish their adherents to have come by their beliefs freely and of their own accord; so why do they insist that religious training begin at an age when the child is not able to think for itself and is incapable of questioning the authority of its parents or other adult figures? As H. P. Lovecraft states:

> We all know that *any* emotional bias—irrespective of truth or falsity—can be implanted by suggestion in the emotions of the young, hence the inherited traditions of an orthodox community are absolutely without evidential value. . . . If religion were true, its followers would not try to bludgeon their young into an artificial conformity; but would merely insist on their unbending quest for *truth*, irrespective of artificial backgrounds or practical consequences. With such an honest and inflexible *openness to evidence*, they could not fail to receive any *real truth* which might be manifesting itself around them. The fact that religionists do *not* follow this honourable course, but cheat at their game by invoking juvenile quasi-hypnosis, is enough to destroy their pretensions in my eyes even if their absurdity were not manifest in every other direction.[2]

Religions have always utilized a variety of rhetorical strategies to stifle criticism of their beliefs and practices. They maintain that religion is really a matter of taste and preference; that it is a "way of life" rather than a set of doctrines; that atheism itself is a dogmatic religion; that skeptics should not "meddle" with people's religious beliefs; that religion nowadays has been purged of all the bad elements that polluted it in the past; that it would be cruel and unfair to "take away" a person's religion from him when he or she finds it such a comfort. Let us examine these contentions a bit more carefully.

The first point need hardly detain us long. If religion is simply a taste or preference—such as one person's fondness for chocolate ice cream and another's fondness for vanilla—then there can indeed be no debate on the matter. But this very assertion undercuts any "truth" that religion may have (my preference for chocolate ice cream cannot be "truer" than your preference for vanilla), and it should accordingly make no difference which religion a person believes, or whether he believes none at all.

The second point—the "way of life" claim—is open to many of the same objections, and is again merely a means of shielding religious dogma from skeptical scrutiny. Surely a Christian "way of life" must differ from a Muslim "way of life" or an atheist "way of life"; if it didn't, it would make no difference if one were a Christian or a Muslim or an atheist. And what can the difference be but a set of doctrines, which can indeed be challenged on intellectual grounds?

As for atheism itself being a religion: no doubt there have been some atheists (and, as with the communists, some entire societies) who have embraced atheism with the fervency and dogmatism of a religion, but they are hardly representative of the rational secularists included in this volume. As Ambrose Bierce wittily stated, "It is the peculiar distinction of atheism to be nothing at all. The atheist, as such, has no belief. To say he believes there is no God is inaccurate; he merely does *not* believe there is a God."[3]

The idea of "meddling" is a bit more interesting. Now that we have reached the stage where religions are no longer permitted to kill or imprison "heretics" or "infidels" merely on the basis of their opinions, all that the devout can do is to whine pitiably about anyone "meddling" with their beliefs. Of course, religions themselves do not "meddle" with people's beliefs, except in encouraging them to indoctrinate their children into their own religious dogma (as opposed to some other dogma, or none at all), or in advocating their religious principles every Saturday or Sunday or on any other occasion that presents itself, or in sending out missionaries to foreign countries to convert the "heathen." This is not considered "meddling," evidently. The notion that a given religious view (which, whatever else it may claim, surely claims to be the "truth") should be, of all the myriad aspects of human life, exempt from criticism—especially when its tenets now appear to be very far from the truth about the universe as we have come to understand it—is, to put it mildly, impertinent.

H. L. Mencken put it most concisely:

> Even a superstitious man has certain inalienable rights. He has a right to harbor and indulge his imbecilities as long as he pleases, provided only he does not try to inflict them upon other men by force. He has a right to argue for them as eloquently as he can, in season and out of season. He has a right to teach them to his children. But certainly he has no right to be protected against the free criticism of those who do not hold them. He has no right to demand that they be treated as sacred. He has no right to preach them without challenge.

Even ridicule of religion is an entirely valid enterprise. Writers as diverse as Aristophanes, Voltaire, Bierce, Mencken, and Gore Vidal have found satire—whose very purpose, let us recall, is to offend, provoke, and annoy—a welcome tool to expose religious folly, hypocrisy, and injustice.

Has religion been "purified" by renunciation of many of the more insane, bizarre, and disgusting features upon which so many contributors to this book expatiate? It would be comforting to think so, although a glance at fundamentalists, whether Christian or Islamic, may make us pause. In any event, it would appear that this "purification" (at least as regards Christianity) has been effected by the simple expedient of ignoring a number of clear and unequivocal statements in the Bible—that witches should not be suffered to live; that those who violate the Sabbath should be killed; that women should not be permitted to speak in church; that slavery is to be condoned; perhaps the very existence of hell. Let it pass that all these things have now become embarrassing only because of the advance of secular knowledge; the true question is whether this kind of procedure—picking and choosing which parts of the Bible to believe in, and brushing the loathsome or embarrassing parts under the rug and hoping no one will notice—has any legitimacy beyond that of practical expediency. I will tactfully leave the matter to more learned theologians than myself.

The whole notion that the secularist wishes to "take away" someone's religion is full of fallacies and paradoxes. No one would chastise a doctor for "taking away" a tumor from someone's brain—presumably the tumor is not something the person needs or wants, so no moral taint is associated with "taking it away." In any case, the argument, when phrased in this way, is misleading: if people, by reading the writings of secularists, come to a rational conclusion that the tenets of religion are false and that they will henceforth put them aside, that is a decision that these people have reached on their own—no one has "taken" anything "away" from them. The frenetic efforts of religionists to silence opposition clearly arises from their fears that this exact procedure will indeed occur, as it has occurred many times in the past.

The idea that religion provides "comfort" is also a red herring. I appeal again to my hypothetical friend who believes he is the reincarnation of Julius Caesar. No doubt he derives great comfort from such a belief, but I trust we are in agreement that it would be better for him if he put aside this belief on the grounds that it is not very likely to be true. Is is not better to accommodate one's beliefs, morals, and actions to what is true (or likely to be true) than to ignore or contradict the truth merely because it does not conform to one's hopes and fears? This latter is the process called wishful thinking, and most people are of the opinion that it is not a very sound guide for belief or conduct. In any event, it does not appear that the lives of atheists, agnostics, or secularists are notably more miserable than those of the pious: perhaps statistics of this kind are not kept, but I do not know of a radically higher rate of depression or suicide in the one group over the other.

So what is the atheist, agnostic, or secularist to do?

In the first place, we should insist on the need to engage in a meaningful debate on the entire issue of the truth or falsity (or probability or improbability) of religious tenets, without being subject to accusations of impiety, immorality, impoliteness, or any of the other smokescreens used by the pious to deflect attention from the central issues at hand.

Secondly, we should guard against the encroachment of religion in areas where it has no place, and in particular the control of education by religious authority. The attempts to ban the teaching of evolution or other scientific theories—a feeble echo of medieval church tyranny and hostility to learning, but an echo nonetheless—are serious threats to freedom of inquiry and should be vigorously combated.

Thirdly, we should not be cowed by exaggerated sensitivity to people's religious beliefs and fail to speak vigorously and pointedly when the devout put forth arguments manifestly contrary to all the acquired knowledge of the past two or three millennia. Those who advocate a piece of folly like the theory of an "intelligent creator" should be held accountable for their folly; they have no right to be offended for being called fools until they establish that they are not in fact fools. Religiously inclined writers like Stephen L. Carter may plead that "respect" should be accorded to religious views in public discourse, but he neglects to demonstrate that those views are worthy of respect. All secularists—scientists, literary figures, even politicians (if there are any such with the requisite courage)—should speak out on the issue when the opportunity presents itself.

I myself am not comfortable with the notion of secularists congregating in groups, except perhaps for defensive purposes: the last thing a secularist should wish to do is to act like a religion, with its rigid hierarchies, its suppression of divergent opinion, and, above all, its ruthless attempts (now mercifully inhibited by laws) to outlaw "heresy" by brute force. Opinions must be changed, one at a time if necessary, but if there are those who wish to persist in religious belief, they should certainly be allowed to do so. The intellectual world is already largely secular, and there is now no going back to irrational piety; whether the great mass of people ever gain sufficient intelligence and courage to follow is a distinctly secondary matter.

—S. T. JOSHI

A NOTE ON THIS EDITION

I have striven to print the selections contained in this volume as accurately as possible from original editions of the works in question, preserving many archaisms and idiosyncrasies of spelling, punctuation, and style. I have silently corrected apparent typographical and other errors in the texts. In the articles by Lucretius and Holbach, I have revised the somewhat antiquated translations by an overall modernization of style, spelling, and syntax, and also by checking the accuracy of the translations with the original Latin and French texts. The translation of Holbach was not very close to the original; I believe my version is somewhat more so. I have added explanatory notes to some of the essays, to clarify allusions to now obscure individuals and issues. These notes are enclosed in brackets in the section of notes at the end of each chapter. Notes by the authors themselves are not enclosed in brackets. I have not felt the need to preserve all notes found in the original texts, since many are lengthy asides not germane to the central issues under discussion.

I have done most of my research at the New York University Library and the New York Public Library. I am grateful to the staffs of these institutions for their kind assistance.

NOTES

1. I am fully aware that these terms are by no means synonymous; but as they all indicate a common skepticism in regard to religious orthodoxy, I feel justified in using them interchangeably in this introduction.

2. H. P. Lovecraft, Letter to Maurice W. Moe, 3 August 1931, in *Selected Letters 1929–1931*, ed. August Derleth and Donald Wandrei (Sauk City, WI: Arkham House, 1971), pp. 390–91.

3. Ambrose Bierce, "Prattle" (*San Francisco Examiner*, 19 January 1890); reprinted in *A Sole Survivor: Bits of Autobiography*, ed. S. T. Joshi and David E. Schultz (Knoxville: University of Tennessee Press, 1998), p. 224.

PART 1

SOME OVERVIEWS

FAITH, n. *Belief without evidence in what is told by one who speaks without knowledge, of things without parallel.*

—Ambrose Bierce
The Devil's Dictionary (1906)

1

AGNOSTICISM
(1889)

Thomas Henry Huxley

Thomas Henry Huxley (1825–1895) studied medicine at London University, then sailed aboard the H.M.S. Rattlesnake *as a surgeon; his important observations of flora and fauna in the southern hemisphere established his early scientific reputation. Huxley was greatly influenced by Darwin's* Origin of Species, *but—although he gained the nickname "Darwin's bulldog" for his vigorous advocacy of evolution—he differed from Darwin in several important particulars, downplaying the element of natural selection in evolution and also expressing skepticism in regard to Darwin's theory of the gradual evolution of species. Although he made several notable contributions to biology and physiology, Huxley gained greatest celebrity as a popularizer of science, especially in such works as* Evidences as to Man's Place in Nature *(1863),* Science and Culture *(1881), and* Evolution and Ethics *(1893). In 1869 he coined the term "agnosticism," claiming that the advance of science had rendered many religious conceptions of the universe invalid or at best highly unlikely. This stance embroiled Huxley in numerous controversies with theologians, into which he entered with vigor and enthusiasm. His writings on the subject are found in* Science and Hebrew Tradition *(1894) and* Science and Christian Tradition *(1894). His* Scientific Memoirs *(1898–1903; 5 vols.),* Life and Letters *(1900; 2 vols.), and* Autobiography and Selected Essays *(1909) appeared posthumously. The following extracts from his celebrated essay "Agnosticism" (1889) present a defense of his views on both intellectual and moral grounds.*

From Thomas Henry Huxley, "Agnosticism" (1889), *Science and Christian Tradition* (New York: D. Appleton & Co., 1894), pp. 209–14, 228–30, 233–35, 240–46.

WITHIN THE LAST FEW MONTHS, the public has received much and varied information on the subject of agnostics, their tenets, and even their future. Agnosticism exercised the orators of the Church Congress at Manchester.[1] It has been furnished with a set of "articles" fewer, but not less rigid, and certainly not less consistent than the thirty-nine; its nature has been analysed, and its future severely predicted by the most eloquent of that prophetical school whose Samuel is Auguste Comte.[2] It may still be a question, however, whether the public is as much the wiser as might be expected, considering all the trouble that has been taken to enlighten it. Not only are the three accounts of the agnostic position sadly out of harmony with one another, but I propose to show cause for my belief that all three must be seriously questioned by any one who employs the term "agnostic" in the sense in which it was originally used. The learned Principal of King's College,[3] who brought the topic of Agnosticism before the Church Congress, took a short and easy way of settling the business:—

> But if this be so, for a man to urge, as an escape from this article of belief, that he has no means of a scientific knowledge of the unseen world, or of the future, is irrelevant. His difference from Christians lies not in the fact that he has no knowledge of these things, but that he does not believe the authority on which they are stated. He may prefer to call himself an Agnostic; but his real name is an older one—he is an infidel; that is to say, an unbeliever. The word infidel, perhaps, carries an unpleasant significance. Perhaps it is right that it should. It is, and ought to be, an unpleasant thing for a man to have to say plainly that he does not believe in Jesus Christ.

So much of Dr. Wace's address either explicitly or implicitly concerns me, that I take upon myself to deal with it; but, in so doing, it must be understood that I speak for myself alone. I am not aware that there is any sect of Agnostics; and if there be, I am not its acknowledged prophet or pope. I desire to leave to the Comtists the entire monopoly of the manufacture of imitation ecclesiasticism.

Let us calmly and dispassionately consider Dr. Wace's appreciation of agnosticism. The agnostic, according to his view, is a person who says he has no means of attaining a scientific knowledge of the unseen world or of the future; by which somewhat loose phraseology Dr. Wace presumably means the theological unseen world and future. I cannot think this description happy, either in form or substance, but for the present it may pass. Dr. Wace continues, that it is not "his difference from Christians." Are there then any Christians who say that they know nothing about the unseen world and the future? I was ignorant of the fact, but I am ready to accept it on the authority of a professional theologian, and I proceed to Dr. Wace's next proposition.

The real state of the case, then, is that the agnostic "does not believe the authority" on which "these things" are stated, which authority is Jesus Christ. He is simply an old-fashioned "infidel" who is afraid to own to his right name. As "Presbyter is priest writ large," so is "agnostic" the mere Greek equivalent for the Latin "infidel." There is an attractive simplicity about this solution of the problem; and it has that advantage of being somewhat offensive to the persons attacked, which is so dear to the less refined sort of controversialist. The agnostic says, "I cannot find good evidence that so and so is true." "Ah," says his adversary, seizing his opportunity, "then you declare that Jesus Christ was untruthful, for he said so and so;" a very telling method of rousing prejudice. But suppose that the value of the evidence as to what Jesus Christ may have said and done, and as to the exact nature and scope of his authority, is just that which the agnostic finds most difficult to determine. If I venture to doubt that the Duke of Wellington gave the command "Up, Guards, and at 'em!" at Waterloo, I do not think that even Dr. Wace would accuse me of disbelieving the Duke. Yet it would be just as reasonable to do this as to accuse any one of denying what Jesus said, before the preliminary question of what he did say is settled.

Now, the question as to what Jesus really said and did is strictly a scientific problem, which is capable of solution by no other methods than those practised by the historian and the literary critic. It is a problem of immense difficulty, which has occupied some of the best heads in Europe for the last century; and it is only of late years that their investigations have begun to converge towards one conclusion.

That kind of faith which Dr. Wace describes and lauds is of no use here. Indeed, he himself takes pains to destroy its evidential value.

"What made the Mahommedan world? Trust and faith in the declarations and assurances of Mahommed. And what made the Christian world? Trust and faith in the declarations and assurances of Jesus Christ and His Apostles" (*l. c.* p. 253). The triumphant tone of this imaginary catechism leads me to suspect that its author has hardly appreciated its full import. Presumably, Dr. Wace regards Mahommed as an unbeliever, or, to use the term which he prefers, infidel; and considers that his assurances have given rise to a vast delusion which has led, and is leading, millions of men straight to everlasting punishment. And this being so, the "Trust and faith" which have "made the Mahommedan world," in just the same sense as they have "made the Christian world," must be trust and faith in falsehoods. No man who has studied history, or even attended to the occurrences of everyday life, can doubt the enormous practical value of trust and faith; but as little will he be inclined to deny that this practical value has not the least relation to the reality of the objects of that trust and faith. . . .

I was brought up in the strictest school of evangelical orthodoxy; and when I was old enough to think for myself, I started upon my journey of inquiry with little doubt about the general truth of what I had been taught; and with that feeling of the unpleasantness of being called an "infidel" which, we are told, is so right and proper. Near my journey's end, I find myself in a condition of something more than mere doubt about these matters.

In the course of other inquiries, I have had to do with fossil remains which looked quite plain at a distance, and became more and more indistinct as I tried to define their outline by close inspection. There was something there—something which, if I could win assurance about it, might mark a new epoch in the history of the earth; but, study as long as I might, certainty eluded my grasp. So had it been with me in my efforts to define the grand figure of Jesus as it lies in the primary strata of Christian literature. Is he the kindly, peaceful Christ depicted in the Catacombs? Or is he the stern Judge who frowns upon the altar of SS. Cosmas and Damianus? Or can he be rightly represented by the bleeding ascetic, broken down by physical pain, of too many mediæval pictures? Are we to accept the Jesus of the second, or the Jesus of the fourth Gospel, as the true Jesus? What did he really say and do; and how much that is attributed to him, in speech and action, is the embroidery of the various parties into which his followers tended to split themselves within twenty years of his death, when even the three-fold tradition was only nascent?

If any one will answer these questions for me with something more to the point than feeble talk about the "cowardice of agnosticism," I shall be deeply his debtor. Unless and until they are satisfactorily an-swered, I say of agnosticism in this matter, *"J'y suis, and j'y reste."*[4] . . .

"Infidel" is a term of reproach, which Christians and Mahomme-dans, in their modesty, agree to apply to those who differ from them. If he had only thought of it, Dr. Wace might have used the term "mis-creant," which, with the same etymological significance, has the advan-tage of being still more "unpleasant" to the persons to whom it is applied.[5] But why should a man be expected to call himself a "mis-creant" or an "infidel"? That St. Patrick "had two birthdays because he was a twin" is a reasonable and intelligible utterance beside that of the man who should declare himself to be an infidel on the ground of denying his own belief. It may be logically, if not ethically, defensible that a Christian should call a Mahommedan an infidel and *vice versâ*; but, on Dr. Wace's principles, both ought to call themselves infidels, because each applies the term to the other.

Now I am afraid that all the Mahommedan world would agree in reciprocating that appellation to Dr. Wace himself. I once visited the Hazar Mosque, the great University of Mohammedanism, in Cairo, in ignorance of the fact that I was unprovided with proper authority. A swarm of angry undergraduates, as I suppose I ought to call them, came buzzing about me and my guide; and if I had known Arabic, I suspect that "dog of an infidel" would have been by no means the most "unpleasant" of the epithets showered upon me, before I could explain and apologise for the mistake. If I had had the pleasure of Dr. Wace's company on that occasion, the undiscriminative followers of the Prophet would, I am afraid, have made no difference between us; not even if they had known that he was the head of an orthodox Christian seminary. And I have not the smallest doubt that even one of the learned mollahs, if his grave courtesy would have permitted him to say anything offensive to men of another mode of belief, would have told us that he wondered we did not find it "very unpleasant" to disbelieve in the Prophet of Islam.

From what precedes, I think it becomes sufficiently clear that Dr. Wace's account of the origin of the name of "Agnostic" is quite wrong. . . .

The last objection (I rejoice as much as my readers must do, that it is the last) which I have to take to Dr. Wace's deliverance before the Church Congress arises, I am sorry to say, on a question of morality.

"It is, and it ought to be," authoritatively declares this official representative of Christian ethics, "an unpleasant thing for a man to have to say plainly that he does not believe in Jesus Christ" (*l. c.* p. 254).

Whether it is so depends, I imagine, a good deal on whether the man was brought up in a Christian household or not. I do not see why it should be "unpleasant" for a Mahommedan or Buddhist to say so. But that "it ought to be" unpleasant for any man to say anything which he sincerely, and after due deliberation, believes, is, to my mind, a proposition of the most profoundly immoral character. I verily believe that the great good which has been effected in the world by Christianity has been largely counteracted by the pestilent doctrine on which all the Churches have insisted, that honest disbelief in their more or less astonishing creeds is a moral offence, indeed a sin of the deepest dye, deserving and involving the same future retribution as murder and robbery. If we could only see, in one view, the torrents of hypocrisy and cruelty, the lies, the slaughter, the violations of every obligation of humanity, which have flowed from this source along the course of the history of Christian nations, our worst imaginations of Hell would pale beside the vision.

A thousand times, no! It ought *not* to be unpleasant to say that which one honestly believes or disbelieves. That it so constantly is painful to do so, is quite enough obstacle to the progress of mankind in that most valuable of all qualities, honesty of word or of deed, without erecting a sad concomitant of human weakness into something to be admired and cherished. The bravest of soldiers often, and very naturally, "feel it unpleasant" to go into action; but a court-martial which did its duty would make short work of the officer who promulgated the doctrine that his men *ought* to feel their duty unpleasant.

I am very well aware, as I suppose most thoughtful people are in these times, that the process of breaking away from old beliefs is extremely unpleasant; and I am much disposed to think that the encouragement, the consolation, and the peace afforded to earnest believers in even the worst forms of Christianity are of great practical advantage to them. What deductions must be made from this gain on the score of the harm done to the citizen by the ascetic other-worldliness of logical Christianity; to the ruler, by the hatred, malice, and all uncharitableness of sectarian bigotry; to the legislator, by the spirit of exclusiveness and domination of those that count themselves pillars of orthodoxy; to the philosopher, by the restraints on the freedom of learning and teaching which every Church exercises, when it is strong enough; to the conscientious soul, by the introspective hunting after sins of the mint and cummin type, the fear of theological error, and the overpowering terror of possible damnation, which have accompanied the Churches like their shadow, I need not now consider; but they are assuredly not small. If agnostics lose heavily on the one side, they gain a good deal on the other. People who talk about the comforts of belief appear to forget its discomforts; they ignore the fact that the Christianity of the Churches is something more than faith in the ideal personality of Jesus, which they create for themselves, *plus* so much as can be carried into practice, without disorganising civil society, of the maxims of the Sermon on the Mount. Trip in morals or in doctrine (especially in doctrine), without due repentance or retraction, or fail to get properly baptized before you die, and a *plébiscite* of the Christians of Europe, if they were true to their creeds, would affirm your everlasting damnation by an immense majority.

Preachers, orthodox and heterodox, din into our ears that the world cannot get on without faith of some sort. There is a sense in which that is as eminently as obviously true; there is another, in which, in my judgment, it is as eminently as obviously false, and it seems to me that the hortatory, or pulpit, mind is apt to oscillate between the false and the true meanings, without being aware of the fact.

It is quite true that the ground of every one of our actions, and the validity of all our reasonings, rest upon the great act of faith, which leads us to take the experience of the past as a safe guide in our dealings with the present and the future. From the nature of ratiocination, it is obvious that the axioms, on which it is based, cannot be demonstrated by ratiocination. It is also a trite observation that, in the business of life, we constantly take the most serious action upon evidence of an utterly insufficient character. But it is surely plain that faith is not necessarily entitled to dispense with ratiocination because ratiocination cannot dispense with faith as a starting-point; and that because we are often obliged, by the pressure of events, to act on very bad evidence, it does not follow that it is proper to act on such evidence when the pressure is absent.

The writer of the epistle to the Hebrews tells us that "faith is the assurance of things hoped for, the proving of things not seen."[6] In the authorised version, "substance" stands for "assurance," and "evidence" for "proving." The question of the exact meaning of the two words, *hypostasis* and *elenchos*, affords a fine field of discussion for the scholar and the metaphysician. But I fancy we shall not be far from the mark if we take the writer to have had in his mind the profound psychological truth, that men constantly feel certain about things for which they strongly hope, but have no evidence, in the legal or logical sense of the word; and he calls this feeling "faith." I may have the most absolute faith that a friend has not committed the crime of which he is accused. In the early days of English history, if my friend could have obtained a few more compurgators of a like robust faith, he would have been acquitted. At the present day, if I tendered myself as a witness on that score, the judge would tell me to stand down, and the youngest barrister would smile at my simplicity. Miserable indeed is the man who has not such faith in some of his fellow-men—only less miserable than the man who allows himself to forget that such faith is not, strictly speaking, evidence; and when his faith is disappointed, as will happen now and again, turns Timon and blames the universe for his own blunders. And so, if a man can find a friend, the hypostasis of all his hopes, the mirror of his ethical ideal, in the Jesus of any, or all, of the Gospels, let him live by faith in that ideal. Who shall or can forbid him? But let him not delude himself with the notion that his faith is evidence of the objective reality of that in which he trusts. Such evidence is to be obtained only by the use of the methods of science, as applied to history and to literature, and it amounts at present to very little.

It appears that Mr. Gladstone some time ago asked Mr. Laing if he could draw up a short summary of the negative creed; a body of negative propositions, which have so far been adopted on the negative side as to be what the Apostles' and other accepted creeds are on the positive; and Mr. Laing at once kindly obliged Mr. Gladstone with the desired articles—eight of them.[7]

If any one had preferred this request to me, I should have replied that, if he referred to agnostics, they have no creed; and, by the nature of the case, cannot have any. Agnosticism, in fact, is not a creed, but a method, the essence of which lies in the rigorous application of a single principle. That principle is of great antiquity; it is as old as Socrates; as old as the writer who said, "Try all things, hold fast by that which is good;"[8] it is the foundation of the Reformation, which simply illustrated the axiom that every man should be able to give a reason for the faith that is in him; it is the great principle of Descartes; it is the fundamental axiom of modern science. Positively the principle may be expressed: In matters of the intellect, follow your reason as far as it will take you, without regard to any other consideration. And negatively: In matters of the intellect do not pretend that conclusions are certain which are not demonstrated or demonstrable. That I take to be the agnostic faith, which if a man keep whole and undefiled, he shall not be ashamed to look the universe in the face, whatever the future may have in store for him.

NOTES

1. See the *Official Report of the Church Congress held at Manchester,* October 1888, pp. 253, 254.

2. [Auguste Comte (1798–1857), French philosopher and founder of Positivism, who asserted that human knowledge would progress from a theological stage through a metaphysical stage to the "positive" stage, wherein the limitations of human knowledge are recognized and emphasis is placed on those aspects of natural phenomena that can be definitely known.]

3. [Henry Wace (1836–1924), principal of King's College, Oxford, later dean of Canterbury, and one of the more conservative theologians of the later nineteenth century.]

4. ["I am here, and I stay here."]

5. ["Miscreant" is derived from the Latin *credo* (to believe), hence an unbeliever.]

6. [Hebrews 11:1: "Now faith is the substance of things hoped for, the evidence of things not seen" (KJV); "Now faith is the assurance of things hoped for, the conviction of things not seen" (RSV).]

7. [William Ewart Gladstone (1809–1898), prime minister of England (1868–74, 1880–85, 1886, 1892–94) and vigorous defender of Christianity. Samuel Laing (1812–1897), freethinker and author of *Modern Science and Modern Thought* (1885), *Human Origins* (1892), and other works.]

8. [Thessalonians 5:21 ("Prove" for "Try" in KJV).]

2

AN AGNOSTIC'S APOLOGY
(1876)

Leslie Stephen

Leslie Stephen (1832–1904), the father of Virginia Woolf, was among the leading British intellectuals of his time. He was educated at Trinity Hall, Cambridge, where he later received a fellowship as a tutor. One of the requirements of the position was that Stephen take holy orders within a year, and accordingly he became an ordained deacon in 1855. But his readings of Mill, Comte, and Kant led him to reject the historical bases of Christianity, and he resigned his tutorship. Stephen went on to write pioneering works of literary criticism, notably Hours in a Library *(1874–79) and* History of English Thought in the Eighteenth Century *(1876), as well as biographies of Samuel Johnson, Alexander Pope, Jonathan Swift, George Eliot, and Thomas Hobbes for the English Men of Letters series. He was knighted in 1902. As early as 1873 he had published* Essays on Free Thinking and Plain Speaking, *and his "An Agnostic's Apology" appeared in the* Fortnightly Review *for June 1876. In this essay, Stephen trenchantly defends Huxley's agnosticism, deprecating dogmatism in matters beyond the scope of human knowledge.*

THE NAME AGNOSTIC, ORIGINALLY COINED by Professor Huxley about 1869, has gained general acceptance. It is sometimes used to indicate the philosophical theory which Mr. Herbert Spencer, as he tells

From Leslie Stephen, "An Agnostic's Apology" (1876), in *An Agnostic's Apology and Other Essays* (New York: G. P. Putnam's Sons; London: Smith, Elder & Co., 1903), pp. 1–18, 28–41.

us, developed from the doctrine of Hamilton and Mansel.[1] Upon that theory I express no opinion. I take the word in a vaguer sense, and am glad to believe that its use indicates an advance in the courtesies of controversy. The old theological phrase for an intellectual opponent was Atheist—a name which still retains a certain flavour as of the stake in this world and hell-fire in the next, and which, moreover, implies an inaccuracy of some importance. Dogmatic Atheism—the doctrine that there is no God, whatever may be meant by God—is, to say the least, a rare phase of opinion. The word Agnosticism, on the other hand, seems to imply a fairly accurate appreciation of a form of creed already common and daily spreading. The Agnostic is one who asserts—what no one denies—that there are limits to the sphere of human intelligence. He asserts, further, what many theologians have expressly maintained, that those limits are such as to exclude at least what Lewes[2] called "metempirical" knowledge. But he goes further, and asserts, in opposition to theologians, that theology lies within this forbidden sphere. This last assertion raises the important issue; and, though I have no pretension to invent an opposition nickname, I may venture, for the purposes of this article, to describe the rival school as Gnostics.

The Gnostic holds that our reason can, in some sense, transcend the narrow limits of experience. He holds that we can attain truths not capable of verification, and not needing verification, by actual experiment or observation. He holds, further, that a knowledge of those truths is essential to the highest interests of mankind, and enables us in some sort to solve the dark riddle of the universe. A complete solution, as everyone admits, is beyond our power. But some answer may be given to the doubts which harass and perplex us when we try to frame any adequate conception of the vast order of which we form an insignificant portion. We cannot say why this or that arrangement is what it is; we can say, though obscurely, that some answer exists, and would be satisfactory, if we could only find it. Overpowered, as every honest and serious thinker is at times overpowered, by the sight of pain, folly, and helplessness, by the jarring discords which run through the vast harmony of the universe, we are yet enabled to hear at times a whisper that all is well, to trust to it as coming from the most authentic source, and to know that only the temporary bars of sense prevent us from recognising with certainty that the harmony beneath the discords is a reality and not a dream. This knowledge is embodied in the central dogma of theology. God is the name of the harmony; and God is knowable. Who would not be happy in accepting this belief, if he could accept it honestly? Who would not be glad if he could say with confidence: "the evil is transitory, the good eternal: our doubts are due to limitations destined to be abolished, and the world is really an embodiment of love and wisdom, however dark it may appear to our faculties"? And yet, if the so-called knowledge be illusory, are we not bound by the most sacred obligations to recognise the facts? Our brief path is dark enough on any hypothesis. We cannot afford to turn aside after every *ignis fatuus*[3] without asking whether it leads to sounder footing or to hopeless quagmires. Dreams may be pleasanter for the moment than realities; but happiness must be won by adapting our lives to the realities. And who, that has felt the burden of existence, and suffered under wellmeant efforts at consolation, will deny that such consolations are the bitterest of mockeries? Pain is not an evil; death is not a separation; sickness is but a blessing in disguise. Have the gloomiest speculations of avowed pessimists ever tortured sufferers like those kindly platitudes? Is there a more cutting piece of satire in the language than the reference in our funeral service to the "sure and certain hope of a blessed resurrection"? To dispel genuine hopes might be painful, however salutary. To suppress these spasmodic efforts to fly in the face of facts would be some comfort, even in the distress which they are meant to alleviate.

Besides the important question whether the Gnostic can prove his dogmas, there is, therefore, the further question whether the dogmas, if granted, have any meaning. Do they answer our doubts, or mock us with the appearance of an answer? The Gnostics rejoice in their knowledge. Have they anything to tell us? They rebuke what they call the "pride of reason" in the name of a still more exalted pride. The scientific reasoner is arrogant because he sets limits to the faculty in which he trusts, and denies the existence of any other faculty. They are humble because they dare to tread in the regions which he declares to be inaccessible. But without bandying such accusations, or asking which pride is the greatest, the Gnostics are at least bound to show some ostensible justification for their complacency. Have they discovered a firm restingplace from which they are entitled to look down in compassion or contempt upon those who hold it to be a mere edifice of moonshine? If they have diminished by a scruple the weight of one passing doubt, we should be grateful: perhaps we should be converts. If not, why condemn Agnosticism?

I have said that our knowledge is in any case limited. I may add that, on any showing, there is a danger in failing to recognise the limits of possible knowledge. The word Gnostic has some awkward associations. It once described certain heretics who got into trouble from fancying that men could frame theories of the Divine mode of existence. The sects have been dead for many centuries. Their fundamental assumptions can hardly be quite extinct. Not long ago, at least, there appeared in the papers a string of propositions framed—so we were assured—by some of the most candid and most learned of living theologians. These propositions defined by the help of various languages the precise relations which exist between the persons of the Trinity. It is an odd, though far from an unprecedented, circumstance that the unbeliever cannot quote them for fear of profanity. If they were transplanted into the pages of the *Fortnightly Review*, it would be impossible to convince anyone that the intention was not to mock the simple-minded persons who, we must suppose, were not themselves intentionally irreverent. It is enough to say that they defined the nature of God Almighty with an accuracy from which modest naturalists would shrink in describing the genesis of a black-beetle. I know not whether these dogmas were put forward as articles of faith, as pious conjectures, or as tentative contributions to sound theory. At any rate, it was supposed that they were interesting to beings of flesh and blood. If so, one can only ask in wonder whether an utter want of reverence is most strongly implied in this mode of dealing with sacred mysteries; or an utter ignorance of the existing state of the world in the assumption that the question which really divides mankind is the double procession of the Holy Ghost; or an utter incapacity for speculation in the confusion of these dead exuviæ of long-past modes of thought with living intellectual tissue; or an utter want of imagination, or of even a rudimentary sense of humour, in the hypothesis that the promulgation of such dogmas could produce anything but the laughter of sceptics and the contempt of the healthy human intellect?

The sect which requires to be encountered in these days is not one which boggles over the *filioque*,[4] but certain successors of those Ephesians who told Paul that they did not even know "whether there were any Holy Ghost." But it explains some modern phenomena when we find that the leaders of theology hope to reconcile faith and reason, and to show that the old symbols have still a right to the allegiance of our hearts and brains, by putting forth these portentous propositions. We are struggling with hard facts, and they would arm us with the forgotten tools of scholasticism. We wish for spiritual food, and are to be put off with these ancient mummeries of forgotten dogma. If Agnosticism is the frame of mind which summarily rejects these imbecilities, and would restrain the human intellect from wasting its powers on the attempt to galvanise into sham activity this *caput mortuum*[5] of old theology, nobody need be afraid of the name. Argument against such adversaries would be itself a foolish waste of time. Let the dead bury their dead, and Old Catholics decide whether the Holy Ghost proceeds from the Father and the Son, or from the Father alone. Gentlemen, indeed, who still read the Athanasian Creed,[6] and profess to attach some meaning to its statements, have no right to sneer at their brethren who persist in taking things seriously. But for men who long for facts instead of phrases, the only possible course is to allow such vagaries to take their own course to the limbo to which they are naturally destined, simply noting, by the way, that modern Gnosticism may lead to puerilities which one blushes even to notice.

It is not with such phenomena that we have seriously to deal. Nobody maintains that the unassisted human intellect can discover the true theory of the Trinity; and the charge of Agnosticism refers, of course, to the sphere of reason, not to the sphere of revelation. Yet those who attack the doctrine are chiefly believers in revelation; and as such they should condescend to answer one important question. Is not the denunciation of reason a commonplace with theologians? What could be easier than to form a catena of the most philosophical defenders of Christianity who have exhausted language in declaring the impotence of the unassisted intellect? Comte has not more explicitly enounced the incapacity of man to deal with the Absolute and the Infinite than a whole series of orthodox writers. Trust your reason, we have been told till we are tired of the phrase, and you will become Atheists or Agnostics. We take you at your word: we become Agnostics. What right have you to turn round and rate us for being a degree more logical than yourselves? Our right, you reply, is founded upon a Divine revelation to ourselves or our Church. Let us grant—it is a very liberal concession—that the right may conceivably be established; but still you are at one with us in philosophy. You say, as we say, that the natural man can know nothing of the Divine nature. That is Agnosticism. Our fundamental principle is not only granted, but asserted. By what logical device you succeed in over-leaping the barriers which you have declared to be insuperable is another question. At least you have no *primâ facie* ground for attacking our assumption that the limits of the human intellect are what you declare them to be. This is no mere verbal retort. Half, or more than half, of our adversaries agree formally with our leading principle. They cannot attack us without upsetting the very ground upon which the ablest advocates of their own case rely. The last English writer who professed to defend Christianity with weapons drawn from wide and genuine philosophical knowledge was Dean Mansel. The whole substance of his argument was simply and solely the assertion of the first principles of Agnosticism. Mr. Herbert Spencer, the prophet of the Unknowable, the foremost representative of Agnosticism, professes in his programme to be carrying "a step further the doctrine put into shape by Hamilton and Mansel." Nobody, I suspect, would now deny, nobody except Dean Mansel himself, and the "religious" newspapers, ever denied very seriously, that the "further step" thus taken was the logical step. Opponents both from within and without the Church, Mr. Maurice and Mr. Mill,[7] agreed that this affiliation was legitimate. The Old Testament represents Jehovah as human, as vindictive, as prescribing immoralities; therefore, Jehovah was not the true God; that was the contention of the infidel. We know nothing whatever about the true God was the reply, for God means the Absolute and the Infinite. Any special act may come from God, for it may be a moral miracle; any attribute may represent the character of God to man, for we know nothing whatever of His real attributes, and cannot even conceive Him as endowed with attributes. The doctrine of the Atonement cannot be revolting, because it cannot have any meaning. Mr. Spencer hardly goes a step beyond his original, except, indeed, in candour.

Most believers repudiate Dean Mansel's arguments. They were an anachronism. They were fatal to the decaying creed of pure Theism, and powerless against the growing creed of Agnosticism. When theology had vital power enough to throw out fresh branches, the orthodox could venture to attack the Deist, and the Deist could assail the traditional beliefs. As the impulse grows fainter, it is seen that such a warfare is suicidal. The old rivals must make an alliance against the common enemy. The theologian must appeal for help to the metaphysician whom he reviled. Orthodoxy used to call Spinoza an Atheist; it is now glad to argue that even Spinoza is a witness on its own side. Yet the most genuine theology still avows its hatred of reason and distrusts sham alliances. Newman[8] was not, like Dean Mansel, a profound metaphysician, but his admirable rhetoric expressed a far finer religious instinct. He felt more keenly, if he did not reason so systematically; and the force of one side of his case is undeniable. He holds that the unassisted reason cannot afford a sufficient support for a belief in God. He declares, as innumerable writers of less power have declared, that there is "no medium, in true philosophy, between Atheism and Catholicity, and that a perfectly consistent mind, under those circumstances in which it finds itself here below, must embrace either the one or the other."[9] He looks in vain for any antagonist, except the Catholic Church, capable of baffling and withstanding "the fierce energy of passion, and the all-corroding, all-dissolving scepticism of the intellect in religious matters."[10] Some such doctrine is in fact but a natural corollary from the doctrine of human corruption held by all genuine theologians. The very basis of orthodox theology is the actual separation of the creation from the Creator. In the *Grammar of Assent*, Newman tells us that we "can only glean from the surface of the world some faint and fragmentary views" of God. "I see," he proceeds, "only a choice of alternatives in view of so critial a fact; either there is no Creator, or He has disowned His creatures."[11] The absence of God from His own world is the one prominent fact which startles and appals him. Newman, of course, does not see or does not admit the obvious consequence. He asserts most emphatically that he believes in the existence of God as firmly as in his own existence; and he finds the ultimate proof of this doctrine—a proof not to be put into mood and figure—in the testimony of the conscience. But he apparently admits that Atheism is as logical, that is, as free from self-contradiction, as Catholicism. He certainly delares that though the ordinary arguments are conclusive, they are not in practice convincing. Sound reason would, of course, establish theology; but corrupt man does not and cannot reason soundly. Newman, however, goes further than this. His Theism can only be supported by help of his Catholicity. If, therefore, Newman had never heard of the Catholic Church—if, that is, he were in the position of the great majority of men now living, and of the overwhelming majority of the race which has lived since its first appearance, he would be driven to one of two alternatives. Either he would be an Atheist or he would be an Agnostic. His conscience might say, there is a God; his observation would say, there is no God. Moreover, the voice of conscience has been very differently interpreted. Newman's interpretation has no force for anyone who, like most men, does not share his intuitions. To such persons, therefore, there can be, on Newman's own showing, no refuge except the admittedly logical refuge of Atheism. Even if they shared his intuitions, they would be necessarily sceptics until the Catholic Church came to their aid, for their intuitions would be in hopeless conflict with their experience. I need hardly add that, to some minds, the proposed alliance with reason of a Church which admits that its tenets are corroded and dissolved wherever free reason is allowed to play upon them, is rather suspicious. At any rate, Newman's arguments go to prove that man, as guided by reason, ought to be an Agnostic, and that, at the present moment, Agnosticism is the only reasonable faith for at least three-quarters of the race.

All, then, who think that men should not be dogmatic about matters beyond the sphere of reason or even conceivability, who hold that reason, however weak, is our sole guide, or who find that their conscience does not testify to the divinity of the Catholic God, but declares the moral doctrines of Catholicity to be demonstrably erroneous, are entitled to claim such orthodox writers as sharing their fundamental principles, though refusing to draw the legitimate inferences. The authority of Dean Mansel and Newman may of course be repudiated. In one sense, however, they are simply stating an undeniable fact. The race collectively is agnostic, whatever may be the case with individuals. Newton might be certain of the truth of his doctrines, whilst other thinkers were still convinced of their falsity. It could not be said that the doctrines were certainly true, so long as they were doubted in good faith by competent reasoners. Newman may be as much convinced of the truth of his theology as Professor Huxley of its error. But speaking of the race, and not of the individual, there is no plainer fact in history than the fact that hitherto no knowledge has been attained. There is not a single proof of natural theology of which the negative has not been maintained as vigorously as the affirmative.

You tell us to be ashamed of professing ignorance. Where is the shame of ignorance in matters still involved in endless and hopeless controversy? Is it not rather a duty? Why should a lad who has just run the gauntlet of examinations and escaped to a country parsonage be dogmatic, when his dogmas are denounced as erroneous by half the philosophers of the world? What theory of the universe am I to accept as demonstrably established? At the very earliest dawn of philosophy men were divided by earlier forms of the same problems which divide them now. Shall I be a Platonist or an Aristotelian? Shall I admit or deny the existence of innate ideas? Shall I believe in the possibility or in the impossibility of transcending experience? Go to the mediæval philosophy, says one controversialist. To which mediæval philosophy, pray? Shall I be a nominalist or a realist? And why should I believe you rather than the great thinkers of the seventeenth century, who agreed with one accord that the first condition of intellectual progress was the destruction of that philosophy? There would be no difficulty if it were a question of physical science. I might believe in Galileo and Newton and their successors down to Adams and Leverrier without hesitation, because they all substantially agree. But when men deal with the old problems there are still the old doubts. Shall I believe in Hobbes or in Descartes? Can I stop where Descartes stopped, or must I go on to Spinoza? Or shall I follow Locke's guidance, and end with Hume's scepticism? Or listen to Kant, and, if so, shall I decide that he is right in destroying theology, or in reconstructing it, or in both performances? Does Hegel hold the key of the secret, or is he a mere spinner of jargon? May not Feuerbach or Schopenhauer represent the true development of metaphysical inquiry? Shall I put faith in Hamilton and Mansel, and, if so, shall I read their conclusions by the help of Mr. Spencer, or shall I believe in Mill or in Green? State any one proposition in which all philosophers agree, and I will admit it to be true; or any one which has a manifest balance of authority, and I will agree that it is probable. But so long as every philosopher flatly contradicts the first principles of his predecessors, why affect certainty? The only agreement I can discover is, that there is no philosopher of whom his opponents have not said that his opinions lead logically either to Pantheism or to Atheism.

When all the witnesses thus contradict each other, the *primâ facie* result is pure scepticism. There is no certainty. Who am I, if I were the ablest of modern thinkers, to say summarily that all the great men who differed from me are wrong, and so wrong that their difference should not even raise a doubt in my mind? From such scepticism there is indeed one, and, so far as I can see, but one, escape. The very hopelessness of the controversy shows that the reasoners have been transcending the limits of reason. They have reached a point where, as at the pole, the compass points indifferently to every quarter. Thus there is a chance that I may retain what is valuable in the chaos of speculation, and reject what is bewildering by confining the mind to its proper limits. But has any limit ever been suggested, except a limit which comes in substance to an exclusion of all ontology? In short, if I would avoid utter scepticism, must I not be an Agnostic?

Let us suppose, however, that this difficulty can be evaded. Suppose that, after calling witnesses from all schools and all ages, I can find ground for excluding all the witnesses who make against me. Let me say, for example, that the whole school which refuses to transcend experience errs from the wickedness of its heart and the consequent dulness of its intellect. Some people seem to think that a plausible and happy suggestion. Let the theologian have his necessary laws of thought, which enable him to evolve truth beyond all need of verification from experience. Where will the process end? The question answers itself. The path has been trodden again and again, till it is as familiar as the first rule of arithmetic. Admit that the mind can reason about the Absolute and the Infinite, and you will get to the position of Spinoza, or to a position substantially equivalent. In fact, the chain of reasoning is substantially too short and simple to be for a moment doubtful. Theology, if logical, leads straight to Pantheism. The Infinite God is everything. All things are bound together as cause and effect. God, the first cause, is the cause of all effects down to the most remote. In one form or other, that is the conclusion to which all theology approximates as it is pushed to its legitimate result.

Here, then, we have an apparent triumph over Agnosticism. But nobody can accept Spinoza without rejecting all the doctrines for which the Gnostics really contend. In the first place, revelation and the God of revelation disappear. The argument according to Spinoza against supernaturalism differs from the argument according to Hume in being more peremptory. Hume only denies that a past miracle can be proved by evidence: Spinoza denies that it could ever have happened. As a fact, miracles and a local revelation were first assailed by Deists more effectually than by sceptics. The old Theology was seen to be unworthy of the God of nature, before it was said that nature could not be regarded through the theological representation. And, in the next place, the orthodox assault upon the value of Pantheism is irresistible. Pantheism can give no ground for morality, for nature is as much the cause of vice as the cause of virtue; it can give no ground for an optimist view of the universe, for nature causes evil as much as it causes good. We no longer doubt, it is true, whether there be a God, for our God means all reality; but every doubt which we entertained about the universe is transferred to the God upon whom the universe is moulded. The attempt to transfer to pure being or to the abstraction Nature the feelings with which we are taught to regard a person of transcendent wisdom and benevolence is, as theologians assert, hopeless. To deny the existence of God is in this sense the same as to deny the existence of no-God. We keep the old word; we have altered the whole of its contents. A Pantheist is, as a rule, one who looks upon the universe through his feelings instead of his reason, and who regards it with love because his habitual frame of mind is amiable. But he has no logical argument as against the Pessimist, who regards it with dread unqualified by love, or the Agnostic, who finds it impossible to regard it with any but a colourless emotion. . . .

There are two questions, in short, about the universe which must be answered to escape from Agnosticism. The great fact which puzzles the mind is the vast amount of evil. It may be answered that evil is an illusion, because God is benevolent; or it may be answered that evil is deserved, because God is just. In one case the doubt is removed by denying the existence of the difficulty, in the other it is made tolerable by satisfying our consciences. We have seen what natural reason can do towards justifying these answers. To escape from Agnosticism we become Pantheists; then the divine reality must be the counterpart of phenomenal nature, and all the difficulties recur. We escape from Pantheism by the illogical device of free-will. Then God is indeed good and wise, but God is no longer omnipotent. By His side we erect a fetish called free-will, which is potent enough to defeat all God's good purposes, and to make His absence from His own universe the most conspicuous fact given by observation; and which, at the same time, is by its own nature intrinsically arbitrary in its action. Your Gnosticism tells us that an almighty benevolence is watching over everything, and bringing good out of all evil. Whence, then, comes the evil? By free-will; that is, by chance! It is an exception, an exception which covers, say, half the phenomena, and includes all that puzzle us. Say boldly at once no explanation can be given, and then proceed to denounce Agnosticism. If, again, we take the moral problem, the Pantheist view shows desert as before God to be a contradiction in terms. We are what He has made us; nay, we are but manifestations of Himself—how can He complain? Escape from the dilemma by making us independent of God, and God, so far as the observed universe can tell us, becomes systematically unjust. He rewards the good and the bad, and gives equal reward to the free agent and the slave of fate. Where are we to turn for a solution?

Let us turn to revelation; that is the most obvious reply. By all means, though this is to admit that natural reason cannot help us; or, in other words, it directly produces more Agnosticism, though indirectly it makes an opening for revelation. There is, indeed, a difficulty here. Pure theism, as we have observed, is in reality as vitally opposed to historical revelation as simple scepticism. The word God is used by the metaphysician and the savage. It may mean anything, from "pure Being" down to the most degraded fetish. The "universal consent" is a consent to use the same phrase for antagonistic conceptions—for order and chaos, for absolute unity or utter heterogeneity, for a universe governed by a human will, or by a will of which man cannot form the slightest conception. This is, of course, a difficulty which runs off the orthodox disputant like water from a duck's back. He appeals to his conscience, and his conscience tells him just what he wants. It reveals a Being just at that point in the scale between the two extremes which is convenient for his purposes. I open, for example, a harmless little treatise by a divine who need not be named. He knows intuitively, so he says, that there is a God, who is benevolent and wise, and endowed with personality, that is to say, conceived anthropomorphically enough to be capable of acting upon the universe, and yet so far different from man as to be able to throw a decent veil of mystery over His more questionable actions. Well, I reply, my intuition tells me of no such Being. Then, says the divine, I can't prove my statements, but you would recognise their truth if your heart or your intellect were not corrupted: that is, you must be a knave or a fool. This is a kind of argument to which one is perfectly accustomed in theology. I am right, and you are wrong; and I am right because I am good and wise. By all means; and now let us see what your wisdom and goodness can tell us.

The Christian revelation makes statements which, if true, are undoubtedly of the very highest importance. God is angry with man. Unless we believe and repent we shall all be damned. It is impossible, indeed, for its advocates even to say this without instantly contradicting themselves. Their doctrine frightens them. They explain in various ways that a great many people will be saved without believing, and that eternal damnation is not eternal nor damnation. It is only the vulgar who hold such views, and who, of course, must not be disturbed in them; but they are not for the intelligent. God grants "uncovenanted mercies"—that is, He sometimes lets a sinner off, though He has not made a legal bargain about it—an explanation calculated to exalt our conceptions of the Deity! But let us pass over these endless shufflings from the horrible to the meaningless. Christianity tells us in various ways how the wrath of the Creator may be appeased and His goodwill ensured. The doctrine is manifestly important to believers; but does it give us a clearer or happier view of the universe? That is what is required for the confusion of Agnostics; and, if the mystery were in part solved, or the clouds thinned in the slightest degree, Christianity would triumph by its inherent merits. Let us, then, ask once more, Does Christianity exhibit the ruler of the universe as benevolent or as just?

If I were to assert that of every ten beings born into this world nine would be damned, that all who refused to believe what they did not hold to be proved, and all who sinned from overwhelming temptation, and all who had not had the good-fortune to be the subjects of a miraculous conversion or the recipients of a grace conveyed by a magical charm, would be tortured to all eternity, what would an orthodox theologian reply? He could not say, "That is false"; I might appeal to the highest authorities for my justification; nor, in fact, could he on his own showing deny the possibility. Hell, he says, exists; he does not know who will be damned; though he does know that all men are by nature corrupt and liable to be damned if not saved by supernatural grace. He might, and probably would, now say, "That is rash. You have no authority for saying how many will be lost and how many saved: you cannot even say what is meant by hell or heaven: you cannot tell how far God may be better than His word, though you may be sure that He won't be worse than His word." And what is all this but to say, We know nothing about it? In other words, to fall back on Agnosticism. The difficulty, as theologians truly say, is not so much that evil is eternal, as that evil exists. That is in substance a frank admission that, as nobody can explain evil, nobody can explain anything. Your revelation, which was to prove the benevolence of God, has proved only that God's benevolence may be consistent with the eternal and infinite misery of most of His creatures; you escape only by saying that it is also consistent with their not being eternally and infinitely miserable. That is, the revelation reveals nothing.

But the revelation shows God to be just. Now, if the free-will hypothesis be rejected—and it is rejected, not only by infidels, but by the most consistent theologians—this question cannot really arise at all. Jonathan Edwards will prove that there cannot be a question of justice as between man and God.[12] The creature has no rights against his Creator. The question of justice merges in the question of benevolence; and Edwards will go on to say that most men are damned, and that the blessed will thank God for their tortures. That is logical, but not consoling. Passing this over, can revelation prove that God is just, assuming that justice is a word applicable to dealings between the potter and the pot?

And here we are sent to the "great argument of Butler."[13] Like some other theological arguments already noticed, that great argument is to many minds—those of James Mill and of Dr. Martineau,[14] for example—a direct assault upon Theism, or, in other words, an argument for Agnosticism. Briefly stated, it comes to this. The God of revelation cannot be the God of nature, said the Deists, because the God of revelation is unjust. The God of revelation, replied Butler, may be the God of nature, for the God of nature is unjust. Stripped of its various involutions, that is the sum and substance of this celebrated piece of reasoning. Butler, I must say in passing, deserves high credit for two things. The first is that he is the only theologian who has ever had the courage to admit that any difficulty existed when he was struggling most desperately to meet the difficulty; though even Butler could not admit that such a difficulty should affect a man's conduct. Secondly, Butler's argument really rests upon a moral theory, mistaken indeed in some senses, but possessing a stoical grandeur. To admit, however, that Butler was a noble and a comparatively candid thinker is not to admit that he ever faced the real difficulty. It need not be asked here by what means he evaded it. His position is in any case plain. Christianity tells us, as he thinks, that God damns men for being bad, whether they could help it or not; and that He lets them off, or lets some of them off, for the sufferings of others. He damns the helpless and punishes the innocent. Horrible! exclaims the infidel. Possibly, replies Butler, but nature is just as bad. All suffering is punishment. It strikes the good as well as the wicked. The father sins, and the son suffers. I drink too much, and my son has the gout. In another world we may suppose that the same system will be carried out more thoroughly. God will pardon some sinners because He punished Christ, and He will damn others everlastingly. That is His way. A certain degree of wrongdoing here leads to irremediable suffering, or rather to suffering remediable by death alone. In the next world there is no death; therefore, the suffering won't be remediable at all. The world is a scene of probation, destined to fit us for a better life. As a matter of fact, most men make it a discipline of vice instead of a discipline of virtue; and most men, therefore, will presumably be damned. We see the same thing in the waste of seeds and animal life, and may suppose, therefore, that it is part of the general scheme of Providence.

This is the Christian revelation according to Butler. Does it make the world better? Does it not, rather, add indefinitely to the terror produced by the sight of all its miseries, and justify James Mill for feeling that rather than such a God he would have no God? What escape can be suggested? The obvious one: it is all a mystery; and what is mystery but the theological phrase for Agnosticism? God has spoken, and endorsed all our most hideous doubts. He has said, let there be light, and there is no light—no light, but rather darkness visible, serving only to discover sights of woe.

The believers who desire to soften away the old dogmas—in other words, to take refuge from the unpleasant results of their doctrine with the Agnostics, and to retain the pleasant results with the Gnostics—have a different mode of escape. They know that God is good and just; that evil will somehow disappear and apparent injustice be somehow redressed. The practical objection to this amiable creed suggests a sad comment upon the whole controversy. We fly to religion to escape from our dark forebodings. But a religion which stifles these forebodings always fails to satisfy us. We long to hear that they are groundless. As soon as we are told that they are groundless we mistrust our authority. No poetry lives which reflects only the cheerful emotions. Our sweetest songs are those which tell of saddest thought. We can bring harmony out of melancholy; we cannot banish melancholy from the world. And the religious utterances, which are the highest form of poetry, are bound by the same law. There is a deep sadness in the world. Turn and twist the thought as you may, there is no escape. Optimism would be soothing if it were possible; in fact, it is impossible, and therefore a constant mockery; and of all dogmas that ever were invented, that which has least vitality is the dogma that whatever is, is right.

Let us, however, consider for a moment what is the net result of this pleasant creed. Its philosophical basis may be sought in pure reason or in experience; but, as a rule, its adherents are ready to admit that the pure reason requires the support of the emotions before such a doctrine can be established, and are therefore marked by a certain tinge of mysticism. They feel rather than know. The awe with which they regard the universe, the tender glow of reverence and love with which the bare sight of nature affects them, is to them the ultimate guarantee of their beliefs. Happy those who feel such emotions! Only, when they try to extract definite statements of fact from these impalpable sentiments, they should beware how far such statements are apt to come into terrible collision with reality. And, meanwhile, those who have been disabused with Candide, who have felt the weariness and pain of all "this unintelligible world," and have not been able to escape into any mystic rapture, have as much to say for their own version of the facts. Is happiness a dream, or misery, or is it all a dream? Does not our answer vary with our health and with our condition? When, rapt in the security of a happy life, we cannot even conceive that our happiness will fail, we are practical optimists. When some random blow out of the dark crushes the pillars round which our life has been entwined as recklessly as a boy sweeps away a cobweb, when at a single step we plunge through the flimsy crust of happiness into the deep gulfs beneath, we are tempted to turn to Pessimism. Who shall decide, and how? Of all questions that can be asked, the most important is surely this: Is the tangled web of this world composed chiefly of happiness or of misery? And of all questions that can be asked, it is surely the most unanswerable. For in no other problem is the difficulty of discarding the illusions arising from our own experience, of eliminating "the personal error" and gaining an outside standing-point, so hopeless.

In any case the real appeal must be to experience. Ontologists may manufacture libraries of jargon without touching the point. They have never made, or suggested the barest possibility of making, a bridge from the world of pure reason to the contingent world in which we live. To the thinker who tries to construct the universe out of pure reason, the actual existence of error in our minds and disorder in the outside world presents a difficulty as hopeless as that which the existence of vice and misery presents to the optimist who tries to construct the universe out of pure goodness. To say that misery does not exist is to contradict the primary testimony of consciousness; to argue on *à priori* grounds that misery or happiness predominates, is as hopeless a task as to deduce from the principle of the excluded middle the distance from St. Paul's to Westminster Abbey. Questions of fact can only be solved by examining facts. Perhaps such evidence would show—and if a guess were worth anything, I should add that I guess that it would show—that happiness predominates over misery in the composition of the known world. I am, therefore, not prejudiced against the Gnostic's conclusion; but I add that the evidence is just as open to me as to him. The whole world in which we live may be an illusion—a veil to be withdrawn in some higher state of being. But be it what it may, it supplies all the evidence upon which we can rely. If evil predominates here, we have no reason to suppose that good predominates elsewhere. All the ingenuity of theologians can never shake our conviction that facts are what we feel them to be, nor invert the plain inference from facts; and facts are just as open to one school of thought as to another.

What, then, is the net result? One insoluble doubt has haunted men's minds since thought began in the world. No answer has ever been suggested. One school of philosophers hands it to the next. It is denied in one form only to reappear in another. The question is not which system excludes the doubt, but how it expresses the doubt. Admit or deny the competence of reason in theory, we all agree that it fails in practice. Theologians revile reason as much as Agnostics; they then appeal to it, and it decides against them. They amend their plea by excluding certain questions from its jurisdiction, and those questions include the whole difficulty. They go to revelation, and revelation replies by calling doubt, mystery. They declare that their consciousness declares just what they want it to declare. Ours declares something else. Who is to decide? The only appeal is to experience, and to appeal to experience is to admit the fundamental dogma of Agnosticism.

Is it not, then, the very height of audacity, in face of a difficulty which meets us at every turn, which has perplexed all the ablest thinkers in proportion to their ability, which vanishes in one shape only to show itself in another, to declare roundly, not only that the difficulty can be solved, but that it does not exist? Why, when no honest man will deny in private that every ultimate problem is wrapped in the profoundest mystery, do honest men proclaim in pulpits that unhesitating certainty is the duty of the most foolish and ignorant? Is it not a spectacle to make the angels laugh? We are a company of ignorant beings, feeling our way through mists and darkness, learning only by incessantly-repeated blunders, obtaining a glimmering of truth by falling into every conceivable error, dimly discerning light enough for our daily needs, but hopelessly differing whenever we attempt to describe the ultimate origin or end of our paths; and yet, when one of us ventures to declare that we don't know the map of the universe as well as the map of our infinitesimal parish, he is hooted, reviled, and perhaps told that he will be damned to all eternity for his faithlessness. Amidst all the endless and hopeless controversies which have left nothing but bare husks of meaningless words, we have been able to discover certain reliable truths. They don't take us very far, and the condition of discovering them has been distrust of *à priori* guesses, and the systematic interrogation of experience. Let us, say some of us, follow at least this clue. Here we shall find sufficient guidance for the needs of life, though we renounce for ever the attempt to get behind the veil which no one has succeeded in raising; if, indeed, there be anything behind. You miserable Agnostics! is the retort; throw aside such rubbish, and cling to the old husks. Stick to the words which profess to explain everything; call your doubts mysteries, and they won't disturb you any longer; and believe in those necessary truths of which no two philosophers have ever succeeded in giving the same version.

Gentlemen, we can only reply, wait till you have some show of agreement amongst yourselves. Wait till you can give some answer, not palpably a verbal answer, to some one of the doubts which oppress us as they oppress you. Wait till you can point to some single truth, however trifling, which has been discovered by your method, and will stand the test of discussion and verification. Wait till you can appeal to reason without in the same breath vilifying reason. Wait till your Divine revelations have something more to reveal than the hope that the hideous doubts which they suggest may possibly be without foundation. Till then we shall be content to admit openly, what you whisper under your breath or hide in technical jargon, that the ancient secret is a secret still; that man knows nothing of the Infinite and Absolute; and that, knowing nothing, he had better not be dogmatic about his ignorance. And, meanwhile, we will endeavour to be as charitable as possible, and whilst you trumpet forth officially your contempt for our scepticism, we will at least try to believe that you are imposed upon by your own bluster.

NOTES

1. [Herbert Spencer (1820–1903), English philosopher who sought to apply the principles of Darwin's theory of evolution to many aspects of human life. Sir William Hamilton (1788–1856), Scottish thinker who fused Scottish "common-sense" philosophy with the skepticism of Kant. Henry Mansel (1820–1871), agnostic philosopher who nonetheless affirmed his faith in an omnipotent and benevolent God.]

2. [George Henry Lewes (1817–1878), British empiricist philosopher, follower of Comte, and companion to George Eliot.]

3. [A will-o'-the-wisp (lit., "foolish fire").]

4. ["And the Son": a reference to the standard formulation "The Father and the Son and the Holy Ghost (Spirit)."]

5. [Lit., "dead head."]

6. [A creed formerly attributed to St. Athanasius (296?-373) and devoted to the doctrines of the Trinity and the Incarnation.]

7. [Frederick Denison Maurice (1805–1872), a leading British theologian who stressed the fundamental unity of all Christian sects. For Mill see below (p. 118).]

8. [John Henry Newman (1801–1890), British theologian who was initially a leader of the Oxford Movement but later converted from Anglicanism to Catholicism and eventually became a cardinal.]

9. *History of My Religious Opinions,* pp. 322–23.

10. Ibid., p. 379.

11. *Grammar of Assent,* p. 392.

12. [Jonathan Edwards (1703–1758), American theologian who became notorious for the fire-and-brimstone sermon "Sinners in the Hands of an Angry God" (1741), although this is not believed to be representative of his thought.]

13. [Joseph Butler (1692–1752), British theologian and author of *The Analogy of Religion* (1736). See also Antony Flew's discussion (pp. 125–27).]

14. [James Mill (1773–1836), Scottish utilitarian philosopher and father of John Stuart Mill. James Martineau (1805–1900), British Unitarian theologian.]

3

THE PHILOSOPHY OF ATHEISM
(1916)

Emma Goldman

Emma Goldman (1869–1940) was born in Russia but emigrated to the United States in the 1880s, when she converted to anarchism and participated frequently in labor agitation to bring about fairer treatment to workers. She edited an anarchist magazine, Mother Earth *(1906–17), and wrote prolifically; some of her work was gathered in* Anarchism and Other Essays *(1910). During World War I she was imprisoned for two years for opposing the draft, and in 1919 she was deported to Russia during the Red Scare. Goldman was convinced that anarchism was the only means to secure individual freedom, and her hostility to capitalism, private property, and religion rested on her perception of their inhibition of human liberty. In the following essay—published in the rare pamphlet,* The Philosophy of Atheism and The Failure of Christianity *(1916)—Goldman sees in atheism a means "to free man from the nightmare of gods."*

TO GIVE AN ADEQUATE EXPOSITION of the philosophy of Atheism, it would be necessary to go into the historical changes of the belief in a Deity, from its earliest beginning to the present day. But that is not within the scope of the present paper. However, it is not out of place to mention, in passing, that the concept God, Supernatural Power, Spirit, Deity, or in whatever other term the essence of Theism may have found

From Emma Goldman, "The Philosophy of Atheism," in *The Philosophy of Atheism and The Failure of Christianity* (New York: Mother Earth Publishing Association, 1916), pp. 1–7.

expression, has become more indefinite and obscure in the course of time and progress. In other words, the God idea is growing more impersonal and nebulous in proportion as the human mind is learning to understand natural phenomena and in the degree that science progressively correlates human and social events.

God, today, no longer represents the same forces as in the beginning of His existence; neither does He direct human destiny with the same iron hand as of yore. Rather does the God idea express a sort of spiritualistic stimulus to satisfy the fads and fancies of every shade of human weakness. In the course of human development the God idea has been forced to adapt itself to every phase of human affairs, which is perfectly consistent with the origin of the idea itself.

The conception of gods originated in fear and curiosity. Primitive man, unable to understand the phenomena of nature and harassed by them, saw in every terrifying manifestation some sinister force expressly directed against him; and as ignorance and fear are the parents of all superstition, the troubled fancy of primitive man wove the God idea.

Very aptly, the world-renowned atheist and anarchist, Michael Bakunin, says in his great work *God and the State*: "All religions, with their demi-gods, and their prophets, their messiahs and their saints, were created by the prejudiced fancy of men who had not attained the full development and full possession of their faculties. Consequently, the religious heaven is nothing but the mirage in which man, exalted by ignorance and faith, discovered his own image, but enlarged and reversed—that is, divinised. The history of religions, of the birth, grandeur, and the decline of the gods who had succeeded one another in human belief, is nothing, therefore, but the development of the collective intelligence and conscience of mankind. As fast as they discovered, in the course of their historically-progressive advance, either in themselves or in external nature, a quality, or even any great defect whatever, they attributed them to their gods, after having exaggerated and enlarged them beyond measure, after the manner of children, by an act of their religious fancy. . . . With all due respect, then, to the metaphysicians and religious idealists, philosophers, politicians or poets: the idea of God implies the abdication of human reason and justice; it is the most decisive negation of human liberty, and necessarily ends in the enslavement of mankind, both in theory and practice."[1]

Thus the God idea revived, readjusted, and enlarged or narrowed, according to the necessity of the time, has dominated humanity and will continue to do so until man will raise his head to the sunlit day, unafraid and with an awakened will to himself. In proportion as man learns to realize himself and mold his own destiny, theism becomes superfluous. How far man will be able to find his relation to his fellows will depend entirely upon how much he can outgrow his dependence upon God.

Already there are indications that theism, which is the theory of speculation, is being replaced by Atheism, the science of demonstration; the one hangs in the metaphysical clouds of the Beyond, while the other has its roots firmly in the soil. It is the earth, not heaven, which man must rescue if he is truly to be saved.

The decline of theism is a most interesting spectacle, especially as manifested in the anxiety of the theists, whatever their particular brand. They realize, much to their distress, that the masses are growing daily more atheistic, more anti-religious; that they are quite willing to leave the Great Beyond and its heavenly domain to the angels and sparrows; because more and more the masses are becoming engrossed in the problems of their immediate existence.

How to bring the masses back to the God idea, the spirit, the First Cause, etc.—that is the most pressing question to all theists. Metaphysical as all these questions seem to be, they yet have a very marked physical background. Inasmuch as religion, "Divine Truth," rewards and punishments are the trade-marks of the largest, the most corrupt and pernicious, the most powerful and lucrative industry in the world, not excepting the industry of manufacturing guns and munitions. It is the industry of befogging the human mind and stifling the human heart. Necessity knows no law; hence the majority of theists are compelled to take up every subject, even if it has no bearing upon a deity or revelation or the Great Beyond. Perhaps they sense the fact that humanity is growing weary of the hundred and one brands of God.

How to raise this dead level of theistic belief is really a matter of life and death for all denominations. Therefore their tolerance; but it is a tolerance not of understanding, but of weakness. Perhaps that explains the efforts fostered in all religious publications to combine variegated religious philosophies and conflicting theistic theories into one denominational trust. More and more, the various concepts "of the only true God, the only pure spirit, the only true religion" are tolerantly glossed over in the frantic effort to establish a common ground to rescue the modern mass from the "pernicious" influence of atheistic ideas.

It is characteristic of theistic "tolerance" that no one really cares what the people believe in, just so they believe or pretend to believe. To accomplish this end, the crudest and vulgarest methods are being used. Religious endeavor meetings and revivals with Billy Sunday[2] as their champion—methods which must outrage every refined sense, and which in their effect upon the ignorant and curious often tend to create a mild state of insanity not infrequently coupled with erotomania. All these frantic efforts find approval and support from the earthly powers; from the Russian despot to the American President; from Rockefeller and Wanamaker down to the pettiest business man. They know that capital invested in Billy Sunday, the YMCA, Christian Science, and various other religious institutions will return enormous profits from the subdued, tamed, and dull masses.

Consciously or unconsciously, most theists see in gods and devils, heaven and hell, reward and punishment, a whip to lash the people into obedience, meekness and contentment. The truth is that theism would have lost its footing long before this but for the combined support of Mammon and power. How thoroughly bankrupt it really is, is being demonstrated in the trenches and battlefields of Europe today.

Have not all theists painted their Deity as the god of love and goodness? Yet after thousands of years of such preachments the gods remain deaf to the agony of the human race. Confucius cares not for the poverty, squalor and misery of the people of China. Buddha remains undisturbed in his philosophical indifference to the famine and starvation of the outraged Hindoos; Jahve continues deaf to the bitter cry of Israel; while Jesus refuses to rise from the dead against his Christians who are butchering each other.

The burden of all song and praise, "unto the Highest" has been that God stands for justice and mercy. Yet injustice among men is ever on the increase; the outrages committed against the masses in this country alone would seem enough to overflow the very heavens. But where are the gods to make an end to all these horrors, these wrongs, this inhumanity to man? No, not the gods, but MAN must rise in his mighty wrath. He, deceived by all the deities, betrayed by their emissaries, he, himself, must undertake to usher in justice upon the earth.

The philosophy of Atheism expresses the expansion and growth of the human mind. The philosophy of theism, if we can call it philosophy, is static and fixed. Even the mere attempt to pierce these mysteries represents, from the theistic point of view, non-belief in the all embracing omnipotence, and even a denial of the wisdom of the divine powers outside of man. Fortunately, however, the human mind never was, and never can be, bound by fixities. Hence it is forging ahead in its restless march towards knowledge and life. The human mind is realizing "that the universe is not the result of a creative fiat by some divine intelligence, out of nothing, producing a masterpiece in perfect operation," but that it is the product of chaotic forces operating through aeons of time, of clashes and cataclysms, of repulsion and attraction crystallizing through the principle of selection into what the theists call "the universe guided into order and beauty." As Joseph McCabe well points out in his *Existence of God*: "a law of nature is not a formula drawn up by a legislator, but a mere summary of the observed facts—a 'bundle of facts.' Things do not act in a particular way because there is a law, but we state the 'law' because they act in that way."[3]

The philosophy of Atheism represents a concept of life without any metaphysical Beyond or Divine Regulator. It is the concept of an actual, real world with its liberating, expanding and beautifying possibilities, as against an unreal world, which, with its spirits, oracles, and mean contentment, has kept humanity in helpless degradation.

It may seem a wild paradox, and yet it is pathetically true, that this real, visible world and our life should have been so long under the influence of metaphysical speculation, rather than of physical demonstrable forces. Under the lash of the theistic idea, this earth has served no other purpose than as a temporary station to test man's capacity for immolation to the will of God. But the moment man attempted to ascertain the nature of that will, he was told that it was utterly futile for "finite human intelligence" to get beyond the all-powerful infinite will. Under the terrific weight of this omnipotence, man has been bowed into the dust,—a will-less creature, broken and swarting in the dark. The triumph of the philosophy of Atheism is to free man from the nightmare of gods; it means the dissolution of the phantoms of the beyond. Again and again the light of reason has dispelled the theistic nightmare, but poverty, misery and fear have recreated the phantoms—though whether old or new, whatever their external form, they differed little in their essence. Atheism, on the other hand, in its philosophic aspect refuses allegiance not merely to a definite concept of God, but it refuses all servitude to the God idea, and opposes the theistic principle as such. Gods in their individual function are not half as pernicious as the principle of theism which represents the belief in a supernatural, or even omnipotent, power to rule the earth and man upon it. It is the absolutism of theism, its pernicious influence upon humanity, its paralyzing effect upon thought and action, which Atheism is fighting with all its power.

The philosophy of Atheism has its root in the earth, in this life; its aim is the emancipation of the human race from all God-heads, be they Judaic, Christian, Mohammedan, Buddhistic, Brahministic, or what not. Mankind has been punished long and heavily for having created its gods; nothing but pain and persecution have been man's lot since gods began. There is but one way out of this blunder: Man must break his fetters which have chained him to the gates of heaven and hell, so that he can begin to fashion out of his reawakened and illumined consciousness a new world upon earth.

Only after the triumph of the Atheistic philosophy in the minds and hearts of man will freedom and beauty be realized. Beauty as a gift from heaven has proved useless. It will, however, become the essence and impetus of life when man learns to see in the earth the only heaven fit for man. Atheism is already helping to free man from his dependence upon punishment and reward as the heavenly bargain-counter for the poor in spirit.

Do not all theists insist that there can be no morality, no justice, honesty or fidelity without the belief in a Divine Power? Based upon fear and hope, such morality has always been a vile product, imbued partly with self-righteousness, partly with hypocrisy. As to truth, justice, and fidelity, who have been their brave exponents and daring proclaimers? Nearly always the godless ones: the Atheists; they lived, fought, and died for them. They knew that justice, truth, and fidelity are not conditioned in heaven, but that they are related to and interwoven with the tremendous changes going on in the social and material life of the human race; not fixed and eternal, but fluctuating, even as life itself. To what heights the philosophy of Atheism may yet attain, no one can prophesy. But this much can already be predicted: only by its regenerating fire will human relations be purged from the horrors of the past.

Thoughtful people are beginning to realize that moral precepts, imposed upon humanity through religious terror, have become stereo-typed and have therefore lost all vitality. A glance at life today, at its dis-integrating character, its conflicting interests with their hatreds, crimes, and greed, suffices to prove the sterility of theistic morality.

Man must get back to himself before he can learn his relation to his fellows. Prometheus chained to the Rock of Ages is doomed to remain the prey of the vultures of darkness. Unbind Prometheus, and you dispel the night and its horrors.

Atheism in its negation of gods is at the same time the strongest affirmation of man, and through man, the eternal yea to life, purpose, and beauty.

NOTES

1. [Mikhail Bakunin (1814–1876), Russian political thinker and founder of anarchism. *God and the State* is an extract from Bakunin's treatise, *L'Empire Knouto-Germanique et la révolution sociale* (1871).]

2. [Billy Sunday (1862–1935), American evangelist who gained notoriety and ridicule by his histrionic behavior during revival meetings.]

3. [*The Existence of God* (1913) by Joseph McCabe (1867–1955), a leading British freethinker of his time.]

4

WHY I AM AN UNBELIEVER
(1926)

Carl Van Doren

Carl Van Doren (1885–1950), longtime professor of English at Columbia University, was a widely published literary critic and author of such works as The American Novel *(1921) and the biography* Benjamin Franklin *(1938), which won the Pulitzer Prize. The following statement—first published in the* Forum *for December 1926 and gathered in the anthology* Twelve Modern Apostles and Their Creeds *(1926)—refutes, with simple eloquence, numerous beliefs regarding atheism: that it is merely "negative," that it is a "bleak" view of the world, and that atheists are less moral than believers.*

LET US BE HONEST. THERE have always been men and women without the gift of faith. They lack it, do not desire it, and would not know what to do with it if they had it. They are apparently no less intelligent than the faithful, and apparently no less virtuous. How great the number of them is it would be difficult to say, but they exist in all communities and are most numerous where there is most enlightenment. As they have no organization and no creed, they can of course have no official spokesman. Nevertheless, any one of them who speaks out can be trusted to speak, in a way, for all of them. Like the mystics, the unbelievers, wherever found, are essentially of one spirit and one language. I cannot, however, pretend to represent more than a single complexion of unbelief.

From Carl Van Doren, "Why I Am an Unbeliever," in *Twelve Modern Apostles and Their Creeds* (New York: Duffield, 1926), pp. 198–209.

The very terms which I am forced to use put me at the outset in a trying position. Belief, being first in the field, naturally took a positive term for itself and gave a negative term to unbelief. As an unbeliever, I am therefore obliged to seem merely to dissent from the believers, no matter how much more I may do. Actually I do more. What they call unbelief, I call belief. Doubtless I was born to it, but I have tested it with reading and speculation, and I hold it firmly. What I have referred to as the gift of faith I do not, to be exact, regard as a gift. I regard it, rather, as a survival from an earlier stage of thinking and feeling: in short, as a form of superstition. It, and not the thing I am forced to name unbelief, seems to me negative. It denies the reason. It denies the evidences in the case, in the sense that it insists upon introducing elements which come not from the facts as shown but from the imaginations and wishes of mortals. Unbelief does not deny the reason and it sticks as closely as it can to the evidences.

I shall have to be more explicit. When I say I am an unbeliever, I do not mean merely that I am no Mormon or no Methodist, or even that I am no Christian or no Buddhist. These seem to me relatively unimportant divisions and subdivisions of belief. I mean that I do not believe in any god that has ever been devised, in any doctrine that has ever claimed to be revealed, in any scheme of immortality that has ever been expounded.

As to gods, they have been, I find, countless, but even the names of most of them lie in the deep compost which is known as civilization, and the memories of few of them are green. There does not seem to me to be good reason for holding that some of them are false and some of them, or one of them, true. Each was created by the imaginations and wishes of men who could not account for the behavior of the universe in any other satisfactory way. But no god has satisfied his worshipers forever. Sooner or later they have realized that the attributes once ascribed to him, such as selfishness or lustfulness or vengefulness, are unworthy of the moral systems which men have evolved among themselves. Thereupon follows the gradual doom of the god, however long certain of the faithful may cling to his cult. In the case of the god who still survives in the loyalty of men after centuries of scrutiny, it can always be noted that little besides his name has endured. His attributes will have been so revised that he is really another god. Nor is this objection met by the argument that the concept of the god has been purified while the essence of him survived. In the concept alone can he be studied; the essence eludes the grasp of the human mind. I may prefer among the various gods that god who seems to me most thoroughly purged of what I regard as undivine elements, but I make my choice, obviously, upon principles which come from observation of the conduct of men. Whether a god has been created in the image of gross desires or of pure desires does not greatly matter. The difference proves merely that different men have desired gods and have furnished themselves with the gods they were able to conceive. Behind all their conceptions still lies the abyss of ignorance. There is no trustworthy evidence as to a god's absolute existence.

Nor does the thing called revelation, as I see it, carry the proof further. All the prophets swear that a god speaks through them, and yet they prophesy contradictions. Once more, men must choose in accordance with their own principles. That a revelation was announced long ago makes it difficult to examine, but does not otherwise attest its soundness. That some revealed doctrine has lasted for ages and has met the needs of many generations proves that it is the kind of doctrine which endures and satisfies, but not that it is divine. Secular doctrines which turned out to be perfectly false have also endured and satisfied. If belief in a god has to proceed from the assumption that he exists, belief in revelation has first to proceed from the assumption that a god exists and then to go further to the assumption that he communicates his will to certain men. But both are mere assumptions. Neither is, in the present state of knowledge, at all capable of proof. Suppose a god did exist, and suppose he did communicate his will to any of his creatures. What man among them could comprehend that language? What man could take that dictation? And what man could overwhelmingly persuade his fellows that he had been selected and that they must accept him as authentic? The best they could do would be to have faith in two assumptions and to test the revealed will by its correspondence to their imaginations and wishes. At this point it may be contended that revelation must be real because it arouses so much response in so many human bosoms. This does not follow without a leap of the reason into the realm of hypothesis. Nothing is proved by this general response except that men are everywhere very much alike. They have the same members, the same organs, the same glands, in varying degrees of activity. Being so much alike, they tend to agree upon a few primary desires. Fortunate the religion by which those desires appear to be gratified.

One desire by which the human mind is often teased is the desire to live after death. It is not difficult to explain. Men live so briefly that their plans far outrun their ability to execute them. They see themselves cut off before their will to live is exhausted. Naturally enough, they wish to survive, and, being men, believe in their chances for survival. But their wishes afford no possible proof. Life covers the earth with wishes, as it covers the earth with plants and animals. No wish, however, is evidence of anything beyond itself. Let millions hold it, and it is still only a wish. Let each separate race exhibit it, and it is still only a wish. Let the wisest hold it as strongly as the foolishest, and it is still only a wish. Whoever says he knows that immortality is a fact is merely hoping that it is. And whoever argues, as men often do, that life would be meaningless without immortality because it alone brings justice into human fate, must first argue, as no man has ever quite convincingly done, that life has an unmistakable meaning and that it is just. I, at least, am convinced on neither of these two points. Though I am, I believe, familiar with all the arguments, I do not find any of them notably better than the others. All I see is that the wish for immortality is wide-spread, that certain schemes of immortality imagined from it have here or there proved more agreeable than rival schemes, and that they have been more generally accepted. The religions which provide these successful schemes I can credit with keener insight into human wishes than other religions have had, but I cannot credit them with greater authority as regards the truth. They are all guesswork.

That I think thus about gods, revelation, and immortality ought to be sufficient answer to the question why I am an unbeliever. It would be if the question were always reasonably asked, but it is not. There is also an emotional aspect to be considered. Many believers, I am told, have the same doubts, and yet have the knack of putting their doubts to sleep and entering ardently into the communion of the faithful. The process is incomprehensible to me. So far as I understand it, such believers are moved by their desires to the extent of letting them rule not only their conduct but their thoughts. An unbeliever's desires have, apparently, less power over his reason. Perhaps this is only another way of saying that his strongest desire is to be as reasonable as he can. However the condition be interpreted, the consequence is the same. An honest unbeliever can no more make himself believe against his reason than he can make himself free of the pull of gravitation. For myself, I feel no obligation whatever to believe. I might once have felt it prudent to keep silence, for I perceive that the race of men, while sheep in credulity, are wolves for conformity; but just now, happily, in this breathing-spell of toleration, there are so many varieties of belief that even an unbeliever may speak out.

In so doing, I must answer certain secondary questions which unbelievers are often asked. Does it not persuade me, one question runs, to realize that many learned men have pondered upon supernatural matters and have been won over to belief? I answer, not in the least. With respect to the gods, revelation, and immortality no man is enough more learned than his fellows to have the right to insist that they follow him into the regions about which all men are ignorant. I am not a particle more impressed by some good old man's conviction that he is in the confidence of the gods than I am by any boy's conviction that there are fish in the horse-pond from which no fish has ever been taken. Does it not impress me to see some good old woman serene in the faith of a blessed immortality? No more than it impresses me to see a little girl full of trust in the universal munificence of a Christmas saint. Am I not moved by the spectacle of a great tradition of worship which has broadened out over continents and which brings all its worshipers punctually together in the observance of noble and dignified rites? Yes, but I am moved precisely by that as I am moved by the spectacle of men everywhere putting their seed seasonably in the ground, tending its increase, and patiently gathering in their harvests.

Finally, do I never suspect in myself some moral obliquity, or do I not at least regret the bleak outlook of unbelief? On these points I am, in my own mind, as secure as I know how to be. There is no moral obligation to believe what is unbelievable, any more than there is a moral obligation to do what is undoable. Even in religion, honesty is a virtue. Obliquity, I should say, shows itself rather in prudent pretense or in voluntary self-delusion. Furthermore, the unbelievers have, as I read history, done less harm to the world than the believers. They have not filled it with savage wars or snarled casuistries, with crusades or persecutions, with complacency or ignorance. They have, instead, done what they could to fill it with knowledge and beauty, with temperance and justice, with manners and laughter. They have numbered among themselves some of the most distinguished specimens of mankind. And when they have been undistinguished, they have surely not been inferior to the believers in the fine art of minding their own affairs and so of enlarging the territories of peace.

Nor is the outlook of unbelief, to my way of thinking, a bleak one. It is merely rooted in courage and not in fear. Belief is still in the plight of those ancient races who out of a lack of knowledge peopled the forest with satyrs and the sea with ominous monsters and the ends of the earth with misshapen anthropophagi. So the pessimists among believers have peopled the void with witches and devils, and the optimists among them have peopled it with angels and gods. Both alike have been afraid to furnish the house of life simply. They have cluttered it with the furniture of faith. Much of this furniture, the most reasonable unbeliever would never think of denying, is very beautiful. There are breathing myths, there are comforting legends, there are consoling hopes. But they have, as the unbeliever sees them, no authority beyond that of poetry. That is, they may captivate if they can, but they have no right to insist upon conquering. Beliefs, like tastes, may differ. The unbeliever's taste and belief are austere. In the wilderness of worlds he does not yield to the temptation to belittle the others by magnifying his own. Among the dangers of chance he does not look for safety to any watchful providence whose special concern he imagines he is. Though he knows that knowledge is imperfect, he trusts it alone. If he takes, therefore, the less delight in metaphysics, he takes the more in physics. Each discovery of a new truth brings him a vivid joy. He builds himself up, so far as he can, upon truth, and barricades himself with it. Thus doing, he never sags into superstition, but grows steadily more robust and blithe in his courage. However many fears he may prove unable to escape, he does not multiply them in his imagination and then combat them with his wishes. Austerity may be simplicity and not bleakness.

Does the unbeliever lack certain of the gentler virtues of the believer, the quiet confidence, the unquestioning obedience? He may, yet it must always be remembered that the greatest believers are the greatest tyrants. If the freedom rather than the tyranny of faith is to better the world, then the betterment lies in the hands, I think, of the unbelievers. At any rate, I take my stand with them.

PART 2

THE
EXISTENCE
OF GOD

If we assume that man actually does resemble God, then we are forced into the impossible theory that God is a coward, an idiot and a bounder.
—H. L. Mencken
"Ad Imaginem Dei Creavit Illum" (1922)

5

A REFUTATION OF DEISM
(1814)

Percy Bysshe Shelley

Percy Bysshe Shelley (1792–1822) was educated at Eton and briefly attended University College, Oxford, but was expelled after a year for publishing the pamphlet The Necessity of Atheism *(1811). At this time he began an association with the freethinker William Godwin, whose daughter Mary he eventually married. Shelley was much influenced both by Godwin and by such eighteenth-century philosophers as baron d'Holbach, Thomas Paine, and Jean-Jacques Rousseau, and he wrote a number of works criticizing religious orthodoxy. He became perhaps the greatest of the Romantic poets, and much of his poetry can be read in the light of his religious skepticism. In the following extract from* "A Refutation of Deism" *(1814), Shelley points out numerous logical fallacies in assuming an "intelligent creator" of the universe.*

DESIGN MUST BE PROVED BEFORE a designer can be inferred. The matter in controversy is the existence of design in the Universe, and it is not permitted to assume the contested premises and thence infer the matter in dispute. Insidiously to employ the words contrivance, design and adaptation before these circumstances are made apparent in the Universe, thence justly inferring a contriver, is a popular sophism against which it behoves us to be watchful.

To assert that motion is an attribute of mind, that matter is inert,

From Percy Bysshe Shelley, "A Refutation of Deism" (1814), in *The Complete Works of Percy Bysshe Shelley*, ed. Roger Ingpen and Walter E. Peck, vol. 6 (London and New York: Julian Editions, 1929), pp. 46–50, 51–55, 56.

that every combination is the result of intelligence is also an assumption of the matter in dispute.

Why do we admit design in any machine of human contrivance? Simply, because innumerable instances of machines having been contrived by human art are present to our mind, because we are acquainted with persons who could construct such machines; but if, having no previous knowledge of any artificial contrivance, we had accidentally found a watch upon the ground, we should have been justified in concluding that it was a thing of Nature, that it was a combination of matter with whose cause we were unacquainted, and that any attempt to account for the origin of its existence would be equally presumptuous and unsatisfactory.

The analogy which you attempt to establish between the contrivances of human art, and the various existences of the Universe, is inadmissible. We attribute these effects to human intelligence, because we know before hand that human intelligence is capable of producing them. Take away this knowledge, and the grounds of our reasoning will be destroyed. Our entire ignorance, therefore, of the Divine Nature leaves this analogy defective in its most essential point of comparison.

What consideration remains to be urged in support of the creation of the Universe by a supreme Being? Its admirable fitness for the production of certain effects, that wonderful consent of all its parts, that universal harmony by whose changeless laws innumerable systems of worlds perform their stated revolutions, and the blood is driven through the veins of the minutest animalcule that sports in the corruption of an insect's lymph: on this account did the Universe require an intelligent Creator, because it exists producing invariable effects, and inasmuch as it is admirably organised for the production of these effects, so the more did it require a creative intelligence.

Thus have we arrived at the substance of your assertion, "That whatever exists, producing certain effects, stands in need of a Creator, and the more conspicuous is its fitness for the production of these effects, the more certain will be our conclusion that it would not have existed from eternity, but must have derived its origin from an intelligent creator."

In what respect then do these arguments apply to the Universe, and not apply to God? From the fitness of the Universe to its end you infer the necessity of an intelligent Creator. But if the fitness of the Universe, to produce certain effects, be thus conspicuous and evident, how much more exquisite fitness to his end must exist in the Author of this Universe? If we find great difficulty from its admirable arrangement, in conceiving that the Universe has existed from all eternity, and to resolve this difficulty suppose a Creator, how much more clearly must we perceive the necessity of this very Creator's creation whose perfections comprehend an arrangement far more accurate and just.

The belief of an infinity of creative and created Gods, each more eminently requiring an intelligent author of his being than the foregoing, is a direct consequence of the premises which you have stated. The assumption that the Universe is a design, leads to a conclusion that there are infinity of creative and created Gods, which is absurd. It is impossible indeed to prescribe limits to learned error, when Philosophy relinquishes experience and feeling for speculation.

Until it is clearly proved that the Universe was created, we may reasonably suppose that it has endured from all eternity. In a case where two propositions are diametrically opposite, the mind believes that which is less incomprehensible: it is easier to suppose that the Universe has existed from all eternity, than to conceive an eternal being capable of creating it. If the mind sinks beneath the weight of one, is it an alleviation to encrease the intolerability of the burthen?

A man knows, not only that he now is, but that there was a time when he did not exist; consequently there must have been a cause. But we can only infer, from effects, causes exactly adequate to those effects. There certainly is a generative power which is effected by particular instruments; we cannot prove that it is inherent in these instruments, nor is the contrary hypothesis capable of demonstration. We admit that the generative power is incomprehensible, but to suppose that the same effects are produced by an eternal Omnipotent and Omniscient Being, leaves the cause in the same obscurity, but renders it more incomprehensible.

We can only infer from effects causes exactly adequate to those effects. An infinite number of effects demand an infinite number of causes, nor is the philosopher justified in supposing a greater connection or unity in the latter, than is perceptible in the former. The same energy cannot be at once the cause of the serpent and the sheep; of the blight by which the harvest is destroyed, and the sunshine by which it is matured; of the ferocious propensities by which man becomes a victim to himself, and of the accurate judgment by which his institutions are improved. The spirit of our accurate and exact philosophy is outraged by conclusions which contradict each other so glaringly.

The greatest, equally with the smallest motions of the Universe, are subjected to the rigid necessity of inevitable laws. These laws are the unknown causes of the known effects perceivable in the Universe. Their effects are the boundaries of our knowledge, their names the expressions of our ignorance. To suppose some existence beyond, or above them, is to invent a second and superfluous hypothesis to account for what has already been accounted for by the laws of motion and the properties of matter. I admit that the nature of these laws is incomprehensible, but the hypothesis of a Deity adds a gratuitous difficulty, which so far from alleviating those which it is adduced to explain, requires new hypotheses for the elucidation of its own inherent contradictions.

The laws of attraction and repulsion, desire and aversion, suffice to account for every phenomenon of the moral and physical world. A precise knowledge of the properties of any object, is alone requisite to determine its manner of action. Let the mathematician be acquainted with the weight and volume of a cannon ball, together with the degree of velocity and inclination with which is which it is impelled, and he will accurately delineate the course it must describe, and determine the force with which it will strike an object at a given distance. Let the influencing motive, present to the mind of any person be given, and the knowledge of his consequent conduct will result. Let the bulk and velocity of a comet be discovered, and the astronomer, by the accurate estimation of the equal and contrary actions of the centripetal and centrifugal forces, will justly predict the period of its return.

The anomalous motions of the heavenly bodies, their unequal velocities and frequent aberrations, are corrected by that gravitation by which they are caused. The illustrious Laplace[1] has shewn, that the approach of the Moon to the Earth, and the Earth to the Sun, is only a secular equation of a very long period, which has its maximum and minimum. The system of the Universe then is upheld solely by physical powers. The necessity of matter is the ruler of the world. It is vain philosophy which supposes more causes than are exactly adequate to explain the phenomena of things. . . .

You assert that the construction of the animal machine, the fitness of certain animals to certain situations, the connexion between the organs of perception and that which is perceived; the relation between every thing which exists, and that which tends to preserve it in its existence, imply design. It is manifest that if the eye could not see, nor the stomach digest, the human frame could not preserve its present mode of existence. It is equally certain, however, that the elements of its composition, if they did not exist in one form, must exist in another; and that the combinations which they would form, must so long as they endured, derive support for their peculiar mode of being from their fitness to the circumstances of their situation.

It by no means follows, that because a being exists, performing catain functions, he was fitted by another being to the performance of these functions. So rash a conclusion would conduct, as I have before shewn, to an absurdity; and it becomes infinitely more unwarrantable from the consideration that the known laws of matter and motion, suffice to unravel, even in the present imperfect state of moral and physical science, the majority of those difficulties which the hypothesis of a Deity was invented to explain.

Doubtless no disposition of inert matter, or matter deprived of qualities, could ever have composed an animal, a tree, or even a stone. But matter deprived of qualities, is an abstraction, concerning which it is impossible to form an idea. Matter, such as we behold it, is not inert. It is infinitely active and subtile. Light, electricity and magnetism are fluids not surpassed by thought itself in tenuity and activity; like thought they are sometimes the cause and sometimes the effect of motion; and, distinct as they are from every other class of substances, with which we are acquainted, seem to possess equal claims with thought to the unmeaning distinction of immateriality.

The laws of motion and the properties of matter suffice to account for every phenomenon, or combination of phenomena exhibited in the Universe. That certain animals exist in certain climates, results from the consentaneity of their frames to the circumstances of their situation: let these circumstances be altered to a sufficient degree, and the elements of their composition must exist in some new combination no less resulting than the former from those inevitable laws by which the Universe is governed. . . .

What then is this harmony, this order which you maintain to have required for its establishment, what it needs not for its maintenance, the agency of a supernatural intelligence? Inasmuch as the order visible in the Universe requires one cause, so does the disorder whose operation is not less clearly apparent demand another. Order and disorder are no more than modifications of our own perceptions of the relations which subsist between ourselves and external objects, and if we are justified in inferring the operation of a benevolent power from the advantages attendant on the former, the evils of the latter bear equal testimony to the activity of a malignant principle, no less pertinacious in inducing evil out of good, than the other is unremitting in procuring good from evil.

If we permit our imagination to traverse the obscure regions of possibility, we may doubtless imagine, according to the complexion of our minds, that disorder may have a relative tendency to unmingled good, or order be relatively replete with exquisite and subtile evil. To neither of these conclusions, which are equally presumptuous and unfounded, will it become the philosopher to assent. Order and disorder are expressions denoting our perceptions of what is injurious or beneficial to ourselves, or to the beings in whose welfare we are compelled to sympathize by the similarity of their conformation to our own.

A beautiful antelope panting under the fangs of a tiger, a defenceless ox, groaning beneath the butcher's axe, is a spectacle which instantly awakens compassion in a virtuous and unvitiated breast. Many there are, however, sufficiently hardened to the rebukes of justice and the precepts of humanity, as to regard the deliberate butchery of thousands of their species, as a theme of exultation and a source of honour, and to consider any failure in these remorseless enterprises as a defect in the system of things. The criteria of order and disorder are as various as those beings from whose opinions and feelings they result.

Populous cities are destroyed by earthquakes, and desolated by pestilence. Ambition is every where devoting its millions to incalculable calamity. Superstition, in a thousand shapes, is employed in brutalizing and degrading the human species, and fitting it to endure without a murmur the oppression of its innumerable tyrants. All this is abstractedly neither good nor evil because good and evil are words employed to designate that peculiar state of our own perceptions, resulting from the encounter of any object calculated to produce pleasure or pain. Exclude the idea of relation, and the words good and evil are deprived of import.

Earthquakes are injurious to the cities which they destroy, beneficial to those whose commerce was injured by their prosperity, and indifferent to others which are too remote to be affected by their influence. Famine is good to the corn-merchant, evil to the poor, and indifferent to those whose fortunes can at all times command a superfluity. Ambition is evil to the restless bosom it inhabits, to the innumerable victims who are dragged by its ruthless thirst for infamy, to expire in every variety of anguish, to the inhabitants of the country it depopulates, and to the human race whose improvement it retards; it is indifferent with regard to the system of the Universe, and is good only to the vultures and the jackals that track the conqueror's career, and to the worms who feast in security on the desolation of his progress. It is manifest that we cannot reason with respect to the universal system from that which only exists in relation to our own perceptions.

You allege some considerations in favor of a Deity from the universality of a belief in his existence.

The superstitions of the savage, and the religion of civilized Europe appear to you to conspire to prove a first cause. I maintain that it is from the evidence of revelation alone that this belief derives the slightest countenance.

That credulity should be gross in proportion to the ignorance of the mind which it enslaves, is in strict consistency with the principles of human nature. The idiot, the child and the savage, agree in attributing their own passions and propensities to the inanimate substances by which they are either benefited or injured. The former become Gods and the latter Demons; hence prayers and sacrifices, by the means of which the rude Theologian imagines that he may confirm the benevolence of the one, or mitigate the malignity of the other. He has averted the wrath of a powerful enemy by supplications and submission; he has secured the assistance of his neighbour by offerings; he has felt his own anger subside before the entreaties of a vanquished foe, and has cherished gratitude for the kindness of another. Therefore does he believe that the elements will listen to his vows. He is capable of love and hatred towards his fellow beings, and is variously impelled by those principles to benefit or injure them. The source of his error is sufficiently obvious. When the winds, the waves and the atmosphere act in such a manner as to thwart or forward his designs, he attributes to them the same propensities of whose existence within himself he is conscious when he is instigated by benefits to kindness, or by injuries to revenge. The bigot of the woods can form no conception of beings possessed of properties differing from his own: it requires, indeed, a mind considerably tinctured with science, and enlarged by cultivation to contemplate itself, not as the centre and model of the Universe, but as one of the infinitely various multitude of beings of which it is actually composed.

There is no attribute of God which is not either borrowed from the passions and powers of the human mind, or which is not a negation. Omniscience, Omnipotence, Omnipresence, Infinity, Immutability, Incomprehensibility, and Immateriality, are all words which designate properties and powers peculiar to organised beings, with the addition of negations, by which the idea of limitation is excluded.[2]

That the frequency of a belief in God (for it is not Universal) should be any argument in its favor, none to whom the innumerable mistakes of men are familiar, will assert. It is among men of genius and science that Atheism alone is found, but among these alone is cherished an hostility to those errors, with which the illiterate and vulgar are infected.

How small is the proportion of whose who really believe in God, to the thousands who are prevented by their occupations from ever bestowing a serious thought upon the subject, and the millions who worship butterflies, bones, feathers, monkeys, calabashes and serpents. The word God, like other abstractions, signifies the agreement of certain propositions, rather than the presence of any idea. If we found our belief in the existence of God on the universal consent of mankind, we are duped by the most palpable of sophisms. The word God cannot mean at the same time an ape, a snake, a bone, a calabash, a Trinity, and a Unity. Nor can that belief be accounted universal against which men of powerful intellect and spotless virtue have in every age protested. . . .

Intelligence is that attribute of the Deity, which you hold to be most apparent in the Universe. Intelligence is only known to us as a mode of animal being. We cannot conceive intelligence distinct from sensation and perception, which are attributes to organized bodies. To assert that God is intelligent, is to assert that he has ideas; and Locke has proved that ideas result from sensation. Sensation can exist only in an organized body, an organized body is necessarily limited both in extent and operation. The God of the rational Theosophist is a vast and wise animal. . . .

Thus, from the principles of that reason to which you so rashly appealed as the ultimate arbiter of our dispute, have I shewn that the popular arguments in favor of the being of God are totally destitute of colour. I have shewn the absurdity of attributing intelligence to the cause of those effects which we perceive in the Universe, and the fallacy which lurks in the argument from design. I have shewn that order is no more than a peculiar manner of contemplating the operation of necessary agents, that mind is the effect, not the cause of motion, that power is the attribute, not the origin of Being. I have proved that we can have no evidence of the existence of a God from the principles of reason.

NOTES

1. [Pierre Simon, marquis de Laplace (1749–1827), French astronomer who devised the nebular hypothesis.]

2. See [Holbach's] *Le Système de la Nature:* this book is one of the most eloquent vindications of Atheism.

6

WHAT IS RELIGION?
(1899)

Robert G. Ingersoll

American lawyer and lecturer Robert G. Ingersoll (1833–1899), often called "the great agnostic," was the son of a fanatical Presbyterian preacher. He practiced law in Peoria, Illinois, and was for a time attorney general of Illinois; but further political offices were denied him because of prejudice against his anti-religious views. He began lecturing in 1877, speaking against religion and promoting humanism, achieving tremendous popularity but also earning the wrath of orthodox religionists. Among his numerous works are The Ghosts and Other Lectures *(1878),* Some Mistakes of Moses *(1879), and* The Christian Religion *(1882). His* Works *were published in 12 volumes in 1900. Recent editions include* On the Gods and Other Essays *(Prometheus Books, 1990) and* Reason, Tolerance, and Christianity: The Ingersoll Debates *(Prometheus Books, 1993). In "What Is Religion?" (his last public address, delivered before the American Free Religious Association in Boston on June 2, 1899), Ingersoll passionately argues that belief in God is chiefly based on fear; that the manifold hardships of human and animal life militate against belief in a benevolent god; and that morality is founded upon social relations, not the existence of God.*

I T IS ASSERTED THAT AN infinite God created all things, governs all things, and that the creature should be obedient and thankful to the creator; that the creator demands certain things, and that the person

From Robert G. Ingersoll, "What Is Religion?" (1899), in *The Works of Robert G. Ingersoll*, vol. 4 (New York: Dresden Publishing Co., 1900), pp. 479–96.

who complies with these demands is religious. This kind of religion has been substantially universal.

For many centuries and by many peoples it was believed that this God demanded sacrifices; that he was pleased when parents shed the blood of their babes. Afterward it was supposed that he was satisfied with the blood of oxen, lambs and doves, and that in exchange for or on account of these sacrifices, this God gave rain, sunshine and harvest. It was also believed that if the sacrifices were not made, this God sent pestilence, famine, flood and earthquake.

The last phase of this belief in sacrifice was, according to the Christian doctrine, that God accepted the blood of his son, and that after his son had been murdered, he, God, was satisfied, and wanted no more blood.

During all these years and by all these peoples it was believed that this God heard and answered prayer, that he forgave sins and saved the souls of true believers. This, in a general way, is the definition of religion.

Now, the questions are, Whether religion was founded on any known fact? Whether such a being as God exists? Whether he was the creator of yourself and myself? Whether any prayer was ever answered? Whether any sacrifice of babe or ox secured the favor of this unseen God?

First.—Did an infinite God create the children of men?

Why did he create the intellectually inferior?

Why did he create the deformed and helpless?

Why did he create the criminal, the idiotic, the insane?

Can infinite wisdom and power make any excuse for the creation of failures?

Are the failures under obligation to their creator?

Second.—Is an infinite God the governor of this world?

Is he responsible for all the chiefs, kings, emperors, and queens?

Is he responsible for all the wars that have been waged, for all the innocent blood that has been shed?

Is he responsible for the centuries of slavery, for the backs that have been scarred with the lash, for the babes that have been sold from the breasts of mothers, for the families that have been separated and destroyed?

Is this God responsible for religious persecution, for the Inquisition, for the thumb-screw and rack, and for all the instruments of torture?

Did this God allow the cruel and vile to destroy the brave and virtuous? Did he allow tyrants to shed the blood of patriots?

Did he allow his enemies to torture and burn his friends?

What is such a God worth?

Would a decent man, having the power to prevent it, allow his enemies to torture and burn his friends?

Can we conceive of a devil base enough to prefer his enemies to his friends?

If a good and infinitely powerful God governs this world, how can we account for cyclones, earthquakes, pestilence and famine?

How can we account for cancers, for microbes, for diphtheria and the thousand diseases that prey on infancy?

How can we account for the wild beasts that devour human beings, for the fanged serpents whose bite is death?

How can we account for a world where life feeds on life?

Were beak and claw, tooth and fang, invented and produced by infinite mercy?

Did infinite goodness fashion the wings of the eagles so that their fleeing prey could be overtaken?

Did infinite goodness create the beasts of prey with the intention that they should devour the weak and helpless?

Did infinite goodness create the countless worthless living things that breed within and feed upon the flesh of higher forms?

Did infinite wisdom intentionally produce the microscopic beasts that feed upon the optic nerve?

Think of blinding a man to satisfy the appetite of a microbe!

Think of life feeding on life! Think of the victims! Think of the Niagara of blood pouring over the precipice of cruelty!

In view of these facts, what, after all, is religion?

It is fear.

Fear builds the altar and offers the sacrifice.

Fear erects the cathedral and bows the head of man in worship.

Fear bends the knees and utters the prayer.

Fear pretends to love.

Religion teaches the slave-virtues—obedience, humility, self-denial, forgiveness, non-resistance.

Lips, religious and fearful, tremblingly repeat this passage: "Though he slay me, yet will I trust him."[1] This is the abyss of degradation.

Religion does not teach self-reliance, independence, manliness, courage, self-defence. Religion makes God a master and man his serf. The master cannot be great enough to make slavery sweet.

II.

If this God exists, how do we know that he is good? How can we prove that he is merciful, that he cares for the children of men? If this God exists, he has on many occasions seen millions of his poor children plowing the fields, sowing and planting the grain, and when he saw them he knew that they depended on the expected crop for life, and yet this good God, this merciful being, withheld the rain. He caused the sun to rise, to steal all moisture from the land, but gave no rain. He saw the seeds that man had planted wither and perish, but he sent no rain. He saw the people look with sad eyes upon the barren earth, and he sent no rain. He saw them slowly devour the little that they had, and saw them when the days of hunger came—saw them slowly waste away, saw their hungry, sunken eyes, heard their prayers, saw them devour the miserable animals that they had, saw fathers and mothers, insane with hunger, kill and eat their shriveled babes, and yet the heaven above them was as brass and the earth beneath as iron, and he sent no rain. Can we say that in the heart of this God there blossomed the flower of pity? Can we say that he cared for the children of men? Can we say that his mercy endureth forever?

Do we prove that this God is good because he sends the cyclone that wrecks villages and covers the fields with the mangled bodies of fathers, mothers and babes? Do we prove his goodness by showing that he has opened the earth and swallowed thousands of his helpless children, or that with the volcanoes he has overwhelmed them with rivers of fire? Can we infer the goodness of God from the facts we know?

If these calamities did not happen, would we suspect that God cared nothing for human beings? If there were no famine, no pestilence, no cyclone, no earthquake, would we think that God is not good?

According to the theologians, God did not make all men alike. He made races differing in intelligence, stature and color. Was there goodness, was there wisdom in this?

Ought the superior races to thank God that they are not the inferior? If we say yes, then I ask another question: Should the inferior races thank God that they are not superior, or should they thank God that they are not beasts?

When God made these different races he knew that the superior would enslave the inferior, knew that the inferior would be conquered, and finally destroyed.

If God did this, and knew the blood that would be shed, the agonies that would be endured, saw the countless fields covered with the corpses of the slain, saw all the bleeding backs of slaves, all the broken hearts of mothers bereft of babes, if he saw and knew all this, can we conceive of a more malicious fiend?

Why, then, should we say that God is good?

The dungeons against whose dripping walls the brave and generous have sighed their souls away, the scaffolds stained and glorified with noble blood, the hopeless slaves with scarred and bleeding backs, the writhing martyrs clothed in flame, the virtuous stretched on racks, their joints and muscles torn apart, the flayed and bleeding bodies of the just, the extinguished eyes of those who sought for truth, the countless patriots who fought and died in vain, the burdened, beaten, weeping wives, the shriveled faces of neglected babes, the murdered millions of the vanished years, the victims of the winds and waves, of flood and flame, of imprisoned forces in the earth, of lightning's stroke, of lava's molten stream, of famine, plague and lingering pain, the mouths that drip with blood, the fangs that poison, the beaks that wound and tear, the triumphs of the base, the rule and sway of wrong, the crowns that cruelty has worn and the robed hypocrites, with clasped and bloody hands, who thanked their God—a phantom fiend—that liberty had been banished from the world, these souvenirs of the dreadful past, these horrors that still exist, these frightful facts deny that any God exists who has the will and power to guard and bless the human race.

III. THE POWER THAT WORKS FOR RIGHTEOUSNESS

Most people cling to the supernatural. If they give up one God, they imagine another. Having outgrown Jehovah, they talk about the power that works for righteousness.

What is this power?

Man advances, and necessarily advances through experience. A man wishing to go to a certain place comes to where the road divides. He takes the left hand, believing it to be the right road, and travels until he finds that it is the wrong one. He retraces his steps and takes the right hand road and reaches the place desired. The next time he goes to the same place, he does not take the left hand road. He has tried that road, and knows that it is the wrong road. He takes the right road, and thereupon these theologians say, "There is a power that works for righteousness."

A child, charmed by the beauty of the flame, grasps it with its dimpled hand. The hand is burned, and after that the child keeps its hand out of the fire. The power that works for righteousness has taught the child a lesson.

The accumulated experience of the world is a power and force that works for righteousness. This force is not conscious, not intelligent. It has no will, no purpose. It is a result.

So thousands have endeavored to establish the existence of God by the fact that we have what is called the moral sense; that is to say, a conscience.

It is insisted by these theologians, and by many of the so-called philosophers, that this moral sense, this sense of duty, of obligation, was imported, and that conscience is an exotic. Taking the ground that it was not produced here, was not produced by man, they then imagine a God from whom it came.

Man is a social being. We live together in families, tribes and nations.

The members of a family, of a tribe, of a nation, who increase the happiness of the family, of the tribe or of the nation, are considered good members. They are praised, admired and respected. They are regarded as good; that is to say, as moral.

The members who add to the misery of the family, the tribe or the nation, are considered bad members. They are blamed, despised, punished. They are regarded as immoral.

The family, the tribe, the nation, creates a standard of conduct, of morality. There is nothing supernatural in this.

The greatest of human beings has said, "Conscience is born of love."

The sense of obligation, of duty, was naturally produced.

Among savages, the immediate consequences of actions are taken into consideration. As people advance, the remote consequences are perceived. The standard of conduct becomes higher. The imagination is cultivated. A man puts himself in the place of another. The sense of duty becomes stronger, more imperative. Man judges himself.

He loves, and love is the commencement, the foundation of the highest virtues. He injures one that he loves. Then comes regret, repentance, sorrow, conscience. In all this there is nothing supernatural.

Man has deceived himself. Nature is a mirror in which man sees his own image, and all supernatural religions rest on the presence that the image, which appears to be behind this mirror, has been caught.

All the metaphysicians of the spiritual type, from Plato to Swedenborg, have manufactured their facts, and all founders of religion have done the same.

Suppose that an infinite God exists, what can we do for him? Being infinite, he is conditionless; being conditionless, he cannot be benefited or injured. He cannot want. He has.

Think of the egotism of a man who believes that an infinite being wants his praise!

IV.

What has our religion done? Of course, it is admitted by Christians that all other religions are false, and consequently we need examine only our own.

Has Christianity done good? Has it made men nobler, more merciful, nearer honest? When the church had control, were men made better and happier?

What has been the effect of Christianity in Italy, in Spain, in Portugal, in Ireland?

What has religion done for Hungary or Austria? What was the effect of Christianity in Switzerland, in Holland, in Scotland, in England, in America? Let us be honest. Could these countries have been worse without religion? Could they have been worse had they had any other religion than Christianity?

Would Torquemada have been worse had he been a follower of Zoroaster? Would Calvin have been more bloodthirsty if he had believed in the religion of the South Sea Islanders?[2] Would the Dutch have been more idiotic if they had denied the Father, Son and Holy Ghost, and worshiped the blessed trinity of sausage, beer and cheese? Would John Knox have been any worse had he deserted Christ and become a follower of Confucius?[3]

Take our own dear, merciful Puritan Fathers. What did Christianity do for them? They hated pleasure. On the door of life they hung the crape of death. They muffled all the bells of gladness. They made cradles by putting rockers on coffins. In the Puritan year there were twelve Decembers. They tried to do away with infancy and youth, with prattle of babes and the song of the morning.

The religion of the Puritan was an unadulterated curse. The Puritan believed the Bible to be the word of God, and this belief has always made those who held it cruel and wretched. Would the Puritan have been worse if he had adopted the religion of the North American Indians?

Let me refer to just one fact showing the influence of a belief in the Bible on human beings.

"On the day of the coronation of Queen Elizabeth she was presented with a Geneva Bible by an old man representing Time, with Truth standing by his side as a child. The Queen received the Bible, kissed it, and pledged herself to diligently read therein. In the dedication of this blessed Bible the Queen was piously exhorted to put all Papists to the sword."

In this incident we see the real spirit of Protestant lovers of the Bible. In other words, it was just as fiendish, just as infamous as the Catholic spirit.

Has the Bible made the people of Georgia kind and merciful? Would the lynchers be more ferocious if they worshiped gods of wood and stone?

V. HOW CAN MANKIND BE REFORMED WITHOUT RELIGION?

Religion has been tried, and in all countries, in all times, has failed.

Religion has never made man merciful.

Remember the Inquisition.

What effect did religion have on slavery?

What effect upon Libby, Salisbury and Andersonville?[4]

Religion has always been the enemy of science, of investigation and thought.

Religion has never made man free.

It has never made man moral, temperate, industrious and honest.

Are Christians more temperate, nearer virtuous, nearer honest than savages?

Among savages do we not find that their vices and cruelties are the fruits of their superstitions?

To those who believe in the Uniformity of Nature, religion is impossible.

Can we affect the nature and qualities of substance by prayer? Can we hasten or delay the tides by worship? Can we change winds by sacrifice? Will kneelings give us wealth? Can we cure disease by supplication? Can we add to our knowledge by ceremony? Can we receive virtue or honor as alms?

Are not the facts in the mental world just as stubborn—just as necessarily produced—as the facts in the material world? Is not what we call mind just as natural as what we call body?

Religion rests on the idea that Nature has a master and that this master will listen to prayer; that this master punishes and rewards; that he loves praise and flattery and hates the brave and free.

Has man obtained any help from heaven?

NOTES

1. [Job 13:15.]
2. [Tomás de Torquemada (1420–1498), leader of the Spanish Inquisition. John Calvin (1509–1564), founder of Calvinism, who asserted that human beings are predestined for heaven or hell regardless of their actions during life.]
3. [John Knox (1515?–1572), leader of the Scottish Reformation.]
4. [The reference is to three notorious prisons in Virginia, North Carolina, and Georgia, respectively, where many prisoners died during the Civil War.]

7

IS THERE A GOD?
(1952)

Bertrand Russell

Bertrand Russell (1872–1970) studied mathematics at Trinity College, Cambridge, and later took up a fellowship there. He began writing in the 1890s, and his Principles of Mathematics *(1903) is a landmark work on the philosophy of mathematics. The brief paper "On Denoting" (1905) created a revolution in philosophy, especially in the realms of epistemology and the philosophy of language; it was followed by such works as* Our Knowledge of the External World *(1914),* An Inquiry into Meaning and Truth *(1940), and* Human Knowledge: Its Scope and Limits *(1948). Russell eventually came to believe that scientific knowledge must be the basis both of philosophical inquiry and of human conduct. A prolific writer, Russell also espoused numerous social and political causes: in his long life he protested both World War I and the Vietnam War. He frequently criticized orthodox religion, and thereby became embroiled in a celebrated controversy in 1940 when his appointment as a visiting lecturer at City College, New York, was withdrawn as a result of protests from Catholics who believed Russell to be an atheist and proponent of free love (a view arrived at by misreadings of such works as* Marriage and Morals, *1929). Ten years later he was awarded the Nobel Prize for literature. Some of Russell's writings on religion can be found in* Skeptical Essays *(1928),* Unpopular Essays *(1950), and* Why I Am Not a Christian *(1957). In the following*

From Bertrand Russell, "Is There a God?" (1952), in *The Collected Papers of Bertrand Russell, Volume 11: Last Philosophical Testament, 1943–68*, ed. John G. Slater and Peter Köllner (London: Routledge, 1997), pp. 543–48. Copyright © 1997 by Routledge. Reprinted by permission of Taylor & Francis Books Ltd. and the Bertrand Russell Peace Foundation.

essay—commissioned by Illustrated, *a London magazine, in 1952 but not published there—Russell refutes many of the standard arguments for the existence of God.*

T HE QUESTION WHETHER THERE IS a God is one which is decided on very different grounds by different communities and different individuals. The immense majority of mankind accept the prevailing opinion of their own community. In the earliest times of which we have definite history everybody believed in many gods. It was the Jews who first believed in only one. The first commandment, when it was new, was very difficult to obey because the Jews had believed that Baal and Ashtaroth and Dagon and Moloch and the rest were real gods but were wicked because they helped the enemies of the Jews. The step from a belief that these gods were wicked to the belief that they did not exist was a difficult one. There was a time, namely that of Antiochus IV, when a vigorous attempt was made to Hellenize the Jews. Antiochus decreed that they should eat pork, abandon circumcision, and take baths. Most of the Jews in Jerusalem submitted, but in country places resistance was more stubborn and under the leadership of the Maccabees the Jews at last established their right to their peculiar tenets and customs. Monotheism, which at the beginning of the Antiochan persecution had been the creed of only part of one very small nation, was adopted by Christianity and later by Islam, and so became dominant throughout the whole of the world west of India. From India eastward, it had no success: Hinduism had many gods; Buddhism in its primitive form had none; and Confucianism had none from the eleventh century onward. But, if the truth of a religion is to be judged by its worldly success, the argument in favor of monotheism is a very strong one, since it possessed the largest armies, the largest navies, and the greatest accumulation of wealth. In our own day this argument is growing less decisive. It is true that the un-Christian menace of Japan was defeated. But the Christian is now faced with the menace of atheistic Muscovite hordes, and it is not so certain as one could wish that atomic bombs will provide a conclusive argument on the side of theism.

But let us abandon this political and geographical way of considering religions, which has been increasingly rejected by thinking people ever since the time of the ancient Greeks. Ever since that time there have been men who were not content to accept passively the religious opinions of their neighbors, but endeavoured to consider what reason and philosophy might have to say about the matter. In the commercial cities of Ionia, where philosophy was invented, there were free-thinkers in the sixth century B.C. Compared to modern free-thinkers they had an easy task, because the Olympian gods, however charming to poetic fancy, were hardly such as could be defended by the metaphysical use of the unaided reason. They were met popularly by Orphism (to which Christianity owes much) and, philosophically, by Plato, from whom the Greeks derived a philosophical monotheism very different from the political and nationalistic monotheism of the Jews. When the Greek world became converted to Christianity it combined the new creed with Platonic metaphysics and so gave birth to theology. Catholic theologians, from the time of Saint Augustine to the present day, have believed that the existence of one God could be proved by the unaided reason. Their arguments were put into final form by Saint Thomas Aquinas in the thirteenth century. When modern philosophy began in the seventeenth century, Descartes and Leibniz took over the old arguments somewhat polished up, and, owing largely to their efforts, piety remained intellectually respectable. But Locke, although himself a completely convinced Christian, undermined the theoretical basis of the old arguments, and many of his followers, especially in France, became Atheists. I will not attempt to set forth in all their subtlety the philosophical arguments for the existence of God. There is, I think, only one of them which still has weight with philosophers, that is the argument of the First Cause. This argument maintains that, since everything that happens has a cause, there must be a First Cause from which the whole series starts. The argument suffers, however, from the same defect as that of the elephant and the tortoise. It is said (I do not know with what truth) that a certain Hindu thinker believed the earth to rest upon an elephant. When asked what the elephant rested upon, he replied that it rested upon a tortoise. When asked what the tortoise rested upon, he said, "I am tired of this. Suppose we change the subject." This illustrates the unsatisfactory character of the First-Cause argument. Nevertheless, you will find it in some ultra-modern treatises on physics, which contend that physical processes, traced backward in time, show that there must have been a sudden beginning and infer that this was due to divine Creation. They carefully abstain from attempts to show that this hypothesis makes matters more intelligible.

The scholastic arguments for the existence of a Supreme Being are now rejected by most Protestant theologians in favor of new arguments which to my mind are by no means an improvement. The scholastic arguments were genuine efforts of thought and, if their reasoning had been sound, they would have demonstrated the truth of their conclusion. The new arguments, which Modernists prefer, are vague; and the Modernists reject with contempt every effort to make them precise. There is an appeal to the heart as opposed to the intellect. It is not maintained that those who reject the new arguments are illogical, but that they are destitute of deep feeling or of moral sense. Let us nevertheless examine the modern arguments and see whether there is anything that they really prove.

One of the favourite arguments is from evolution. The world was once lifeless, and when life began it was a poor sort of life consisting of green slime and other uninteresting things. Gradually by the course of evolution, it developed into animals and plants and at last into MAN. Man, so the theologians assure us, is so splendid a Being that he may well be regarded as the culmination to which the long ages of nebula and slime were a prelude. I think the theologians must have been fortunate in their human contacts. They do not seem to me to have given due weight to Hitler or the Beast of Belsen.[1] If Omnipotence, with all time at its disposal, thought it worth while to lead up to these men through the many millions of years of evolution, I can only say that the moral and aesthetic taste involved is peculiar. However, the theologians no doubt hope that the future course of evolution will produce more men like themselves and fewer men like Hitler. Let us hope so. But, in cherishing this hope, we are abandoning the ground of experience and taking refuge in an optimism which history so far does not support.

There are other objections to this evolutionary optimism. There is every reason to believe that life on our planet will not continue forever so that any optimism based upon the course of terrestrial history must be temporary and limited in its purview. There may, of course, be life elsewhere but, if there is, we know nothing about it and have no reason to suppose that it bears more resemblance to the virtuous theologians than to Hitler. The earth is a very tiny corner of the universe. It is a little fragment of the solar system. The solar system is a little fragment of the Milky Way. And the Milky Way is a little fragment of the many millions of galaxies revealed by modern telescopes. In this little insignificant corner of the cosmos there is a brief interlude between two long lifeless epochs. In this brief interlude, there is a much briefer one containing man. If really man is the purpose of the universe the preface seems a little long. One is reminded of some prosy old gentleman who tells an interminable anecdote all quite uninteresting until the rather small point in which it ends. I do not think theologians show a suitable piety in making such a comparison possible.

It has been one of the defects of theologians at all times to over-estimate the importance of our planet. No doubt this was natural enough in the days before Copernicus when it was thought that the heavens revolve about the earth. But since Copernicus and still more since the modern exploration of distant regions, this pre-occupation with the earth has become rather parochial. If the universe had a Creator, it is hardly reasonable to suppose that He was specially interested in our little corner. And, if He was not, His values must have been different from ours, since in the immense majority of regions life is impossible.

There is a moralistic argument for belief in God, which was popularized by William James.[2] According to this argument, we ought to believe in God because, if we do not, we shall not behave well. The first and greatest objection to this argument is that, at its best, it cannot prove that there is a God but only that politicians and educators ought to try to make people think there is one. Whether this ought to be done or not is not a theological question but a political one. The arguments are of the same sort as those which urge that children should be taught respect for the flag. A man with any genuine religious feeling will not be content with the view that the belief in God is useful, because he will wish to know whether, in fact, there is a God. It is absurd to contend that the two questions are the same. In the nursery, belief in Father Christmas is useful, but grown-up people do not think that this proves Father Christmas to be real.

Since we are not concerned with politics we might consider this sufficient refutation of the moralistic argument, but it is perhaps worthwhile to pursue this a little further. It is, in the first place, very doubtful whether belief in God has all the beneficial moral effects that are attributed to it. Many of the best men known to history have been unbelievers. John Stuart Mill may serve as an instance. And many of the worst men known to history have been believers. Of this there are innumerable instances. Perhaps Henry VIII may serve as typical.

However that may be, it is always disastrous when governments set to work to uphold opinions for their utility rather than for their truth. As soon as this is done it becomes necessary to have a censorship to suppress adverse arguments, and it is thought wise to discourage thinking among the young for fear of encouraging "dangerous thoughts." When such malpractices are employed against religion as they are in Soviet Russia, the theologians can see that they are bad, but they are still bad when employed in defence of what the theologians think good. Freedom of thought and the habit of giving weight to evidence are matters of far greater moral import than the belief in this or that theological dogma. On all these grounds it cannot be maintained that theological beliefs should be upheld for their usefulness without regard to their truth.

There is a simpler and more naive form of the same argument, which appeals to many individuals. People will tell us that without the consolations of religion they would be intolerably unhappy. So far as this is true, it is a coward's argument. Nobody but a coward would consciously choose to live in a fool's paradise. When a man suspects his wife of infidelity, he is not thought the better of for shutting his eyes to the evidence. And I cannot see why ignoring evidence should be contemptible in one case and admirable in the other. Apart from this argument the importance of religion in contributing to individual happiness is very much exaggerated. Whether you are happy or unhappy depends upon a number of factors. Most people need good health and enough to eat. They need the good opinion of their social milieu and the affection of their intimates. They need not only physical health but mental health. Given all these things, most people will be happy whatever their theology. Without them, most people will be unhappy, whatever their theology. In thinking over the people I have known, I do not find that on the average those who had religious beliefs were happier than those who had not.

When I come to my own beliefs, I find myself quite unable to discern any purpose in the universe, and still more unable to wish to discern one. Those who imagine that the course of cosmic evolution is slowly leading up to some consummation pleasing to the Creator, are logically committed (though they usually fail to realize this) to the view that the Creator is not omnipotent or, if He were omnipotent, He could decree the end without troubling about means. I do not myself perceive any consummation toward which the universe is tending. According to the physicists, energy will be gradually more evenly distributed and as it becomes more evenly distributed it will become more useless. Gradually everything that we find interesting or pleasant, such as life and light, will disappear—so, at least, they assure us. The cosmos is like a theatre in which just once a play is performed, but, after the curtain falls, the theatre is left cold and empty until it sinks in ruins. I do not mean to assert with any positiveness that this is the case. That would be to assume more knowledge than we possess. I say only that it is what is probable on present evidence. I will not assert dogmatically that there is no cosmic purpose, but I will say that there is no shred of evidence in favor of there being one.

I will say further that, if there be a purpose and if this purpose is that of an Omnipotent Creator, then that Creator, so far from being loving and kind, as we are told, must be of a degree of wickedness scarcely conceivable. A man who commits a murder is considered to be a bad man. An Omnipotent Deity, if there be one, murders everybody. A man who willingly afflicted another with cancer would be considered a fiend. But the Creator, if He exists, afflicts many thousands every year with this dreadful disease. A man who, having the knowledge and power required to make his children good, chose instead to make them bad, would be viewed with execration. But God, if He exists, makes this choice in the case of very many of His children. The whole conception of an omnipotent God whom it is impious to criticize, could only have arisen under oriental despotisms where sovereigns, in spite of capricious cruelties, continued to enjoy the adulation of their slaves. It is the psychology appropriate to this outmoded political system which belatedly survives in orthodox theology.

There is, it is true, a Modernist form of theism, according to which God is not omnipotent, but is doing His best, in spite of great difficulties. This view, although it is new among Christians, is not new in the history of thought. It is, in fact, to be found in Plato. I do not think this view can be proved to be false. I think all that can be said is that there is no positive reason in its favour.

Many orthodox people speak as though it were the business of sceptics to disprove received dogmas rather than of dogmatists to prove them. This is, of course, a mistake. If I were to suggest that between the Earth and Mars there is a china teapot revolving about the sun in an elliptical orbit, nobody would be able to disprove my assertion provided I were careful to add that the teapot is too small to be revealed even by our most powerful telescopes. But if I were to go on to say that, since my assertion cannot be disproved, it is intolerable presumption on the part of human reason to doubt it, I should rightly be thought to be talking nonsense. If, however, the existence of such a teapot were affirmed in ancient books, taught as the sacred truth every Sunday, and instilled into the minds of children at school, hesitation to believe in its existence would become a mark of eccentricity and entitle the doubter to the attentions of the psychiatrist in an enlightened age or of the Inquisitor in an earlier time. It is customary to suppose that, if a belief is widespread, there must be something reasonable about it. I do not think this view can be held by anyone who has studied history. Practically all the beliefs of savages are absurd. In early civilizations there may be as much as one percent for which there is something to be said. In our own day. . . . But at this point I must be careful. We all know that there are absurd beliefs in Soviet Russia. If we are Protestants, we know that there are absurd beliefs among Catholics. If we are Catholics, we know that there are absurd beliefs among Protestants. If we are Conservatives, we are amazed by the superstitions to be found in the Labour Party. If we are Socialists, we are aghast at the credulity of Conservatives. I do not know, dear reader, what your beliefs may be, but whatever they may be, you must concede that nine-tenths of the beliefs of nine-tenths of mankind are totally irrational. The beliefs in question are, of course, those which you do not hold. I cannot, therefore, think it presumptuous to doubt something which has long been held to be true, especially when this opinion has only prevailed in certain geographical regions, as is the case with all theological opinions.

My conclusion is that there is no reason to believe any of the dogmas of traditional theology and, further, that there is no reason to wish that they were true. Man, in so far as he is not subject to natural forces, is free to work out his own destiny. The responsibility is his, and so is the opportunity.

NOTES

1. ["The Beast of Belsen" refers to Josef Kramer (1907-1945), the notoriously cruel commander of the Nazi concentration camp at Bergen-Belsen.]

2. [William James (1842–1910), American philosopher, founder of Pragmatism, and author of *The Will to Believe* (1897) and *The Varieties of Religious Experience* (1902). See also A. J. Ayer on James (pp. 104–105).]

00

THE CLAIMS OF THEOLOGY
(1973)

A. J. Ayer

Alfred Jules Ayer (1910–1989) spent most of his career lecturing at Oxford, becoming one of the leading philosophers of his time. He was an advocate of logical positivism, a philosophy heavily reliant upon empiricism and focusing on the principle of verification: in order for a proposition about the real world to be true, it must be capable of being verified by experience and observation. This principle was used as the basis for Ayer's attacks on statements relating to metaphysics, ethics, and religion, which in his view were unverifiable; such statements are, accordingly, neither true nor false but nonsensical. Ayer propounded his theories in Language, Truth and Logic *(1936)—one of the seminal philosophical works of the twentieth century—and many other volumes. In the following chapter from* The Central Questions of Philosophy *(1973), Ayer criticizes several arguments frequently used to bolster religious belief, including the argument from design, the connection of religion and morality, and the pragmatist argument that religious belief is beneficial because it is psychologically comforting.*

From A. J. Ayer, *The Central Questions of Philosophy* (1973; reprint, New York: William Morrow, 1974), pp. 211–13, 217–20, 223–26, 233–35. Copyright © 1973 by A. J. Ayer. Reprinted by permission of the Orion Publishing Group Ltd.

THE EXISTENCE OF GOD

I N W. H. MALLOCK'S SATIRE *The New Republic*, which was first published in the eighteen seventies, at a time when the conflict between
science and religion was at its height, a character representing Dr Jowett
is made to admit that an atheist opponent can disprove the existence of
God, as he would define him. "All atheists can do that." This does not,
however, disturb the doctor's faith. "For," he says, "the world has at present no adequate definition of God; and I think we should be able to
define a thing before we can satisfactorily disprove it."[1]

I said this was a satire, but the words which are put into Jowett's
mouth represent a point of view which is still not uncommon. People
who try to justify their belief in the existence of God by saying that it
rests on faith are sometimes maintaining no more than that the proposition that God exists is one which they have the right to accept, in
default of sufficient evidence; but sometimes they look to faith for the
assurance that the words "God exists" express some true proposition,
though they do not know what this proposition is; it is one that sur-
passes human understanding. The first of these positions is discussable,
though I think it misguided, but the second is merely disingenuous.
Until we have an intelligible proposition before us, there is nothing for
faith to get to work on. It can be an article of faith that beings of superhuman intelligence, if there are any, entertain propositions that we
cannot grasp. This requires only that we can make sense of the expression "beings with superhuman intelligence." But if we really cannot
grasp these propositions, if the sentences which purport to express them
have no meaning for us, then the fact, if it were a fact, that they did have
meaning for some other beings would be of little interest to us; for this
meaning might be anything whatsoever. The truth is, however, that those
who take this position do understand, or think they understand, something by the words "God exists." It is only when the account they give of
what they understand appears unworthy of credence that they take
refuge in saying that it falls short of what the words really mean. But
words have no meaning beyond the meaning that is given them, and a
proposition is not made the more credible by being treated as an
approximation to something that we do not find intelligible.

In fact, the world is not without descriptions of Gods, whether or not they severally or collectively count as adequate definitions. Until we are provided with a criterion of adequacy, this is a detail that need not detain us. Thus, those who believe in many Gods tend to ascribe properties to them which fit the human activities over which they are thought to preside. The God of War is martial, the God of Love amorous. In some, though not in all cases, these Gods are at least intermittently corporeal and they operate in space and time. Those who believe that there is just one God are in general agreement that he is an intelligent person, or something like one, that he feels emotions such as love or moral indignation, that he is incorporeal, except in the case of the Christian God, when, for a period of about thirty years, if one assumes the identity of the Son and the Father, he had what are ordinarily supposed to be the incompatible properties of being both corporeal and incorporeal, that, again with this exception, he is not located in space, though capable of acting in space, that he is either eternal or with the same exception not located in time, though capable of acting in time, that he created the world and continues to oversee it, that he is not subject to change, that he is all-powerful and all-knowing, that he is morally perfect and consequently supremely benevolent, and that he necessarily exists.

There may be some doubt whether the predicates that are ascribed to this one God are all of them meaningful or mutually consistent. For instance, we have found reason to think that if the notion of disembodied persons is intelligible at all, they must at least be located in time. Neither is it clear how a being that feels emotions can fail to be subject to change, unless we suppose that he feels the same emotions with the same intensity all the time, in which case there must be some danger of their sometimes lacking their appropriate objects. What is anyhow obvious is that these different predicates are for the most part not logically connected. We shall have to consider later on whether it is possible to make sense of the idea that the world was created. If this is a significant proposition, it may be taken to entail that the creator was intelligent. It may also be taken to entail that he was incorporeal, on the ground that the existence of a physical body could not precede the existence of the universe, though then it is not clear why the same should not apply to the existence of a mind. It surely does not entail that the creator is eternal; he might have come into existence at any time before he created the world or ceased to exist at any time after. Neither does it entail that he is all powerful. He might have wished but been unable to create a different world, and having created the world that he did, he might subsequently have found that it escaped wholly or partly from his control. It might also develop in ways that he was unable to foresee. Clearly also, there is no logical connection between having any degree of power, including the power to create the universe, and being morally good. Indeed, if one thought of the world's history as having been planned by its creator, a strong case could be made for inferring that he was malevolent. Finally, even if the creator could consistently possess all these other properties it would not follow that he necessarily existed. If he was thought to be a God, his possession of them might be necessary, in the sense that they were ascribed to any God by definition, but this would not entail that it was not a contingent proposition that the definition was actually satisfied. . . .

THE ARGUMENT FROM DESIGN

. . . The belief that the world affords sufficient evidence of an ulterior plan is responsible for the argument in favour of the existence of a God which is commonly known as the argument from design. The proponents of this argument do not take it to show that there necessarily is a God, but only that the assumption of his existence is a reasonable hypothesis. Their position is elegantly and fairly stated by one of the participants in Hume's *Dialogues Concerning Natural Religion.* "Look round the world: Contemplate the whole and every part of it: You will find it to be nothing but one great machine, subdivided into an infinite number of lesser machines, which again admit of subdivisions, to a degree beyond what human senses and faculties can trace and explain. All these various machines and even their most minute parts, are adjusted to each other with an accuracy, which ravishes into admiration all men, who have ever contemplated them. The curious adapting of means to ends, throughout all nature, resembles exactly, though it much exceeds, the productions of human contrivance; of human design, thought, wisdom, and intelligence. Since therefore the effects resemble each other, we are led to infer, by all the rules of analogy, that the causes also resemble: and that the Author of nature is somewhat similar to the mind of man: though possessed of much larger faculties, proportioned to the grandeur of the work, which he has executed."

Before we try to evaluate this argument, let us take a closer look at the conclusion. What properties is the author of nature supposed to have, and how is he related to the world for which he is made responsible? In the first place, as one of the other participants in Hume's dialogue remarks, there is nothing in the analogy to favour the assumption of a single author, rather than a multiplicity. There is nothing to favour the assumption that the world as we find it is the fruit of his only attempt to make a world, rather than the outcome of previous experiments on his own part or on that of others; if anything the analogy would point the other way. There is nothing either to license the inference that he is eternal or indeed that he is incorporeal; since all the designers that we have actually observed have been mortal and embodied, the analogy, if it were to be pressed, would again point the other way. It would suggest that his faculties are larger than ours, but not that he is omnipotent, nor yet that he is benevolent. The ascription of benevolence to him would require us to find empirical evidence not merely that the world had an author but that it had an author who meant well by the creatures whom he had put into it.

What now of the designer's relation to the world? If one supposes there to have been an act of creation, I do not see how one can avoid the conclusion that it took place at some time. If one supposes this to be the first instant in time, one will find it difficult to say in what sense the author of nature existed antecedently to its creation. The idea that he existed outside time is one to which it is difficult to attach any meaning. It is true that abstract entities can be said to exist outside time, if they can be said to exist at all, but the activities which are attributed to the deity are hardly such as are consistent with his existing after the fashion of an abstract entity. A more intelligible theory would be that events in his history temporally preceded the act of creation. This would be, in a way, to include him in the universe, but on the assumption of his existence, he would anyhow have to be included, if the universe was taken to comprehend everything that there is. The creation of the world as we know it would then appear more as a transformation, a radical change in the total course of events, though not necessarily as a transformation of preexisting matter. It is, however, to be noted that the analogy with the makers of human artifacts is still further weakened if we suppose the material world to have been created out of nothing at all.

In view of these difficulties, the proponents of this argument might be better advised to lay more stress upon the metaphor of the *author* of nature. Instead of comparing the world to a machine, which needed to be designed and built, they could compare it to a play, which needed to be written and directed. Among other things, this accords better with the ordinary concept of creation. The author, who would also be spectator and critic, would exist in time, but the time in which he existed would be incommensurable with that of the incidents in the play, which would have its own spatio-temporal structure. The participants in the play would not be able to verify the existence of its author, except on the dubious assumption that when they had played their parts they were somehow translated into his world, but it might be maintained that they could attach sense to the hypothesis that he existed, as the fundamental principle of a secondary system which they could use to account for the proceedings on their stage.

But now the question arises whether the character of the world as we know it gives any support to these analogies. The fact that regularities are detectable in it is not sufficient, for we have seen that no describable world can fail to exhibit some regularity. Neither is it sufficient that some processes within it are goal-directed, for the fact that ends are pursued and sometimes attained within a system is not a proof that the system as a whole is directed towards any end. What needs to be shown is that the entire universe presents the appearance of a teleological system. If one prefers the dramatic analogy, the play has to have a moral or at least some discernible plot. Can this requirement be met? It does not seem that it can. None of those who have compared the world to a vast machine has ever made any serious attempt to say what the machine could be for. They have spoken of there being an overall purpose, but have not said what it was. Again it will not do to say that there is a plan, but one too intricate for us to fathom. This answer might pass muster if the existence of a deity had been independently established, but if the sole reason given for believing in his existence is that the book of nature must have had an author, then the grounds for taking this metaphor seriously have to be produced.

Insofar as theists have held any view at all about the purpose for which the world was created, they have generally assumed that it had something to do with the emergence of man. This is a view which it is perhaps natural for men to take but hardly one that would be supported by a dispassionate consideration of the scientific evidence. Not only did man make a very late appearance upon the scene in a very small corner of the universe, but it is not even probable that, having made his appearance, he is there to say. As Russell put it, "The second law of thermodynamics makes it scarcely possible to doubt that the universe is running down, and that ultimately nothing of the slightest interest will be possible anywhere. Of course, it is open to us to say that when that time comes God will wind up the machinery again: but if we say this, we can base our assertion only upon faith, not upon one shred of scientific evidence. So far as scientific evidence goes, the universe has crawled by slow degrees to a somewhat pitiful result on this earth, and is going to crawl by still more pitiful stages to a condition of universal death. If this is to be taken as evidence of purpose, I can only say that the purpose is one that does not appeal to me. I see no reason therefore to believe in any sort of God, however vague and however attenuated."[2] . . .

RELIGION AND MORALITY

Is there any support for religious belief in the fact that men have moral sentiments to which their actions sometimes answer? The view that there is has been quite widely held. The main arguments which have been advanced in its favor are, first, that only the agency of God can account for the existence of morality, and, secondly, that God's authority is needed to give our moral standards some objective validity.

The first of these arguments seems very weak. The assumption which underlies it is that it is natural for men to behave only in a purely selfish manner. Consequently, if they sometimes forgo their interests, or what they believe to be their interests, in order to serve others, or because they think that the action which promotes their interests is wrong, or that some other course of action is morally binding on them, the ability to behave in this unnatural way must have been given to them by a higher power. Even if the starting-point of this argument were true, the reasoning would not be cogent, since it ignores the possibility that moral behaviour can be adequately explained in terms of social conditioning, but in fact it is not true. Antecedently to any actual observations that are made of human behaviour, there is no reason to expect it either to be selfish or to be unselfish; there is no reason to expect it either to conform or not to conform to any particular moral code. If it seems to us more natural for men to pursue their individual interests, this is only because they most commonly do so, at any rate in our own form of society. I believe that there are, or have been, societies in which it is more common for men to pursue the interest of some group of which they are members, their family or clan or tribe. But even if the prevalent tendency in all societies were for men to behave selfishly, it would not follow that unselfish behaviour was unnatural, in the sense of being contrary to nature. Nothing that actually happens is contrary to nature, though there are some actions that we misleadingly call unnatural as a way of expressing our disapproval of them. In fact, I think that a good case can be made for saying that altruistic impulses are innate, though they may be initially weaker in small children than the self-regarding or aggressive impulses. If they are not innate, at least the evidence shows that we have the capacity to acquire them. But how did we obtain this capacity? This question is on a level with any other question about the causes of human behaviour. It is no more and no less difficult than the question how we obtain our capacity to injure one another. If there were any good reason to believe that men were the outcome of a God's creation, their creator would be equally responsible for all their characteristics, however much or little we esteem them. Conversely, if there is otherwise no good reason to believe that men were so created, the fact that they behave unselfishly as well as selfishly to each other does not provide one.

In dealing with the argument that a God is required to ensure the objectivity of moral standards, we need to distinguish carefully between the motives for morality and its possible grounds. There is no doubt that belief in a God has frequently been the source of moral incentives. Sometimes the motive has been the altruistic one of love for a deity or a saint whose wishes one believes oneself to be carrying out, or love for other human beings on the ground that they are equally the children of God. Perhaps more frequently it has been the prudential motive of fear of future punishment or hope of future reward. It was the belief that men were not generally capable of behaving decently without this pru- dential motive that led Voltaire to say that if God did not exist it would be necessary to invent him.[3] This is a good epigram, but like many good epigrams, it probably distorts the truth. I do not know that a scientific study has ever been made of this question, but if one were to be made I doubt if it would reveal any strong correlation either of morally admirable behaviour with religious belief or of morally reprehensible behaviour with its absence. Much good has been done in the name of religion but also very much evil. When the long history of religious intolerance and persecution is taken into account, together with the tendency of religious hierarchies to side with the oppressors rather than the oppressed, it is arguable that the evil has outweighed the good. Many bad men have indeed been irreligious, but many agnostics and atheists have led very decent lives. Neither do those who are sincerely religious always live up to their good principles. My own conjecture is that the factors which make for the observance or disregard of morality are mainly psychological and social, and that religious belief has had a smaller influence either way than is commonly supposed. However this may be, it is clear that to show that belief in God had had a predominantly good effect would not be to show that the belief was true, any more than showing that it had had a predominantly bad effect would be to show that it was false.

I suspect that the widespread assumption that religious belief is necessary for the maintenance of moral standards arises not so much from any assessment of the empirical evidence as from a tacit or explicit acceptance of the proposition that if there is no God there is no reason to be moral. What is meant is that there is then no justification for morality, but because of the ambiguity of the word "reason," the fallacious inference is drawn that there is neither any ground nor any motive. The conclusion sought is that since there is reason to be moral, there is a God. This is the obverse of the Nietzschean idea that since God is dead, everything is permitted.

Whichever way it is taken, this proposition contains two serious errors, apart from the fallacy of thinking that the absence of grounds for morality entails the absence of motives. The first error is to suppose that morality needs an ulterior justification. The second error is to suppose that a God could supply it. The fallacy which is involved in thinking that morals could be founded on divine authority has been exposed by many philosophers, but perhaps most clearly and succinctly by Russell. "Theologians have always taught that God's decrees are good, and that this is not a mere tautology: it follows that goodness is logically independent of God's decrees."[4] The point is that moral standards can never be justified merely by an appeal to authority, whether the authority is taken to be human or divine. There has to be the additional premise that the person whose dictates we are to follow is good, or that what he commands is right, and this cannot be the mere tautology that he is what he is, or that he commands what he commands. This does not mean that we cannot look for guidance in conduct to those whom we judge to be better or wiser or more experienced than ourselves. To a greater or lesser extent, we can and do take our morals on trust but in so doing we are making a moral decision. We are at least implicitly judging that the rules which we have been brought up to respect, or the verdicts of our mentor, are morally right: and again this is not the mere tautology that these rules and verdicts just are what they are. . . .

THE MEANING OF LIFE

. . . There are . . . those who would say that in pursuing the question whether there is adequate evidence for a God's existence, we have been approaching the subject of religion in the wrong way. According to them, the question we should have been asking is not whether the proposition that God exists is true as a matter of fact, or acceptable as an explanatory hypothesis, but rather what function the belief in God fulfils in the lives of those who hold it. The justification for the belief may then be said to be that it makes the lives of those who hold it appear meaningful to them in a way that they otherwise would not.

This is substantially the position taken by the pragmatist William James. Having spoken in one book of "the craving of our nature for an ultimate peace behind all tempests, a blue zenith above all clouds,"[5] he criticizes in another the attempts of what he calls "systematic theology" to define the attributes of God. "Wherein," he asks, "is such a definition really instructive? It means less than nothing in its pompous robe of adjectives. Pragmatism alone can read a positive meaning into it, and for that she turns her back upon the intellectualist point of view altogether. 'God's in his heaven; all's right with the world'. *That's* the real heart of your theology, and for that you need no rationalist definitions."[6] Similarly, in his Gifford lectures on *The Varieties of Religious Experience* he speaks of his wish to vindicate "the instinctive belief of mankind: God is real since he produces real effects,"[7] and what he takes these real effects to be is no more than the feelings of greater energy, security and satisfaction which he thinks are enjoyed by those who hold religious beliefs.

As a psychological hypothesis, this could be questioned. For instance, the thesis of eternal damnation which has been a prominent feature of much Christian teaching is not likely to produce a feeling of greater security. On the other hand, there is no doubt that many people derive solace from the idea of their having a spiritual father who watches over them, especially when it is allied to the hope that he will secure to them in a future life the happiness which they may not have found in this one. To infer from this, however, that there is such a father, one needs to accept James's pragmatic theory that, since it is not to be expected of a religious hypothesis that it will either accord or fail to accord with any observable fact, the criterion for its truth is just that the vague assurance which it gives that "all's right with the world" is a source of emotional satisfaction. This is in line with the view of some contemporary theists that the doctrine associated with the religious practices in which they engage is acceptable as a useful myth. This view is so modest that it is hard to take issue with it, unless one wants to argue that the myth is harmful, but it does appear open to the practical objection that the satisfaction which most believers derive from their acceptance of religious doctrine depends upon their not judging it as mythical. A myth which is generally seen to be a myth must be in some danger of losing its utility.

But without the help of such a myth, can life be seen as having any meaning? The simple answer is that it can have just as much meaning as one is able to put into it. There is, indeed, no ground for thinking that human life in general serves any ulterior purpose but this is no bar to a man's finding satisfaction in many of the activities which make up his life, or to his attaching value to the ends which he pursues, including some that he himself will not live to see realized. One may deplore the fact that life is so short, but if it were not independently worth living there would be no good reason to wish it prolonged. Where the discarding of the Christian myth may have a cruel effect is in the denial to those whose lives have not been happy of any serious hope that they will survive to find the balance redressed.

NOTES

1. [W. H. Mallock (1849–1923) wrote *The New Republic* (1877), a novel that discusses a variety of literary, social, and philosophical subjects through conversations by characters who are thinly disguised versions of leading literary figures of the day. "Dr Jowett" is Benjamin Jowett (1817–1893), professor of Greek at Oxford and controversial religious thinker.]

2. Bertrand Russell, *Why I Am Not a Christian*, pp. 24–25.

3. Voltaire, *Epistles* XCVI.

4. Bertrand Russell, *Human Society in Ethics and Politics*, p. 48.

5. William James, *The Will to Believe*, p. 180.

6. William James, *Pragmatism*, pp. 121–22.

7. William James, *The Varieties of Religious Experience*, p. 517.

PART 3

THE
IMMORTALITY
MYTH

It is easy to remove the mind from harping on the lost illusion of immortality. The disciplined intellect fears nothing and craves no sugar-plum at the day's end, but is content to accept life and serve society as best it may. Personally I should not care for immortality in the least. There is nothing better than oblivion, since in oblivion there is no wish unfulfilled. We had it before we were born, yet did not complain. Shall we then whine because we know it will return? It is Elysium enough for me, at any rate.

—H. P. Lovecraft
In Defence of Dagon (1921)

9

ON THE NATURE OF THINGS
(ca. 60 B.C.E.)

Lucretius

Very little is authentically known of the life of the Latin poet Titus Lucretius Carus aside from the fact that he lived in the first half of the first century B.C.E. *and wrote a poem in six books,* De Rerum Natura *(On the Nature of Things), dedicated to the aristocrat Gaius Memmius. This treatise is not only the most exhaustive exposition of the philosophy of Epicurus that has survived from antiquity but one of the imperishable masterworks of Latin literature. In the following extract from Book 3, Lucretius broaches several arguments for the mortality of the soul (which the Epicureans believed to be material); he concludes with a piquant passage in which personified Nature berates a man for bemoaning his untimely death, pointing out that his conscious mind will not be extant and urging him to "take your departure like a guest filled with life."*

NOW MARK ME: THAT YOU may know that the minds and light souls of living creatures have birth and are mortal, I will go on to set forth verses worthy of your attention, got together by long study and invented with welcome effort. Make sure to link both of them to one name, and when for instance I shall choose to speak of the soul, showing it to be mortal, believe that I speak of the mind as well, inasmuch as both make up one thing and are one united substance. . . .

From Lucretius, *On the Nature of Things*, trans. H. A. J. Munro (1864; reprint London: George Bell & Sons, 1908), pp. 97, 98–101, 102–103, 106–107, 111–17, 118–19 (revised by S. T. Joshi).

Again we perceive that the mind is begotten along with the body and grows up together with it and becomes old along with it. For even as children go about with a tottering and weakly body, so slender sagacity of mind follows along with it; then when their life has reached the maturity of confirmed strength, the judgment too is greater and the power of the mind more developed. Afterwards when the body has been shattered by the mastering might of time and the frame has drooped with its forces dulled, then the intellect halts, the tongue dotes, the mind gives way, all faculties fail and are found wanting at the same time. It naturally follows then that the whole nature of the soul is dissolved, like smoke, into the high air; since we see it is begotten along with the body and grows up along with it and, as I have shown, breaks down at the same time worn out with age.

Moreover we see that even as the body is liable to violent diseases and severe pain, so is the mind to sharp cares and grief and fear; it naturally follows therefore that it is its partner in death as well. Again in diseases of the body the mind often wanders and goes astray; for it loses its reason and drivels in its speech and often in a profound lethargy is carried into deep and never-ending sleep with drooping eyes and head; out of which it neither hears the voices nor can recognise the faces of those who stand round calling it back to life and bedewing face and cheeks with tears. Therefore you must admit that the mind too dissolves, since the infection of disease reaches to it. For pain and disease are both forgers of death: a truth we have fully learned ere now by the death of many. Again, when the pungent strength of wine has entered into a man and its spirit has been infused into and transmitted through his veins, why is it that a heaviness of the limbs follows along with this, his legs are hampered as he reels about, his tongue falters, his mind is besotted, his eyes swim, shouting hiccuping wranglings are rife, together with all the other usual concomitants, why is all this, if not because the overpowering violence of the wine is accustomed to disorder the soul within the body? But whenever things can be disordered and hampered, they give token that if a somewhat more potent cause gained an entrance, they would perish and be robbed of all further existence. Moreover it often happens that someone constrained by the violence of disease suddenly drops down before our eyes, as by a stroke of lightning, and foams at the mouth, moans and shivers through his frame, loses his reason, stiffens his muscles, is racked, gasps for breath fitfully, and wearies his limbs with tossing. Sure enough, because the violence of the disease spreads itself through his frame and disorders him, he foams as he tries to eject his soul, just as in the salt sea the waters boil with the mastering might of the winds. A moan too is forced out, because the limbs are seized with pain, and mainly because seeds of voice are driven forth and are carried in a close mass out by the mouth, the road which they are accustomed to take and where they have a well-paved way. Loss of reason follows, because the powers of the mind and soul are disordered and, as I have shown, are riven and forced asunder, torn to pieces by the same baneful malady. Then after the cause of the disease has bent its course back and the acrid humours of the distempered body return to their hiding-places, then he first gets up like one reeling, and by little and little comes back into full possession of his senses and regains his soul. Since therefore even within the body mind and soul are harassed by such violent distempers and so miserably racked by sufferings, why do you believe that outside the body in the open air they can continue existence battling with fierce winds? And since we perceive that the mind is healed like the sick body, and we see that it can be altered by medicine, this too gives warning that the mind has a mortal existence. For it is natural that whosoever essays and attempts to change the mind or seeks to alter any other nature you like, should add new parts or change the arrangement of the present, or withdraw in short some tittle from the sum. But that which is immortal wills not to have its parts transposed nor any addition to be made nor one tittle to ebb away; for whenever a thing changes and quits its proper limits, this change is at once the death of that which was before. Therefore the mind, whether it is sick or whether it is altered by medicine, as I have shown, gives forth signs of mortality. . . .

And since the mind is one part of a man which remains fixed in a particular spot, just as are the ears and eyes and the other senses which guide and direct life; and just as the hand or eye or nose when separated from us cannot feel and exist apart, but in a very short time wastes away in putrefaction, thus the mind cannot exist by itself without the body and the man himself, which as you see serves for the mind's vessel or anything else you choose to imagine which implies a yet closer union with it, since the body is attached to it by the closest ties.

Again the quickened powers of body and mind by their joint partnership enjoy health and life; for the nature of the mind cannot by itself alone without the body give forth vital motions nor can the body again bereft of the soul continue to exist and make use of its senses: just as the eye itself torn away from its roots cannot see anything when apart from the whole body, thus the soul and mind cannot do anything by themselves. Sure enough, because mixed up through veins and flesh, sinews and bones, their first-beginnings are confined by the entire body and are not free to bound away leaving great spaces between, therefore thus shut in they make those sense-giving motions which they cannot make after death when forced out of the body into the air because they are not then confined in a like manner; for the air will be a body and a living thing, if the soul is able to keep itself together and to enclose in it those motions which it previously used to perform in the sinews and within the body. . . .

Again if the nature of the soul is immortal and makes its way into our body at the time of birth, why are we unable to remember the time already gone, and why do we retain no traces of past actions? If the power of the mind has been so completely changed that all remembrance of past things is lost, that, I think, differs not widely from death; therefore you must admit that the soul which was before has perished and that which now is has now been formed.

Again if the quickened power of the mind is wont to be put into us after our body is fully formed, at the instant of our birth and our crossing the threshold of life, it ought in accordance with this to live not in such a way as to seem to have grown with the body and together with its members within the blood, but as in a den apart by and to itself; for it is so closely united with the body throughout the veins, flesh, sinews, and bones, that the very teeth have a share of sense; as their aching proves and the sharp twinge of cold water and the crunching of a rough stone, when it has got into them out of bread. Wherefore, again and again I say, we must believe souls to be neither without a birth nor exempted from the law of death; for we must not believe that they could have been so completely united with our bodies, if they found their way into them from without, nor, since they are so closely inwoven with them, does it appear that they can get out unharmed and unloose themselves unscathed from all the sinews and bones and joints. But if by chance you believe that the soul finds its way in from without and is wont to ooze through all our limbs, so much the more it will perish thus blended with the body; for what oozes through another is dissolved, and therefore dies. As food distributed through all the cavities of the body, while it is transmitted into the limbs and the whole frame, is destroyed and furnishes out of itself the matter of another nature, thus the soul and mind, though they pass entire into a fresh body, yet in oozing through it are dissolved, while there are transmitted, as it were, into the frame through all the cavities those particles of which this nature of mind is formed, which now is sovereign in our body, being born out of that soul which then perished when dispersed through the frame. Wherefore the nature of the soul is seen to be neither without a birthday nor exempt from death. . . .

Death is therefore nothing to us, concerns us not a jot, since the nature of the mind is proved to be mortal; and as in time gone by we felt no distress, when the Poeni from all sides came together to do battle, and all things shaken by war's fearful uproar shuddered and quaked beneath high heaven, and mortal men were in doubt which of the two peoples it should be to whose empire all must fall by sea and land alike, thus when we shall be no more, when there shall have been a separation of body and soul, out of both of which we are each formed into a single being, to us, you may be sure, who then shall be no more, nothing whatever can happen to excite sensation, not if earth were to be mingled with sea and sea with heaven. And even supposing the nature of the mind and power of the soul do feel, after they have been severed from our body, yet that is nothing to us who by the binding tie of marriage between body and soul are formed each into one single being. And if time should gather up our matter after our death and put it once more into the position in which it now is, and the light of life be given to us again, even this result would concern us not at all, when the chain of our self-consciousness has once been snapped asunder. So now we give ourselves no concern about any self which we have been before, nor do we feel any distress on the score of that self. For when you look back on the whole past course of immeasurable time and think how manifold are the shapes which the motions of matter take, you may easily believe that these very same seeds of which we now are formed have often before been placed in the same order in which they now are; and yet we cannot recover this in memory: a break in our existence has been interposed, and all the motions have wandered to and fro far astray from the sensations they produced. For he upon whom evil is to befall must in his own person exist at the very time it comes, if the misery and suffering are by chance to have any place at all; but since death precludes this, and forbids him to be, upon whom the ills can be brought, you may be sure that we have nothing to fear after death, and that he who does not exist cannot become miserable, and that it matters not a whit whether he has been born into life at any other time, when immortal death has taken away his mortal life.

Therefore when you see a man bemoaning the fact that after death he shall either rot with his body laid in the grave or be devoured by flames or the jaws of wild beasts, you may be sure that his ring betrays a flaw and that there lurks in his heart a secret goad, though he himself declares that he does not believe that any sense will remain to him after death. He does not, I think, really grant the conclusion which he professes to grant nor the principle which he so professes, nor does he take and force himself root and branch out of life, but all unconsciously imagines something of himself to survive. For when anyone in life suggests to himself that birds and beasts will rend his body after death, he pities himself: he does not separate himself from that self, nor withdraws himself fully from the body so thrown out, and fancies himself that other self and stands by and impregnates it with his own sense. Hence he moans that he has been born mortal, and sees not that after real death there will be no other self to remain in life and lament to itself that his own self has met death, and there to stand and grieve that his own self is lying there mangled or burnt. For if it is an evil after death to be pulled about by the devouring jaws of wild beasts, I cannot see why it should not be a cruel pain to be laid on fires and burn in hot flames, or to be placed in honey and stifled, or to stiffen with cold, stretched on the smooth surface of an icy slab of stone, or to be pressed down and crushed by a load of earth above.

"Now no more shall your house admit you with glad welcome, nor an excellent wife and sweet children run to be the first to snatch kisses and touch your heart with a silent joy. No more may you be prosperous in thy doings, a safeguard to your own people. One evil day has taken from you, luckless man, in luckless wise all the many prizes of life." This do men say; but add not thereto, "and now no longer does any craving for these things come upon you either." For if they could rightly perceive this in thought and follow up the thought in words, they would release themselves from great distress and apprehension of mind. "You, even as you now are, sunk in the sleep of death, shall continue so to be for all future time, freed from all distressful pains; but we with an insatiable sorrow wept for you, when close by you turned to an ashen hue on your appalling funeral pile, and no length of days shall pluck from our hearts our ever-enduring grief." This question therefore should be asked of this speaker, what there is in it so passing bitter, if it comes in the end to sleep and rest, that any one should pine in never-ending sorrow.

This too men often, when they have reclined at table with cup in hand and shade their brows with crowns, love to say from the heart, "Short is this enjoyment, for poor weak men; presently it will be over and never after may it be called back." As if after their death it will be one of their chiefest afflictions that thirst and parching drought is to burn up these hapless wretches, or a craving for anything else is to come upon them. No one feels the want of himself and life at the time when mind and body are together sunk in sleep; for all we care this sleep might be everlasting, no craving whatever for ourselves then moves us. And yet by no means do those first-beginnings throughout our frame wander at that time far away from their sense-producing motions, at the moment when a man starts up from sleep and collects himself. Death therefore must be thought to concern us much less, if there can be less than what we see to be nothing; for a greater dispersion of the mass of matter follows after death, and no one wakes up, upon whom the chill cessation of life has once come.

Once more, if the nature of things could suddenly utter a voice and in person could chide any of us in such words as these, "What do you, O mortal, have so much at heart, that you go to such lengths in sickly sorrows? Why bemoan and bewail death? For say your life past and gone has been welcome to you and your blessings have not all, as if they were poured into a perforated vessel, run through and been lost without avail: why not then take your departure like a guest filled with life, and with resignation, you fool, enter upon untroubled rest? But if all that you have enjoyed has been squandered and lost, and life is a grievance, why seek to make any addition, to be wasted perversely in its turn and lost utterly without avail? Why not rather make an end of life and travail? For there is nothing more which I can contrive and discover to give you pleasure: all things are ever the same. Though your body is not yet decayed with years nor your frame worn out and exhausted, yet all things remain the same, even though in length of life you should outlast all races of things now living, nay even more if you should never die," what answer have we to make save this, that nature sets up against us a well-founded claim and puts forth in her pleading a true indictment? If, however, one of greater age and more advanced in years should complain and lament, poor wretch, his death more than is right, would she not with greater cause raise her voice and rally him in sharp accents, "Away from this time forth with your tears, rascal; a truce to your complainings: you decay after full enjoyment of all the prizes of life. But because you always yearn for what is not present, and despise what is, life has slipped from your grasp unfinished and unsatisfying, and unbeknownst to you, death has taken his stand at your pillow, before you could take your departure sated and filled. Now, however, resign all things unsuited to your age, and with a good grace get up and go: you must." With good reason, I think, she would bring her charge, with reason chide and reproach; for old things give way and are supplanted by new without fail, and one thing must ever be replenished out of other things; and no one is given over to the pit and black Tartarus: matter is needed for later generations to grow; all of which, nevertheless, will follow you when they have finished their term of life; and thus it is that all these no less than you have before this come to an end and hereafter will come to an end. Thus one thing will never cease to rise out of another, and life is granted to none in fee-simple, to all in usufruct. Think too how the bygone antiquity of everlasting time before our birth was nothing to us. Nature therefore holds this up to us as a mirror of the time yet to come after our death. Is there anything in this that looks appalling, anything that wears an aspect of gloom? Is it not more untroubled than any sleep? . . .

This too you may sometimes say to yourself, "Even worthy Ancus[1] has quitted the light with his eyes, who was far far better than you, worthless man. And since then many other kings and rulers have been laid low, who lorded it over mighty nations. He too, even he who first paved a way over the great sea and made a path for his legions to march over the deep and taught them to pass on foot over the salt pools and set at naught the roarings of the sea, trampling on them with his horses, had the light taken from him and shed forth his soul from his dying body. The son of the Scipios,[2] thunderbolt of war, terror of Carthage, yielded his bones to earth just as if he were the lowest menial. Think too of the inventors of all sciences and graceful arts, think of the companions of the Heliconian maids; among whom Homer bore the sceptre without a peer, and he now sleeps the same sleep as others. Then there is Democritus,[3] who, when a ripe old age had warned him that the memory-waking motions of his mind were waning, by his own spontaneous act offered up his head to death. Even Epicurus passed away, when his light of life had run its course, he who surpassed in intellect the race of man and quenched the light of all, as the ethereal sun arisen quenches the stars. Will you then hesitate and think it a hardship to die?—you for whom life is well-nigh dead whilst yet you live and see the light, who spend the greater part of your time in sleep and snore wide awake and cease not to see visions and have a mind troubled with groundless terror and cannot often discover what it is that ails you, when, besotted man, you are sore pressed on all sides with many cares and go astray tumbling about in the wayward wanderings of your mind.

NOTES

1. [Ancus Marcius (d. 616 B.C.E.), by tradition the fourth king of Rome, who extended Roman territories to the sea and built the port of Ostia.]

2. [P. Cornelius Scipio Africanus Major (236–184 B.C.E.), Roman general who defeated Hannibal in 202 B.C.E., ending the Punic wars.]

3. [Democritus of Abdera (460?–370? B.C.E.), co-founder with Leucippus of Greek atomism, whose metaphysical theories were adopted with modifications by Epicurus (341–271 B.C.E.).]

10

IMMORTALITY
(1868–70)

John Stuart Mill

John Stuart Mill (1806–1873) was born in London, the son of the Scottish philosopher James Mill. Educated by his father and such of his friends as Jeremy Bentham and David Ricardo, Mill showed tremendous precocity in his youth. He worked with his father in the East India Company beginning in 1823, remaining there until 1858. His System of Logic *(1843) established him as a leading British philosopher; he advocated a radical empiricism, maintaining that all knowledge was derived from experience alone. He also wrote trenchantly on political and social subjects:* On Liberty *(1859) is an imperishable statement of political liberalism;* Utilitarianism *(1861) expands on Bentham's ethical principle of the greatest happiness for the greatest number; and* The Subjection of Women *(1869) is a pioneering feminist tract. Throughout his life Mill developed skepticism in regard to religious doctrine; his views were incorporated in the posthumously published* Three Essays on Religion *(1874). In the following extract—taken from the essay on "Theism," written between 1868 and 1870—Mill maintains that belief in life after death is intellectually unwarranted.*

THE INDICATIONS OF IMMORTALITY MAY be considered in two divisions: those which are independent of any theory respecting the Creator and his intentions, and those which depend upon an antecedent belief on that subject.

From John Stuart Mill, "Immortality," in *Three Essays on Religion: Nature, The Utility of Religion, and Theism* (1874; reprint, Amherst, N.Y.: Prometheus Books, 1998), pp. 196–99, 203–10.

Of the former class of arguments speculative men have in different ages put forward a considerable variety, of which those in the Phaedon of Plato are an example; but they are for the most part such as have no adherents, and need not be seriously refuted, now. They are generally founded upon preconceived theories as to the nature of the thinking principle in man, considered as distinct and separable from the body, and on other preconceived theories respecting death. As, for example, that death, or dissolution, is always a separation of parts; and the soul being without parts, being simple and indivisible, is not susceptible of this separation. Curiously enough, one of the interlocutors in the Phaedon anticipates the answer by which an objector of the present day would meet this argument: namely, that thought and consciousness, though mentally distinguishable from the body, may not be a substance separable from it, but a result of it, standing in a relation to it (the illustration is Plato's) like that of a tune to the musical instrument on which it is played; and that the arguments used to prove that the soul does not die with the body, would equally prove that the tune does not die with the instrument, but survives its destruction and continues to exist apart. In fact, those moderns who dispute the evidences of the immortality of the soul, do not, in general, believe the soul to be a substance *per se*, but regard it as the name of a bundle of attributes, the attributes of feeling, thinking, reasoning, believing, willing, &c., and these attributes they regard as a consequence of the bodily organization, which therefore, they argue, it is as unreasonable to suppose surviving when that organization is dispersed, as to suppose the colour or odour of a rose surviving when the rose itself has perished. Those, therefore, who would deduce the immortality of the soul from its own nature have first to prove that the attributes in question are not attributes of the body but of a separate substance. Now what is the verdict of science on this point? It is not perfectly conclusive either way. In the first place, it does not prove, experimentally, that any mode of organization has the power of producing feeling or thought. To make that proof good it would be necessary that we should be able to produce an organism, and try whether it would feel; which we cannot do; organisms cannot by any human means be produced, they can only be developed out of a previous organism. On the other hand, the evidence is well nigh complete that all thought and feeling has some action of the bodily organism for its immediate antecedent or accompaniment; that the specific variations and especially the different degrees of complication of the nervous and cerebral organization, correspond to differences in the development of the mental faculties; and though we have no evidence, except negative, that the mental consciousness ceases for ever when the functions of the brain are at an end, we do know that diseases of the brain disturb the mental functions and that decay or weakness of the brain enfeebles them. We have therefore sufficient evidence that cerebral action is, if not the cause, at least, in our present state of existence, a condition *sine qua non* of mental operations; and that assuming the mind to be a distinct substance, its separation from the body would not be, as some have vainly flattered themselves, a liberation from trammels and restoration to freedom, but would simply put a stop to its functions and remand it to unconsciousness, unless and until some other set of conditions supervenes, capable of recalling it into activty, but of the existence of which experience does not give us the smallest indication. . . .

The belief, however, in human immortality, in the minds of mankind generally, is probably not grounded on any scientific arguments either physical or metaphysical, but on foundations with most minds much stronger, namely on one hand the disagreeableness of giving up existence, (to those at least to whom it has hitherto been pleasant) and on the other the general traditions of mankind. The natural tendency of belief to follow these two inducements, our own wishes and the general assent of other people, has been in this instance reinforced by the utmost exertion of the power of public and private teaching; rulers and instructors having at all times, with the view of giving greater effect to their mandates whether from selfish or from public motives, encouraged to the utmost of their power the belief that there is a life after death, in which pleasures and sufferings far greater than on earth, depend on our doing or leaving undone while alive, what we are commanded to do in the name of the unseen powers. As causes of belief these various circumstances are most powerful. As rational grounds of it they carry no weight at all.

That what is called the consoling nature of an opinion, that is, the pleasure we should have in believing it to be true, can be a ground for believing it, is a doctrine irrational in itself and which would sanction half the mischievous illusions recorded in history or which mislead individual life. It is sometimes, in the case now under consideration, wrapt up in a quasi-scientific language. We are told that the desire of immortality is one of our instincts, and that there is no instinct which has not corresponding to it a real object fitted to satisfy it. Where there is hunger there is somewhere food, where there is sexual feeling there is somewhere sex, where there is love there is somewhere something to be loved, and so forth: in like manner since there is the instinctive desire of eternal life, eternal life there must be. The answer to this is patent on the very surface of the subject. It is unnecessary to go into any recondite considerations concerning instincts, or to discuss whether the desire in question is an instinct or not. Granting that wherever there is an instinct there exists something such as that instinct demands, can it be affirmed that this something exists in boundless quantity, or sufficient to satisfy the infinite craving of human desires? What is called the desire of eternal life is simply the desire of life; and does there not exist that which this desire calls for? Is there not life? And is not the instinct, if it be an instinct, gratified by the possession and preservation of life? To suppose that the desire of life guarantees to us personally the reality of life through all eternity, is like supposing that the desire of food assures us that we shall always have as much as we can eat through our whole lives and as much longer as we can conceive our lives to be protracted to.

The argument from tradition or the general belief of the human race, if we accept it as a guide to our own belief, must be accepted entire: if so we are bound to believe that the souls of human beings not only survive after death but show themselves as ghosts to the living; for we find no people who have had the one belief without the other. Indeed it is probable that the former belief originated in the latter, and that primitive men would never have supposed that the soul did not die with the body if they had not fancied that it visited them after death. Nothing could be more natural than such a fancy; it is, in appearance, completely realized in dreams, which in Homer and in all ages like Homer's, are supposed to be real apparitions. To dreams we have to add not merely waking hallucinations but the delusions, however baseless, of sight and hearing, or rather the misinterpretations of those senses, sight or hearing supplying mere hints from which imagination paints a complete picture and invests it with reality. These delusions are not to be judged of by a modern standard: in early times the line between imagination and perception was by no means clearly defined; there was little or none of the knowledge we now possess of the actual course of nature, which makes us distrust or disbelieve any appearance which is at variance with known laws. In the ignorance of men as to what were the limits of nature and what was or was not compatible with it, no one thing seemed, as far as physical considerations went, to be much more improbable than another. In rejecting, therefore, as we do, and as we have the best reason to do, the tales and legends of the actual appearance of disembodied spirits, we take from under the general belief of mankind in a life after death, what in all probability was its chief ground and support, and deprive it of even the very little value which the opinion of rude ages can ever have as evidence of truth. If it be said that this belief has maintained itself in ages which have ceased to be rude and which reject the superstitions with which it once was accompanied, the same may be said of many other opinions of rude ages, and especially on the most important and interesting subjects, because it is on those subjects that the reigning opinion, whatever it may be, is the most sedulously inculcated upon all who are born into the world. This particular opinion, moreover, if it has on the whole kept its ground, has done so with a constantly increasing number of dissentients, and those especially among cultivated minds. Finally, those cultivated minds which adhere to the belief ground it, we may reasonably suppose, not on the belief of others, but on arguments and evidences; and those arguments and evidences, therefore, are what it concerns us to estimate and judge.

The preceding are a sufficient sample of the arguments for a future life which do not suppose an antecedent belief in the existence, or any theory respecting the attributes of the Godhead. It remains to consider what arguments are supplied by such lights, or such grounds of conjecture, as natural theology affords, on those great questions.

We have seen that these lights are but faint; that of the existence of a Creator they afford no more than a preponderance of probability; of his benevolence a considerably less preponderance; that there is, however, some reason to think that he cares for the pleasures of his creatures, but by no means that this is his sole care, or that other purposes do not often take precedence of it. His intelligence must be adequate to the contrivances apparent in the universe, but need not be more than adequate to them, and his power is not only not proved to be infinite, but the only real evidences in natural theology tend to show that it is limited, contrivance being a mode of overcoming difficulties, and always supposing difficulties to be overcome.

We have now to consider what inference can legitimately be drawn from these premises, in favor of a future life. It seems to me, apart from express revelation, none at all.

The common arguments are, the goodness of God; the improbability that he would ordain the annihilation of his noblest and richest work, after the greater part of its few years of life had been spent in the acquisition of faculties which time is not allowed him to turn to fruit; and the special improbability that he would have implanted in us an instinctive desire of eternal life, and doomed that desire to complete disappointment.

These might be arguments in a world the constitution of which made it possible without contradiction to hold it for the work of a Being at once omnipotent and benevolent. But they are not arguments in a world like that in which we live. The benevolence of the divine Being may be perfect, but his power being subject to unknown limitations, we know not that he could have given us what we so confidently assert that he must have given; *could* (that is) without sacrificing something more important. Even his benevolence, however justly inferred, is by no means indicated as the interpretation of his whole purpose, and since we cannot tell how far other purposes may have interfered with the exercise of his benevolence, we know not that he *would*, even if he could have granted us eternal life. With regard to the supposed improbability of his having given the wish without its gratification, the same answer may be made; the scheme which either limitation of power, or conflict of purposes, compelled him to adopt, may have *required* that we should have the wish although it were not destined to be gratified. One thing, however, is quite certain in respect to God's government of the world; that he either could not, or would not, grant to us every thing we wish. We wish for life, and he has granted some life: that we wish (or some of us wish) for a boundless extent of life and that it is not granted, is no exception to the ordinary modes of his government. Many a man would like to be a Croesus or an Augustus Caesar, but has his wishes gratified only to the moderate extent of a pound a week or the Secretaryship of his Trades Union. There is, therefore, no assurance whatever of a life after death, on grounds of natural religion.

11

CAN WE SURVIVE
OUR OWN DEATHS?
(1993)

Antony Flew

Antony Flew (b. 1923) is a leading British philosopher. Born in London, he has taught at Oxford, the University of Aberdeen, the University of Keele, and the University of Reading, where he is now emeritus professor of philosophy. Among his numerous works are God and Philosophy *(1966),* An Introduction to Western Philosophy *(1971),* The Presumption of Atheism *(1976; revised as* God, Freedom and Immortality *[Prometheus Books, 1984]),* The Logic of Morality *(1987), and (with Terry Miethe)* Does God Exist? *(1991). In the following chapter from* Atheistic Humanism *(1993), Flew points out the logical fallacies in several recent attempts to justify belief in the immortality of the soul.*

Whether we are to live in a future state, as it is the most important question which can possibly be asked, so it is the most intelligible one which can be expressed in language. Yet strange perplexities have been raised about the meaning of that identity or sameness of person, which is implied in the notion of our living now and hereafter, or in any two successive moments.

Joseph Butler (1692–1752)[1]

I T IS BECAUSE THE IDEA of a life after mortal death, and above all the threat of an eternal life in torment, appears so immediately intelligible, and so overwhelmingly formidable, that Butler and so many others have not been and are not greatly distressed by the indefeasibility in this life of "the religious hypothesis." For they could be confident that in that infinite future all would be made plain. The solution to the Problem of Evil would be revealed, wrongs would all be righted, and the divine justice vindicated.

The promise of such eschatological verification is, of course, paradoxical. Unbelievers are eventually to learn the grim truth, but only when it will be too late for prudent, saving action. To our protests that we never knew, and could not have known, the response will be that made to a parallel protest by an old-time Scots Judge: "Well, ye ken noo!" If however it is the believers who are mistaken, then they will never be embarrassed by a posthumous awareness of their error, any more than we can expect to enjoy the satisfaction of saying to them, "We told you so!" For, as the Epicureans used to urge, it will be for us mortals after death as it was before we were born:

> If it is going to be wretched and miserable for anyone in the future, then he to whom the bad things may happen has also got to exist at that time. Since death prevents that possibility . . . we can know that there is nothing to be feared after death, that he who does not exist cannot be miserable. It makes not a jot of difference . . . when immortal death has taken away his mortal life.[2]

1. SETTING THE PROBLEM: THE GREAT OBSTACLE

Surely Butler was right. "Whether we are to live in a future state, as it is the most important question which can possibly be asked, so it is the most intelligible one which can be expressed in language." Surely we can understand the fears of those warned of the fate of the damned and the hopes of warriors of Allah expecting if they die in Holy Wars to go straight to the arms of the black-eyed houris in Paradise. Of course we can: they both expect—and what could be more intelligible than this?—that, if they do certain things, then they will in consequence enjoy or suffer certain rewards or punishments. And, if this future life is supposed to last forever, then clearly the question of whether or not we shall have it (and, if so, the consequent problem of ensuring that we shall pass it agreeably) is of quite overwhelming existential importance. For what are three-score years and ten compared with all eternity?

Now wait a minute, the skeptic protests. Surely something crucial is being overlooked. For this future life is supposed to continue even *after* physical dissolution, even *after* the slow corruption in the cemetery or the swift consumption in the crematorium. Of course we can understand the myth of Er[3] or stories of Valhalla. But to expect that after my death and dissolution such things might happen to me is to overlook that I shall not then exist. To expect such things, through overlooking this, is surely like accepting a fairy tale as history, through ignoring the prefatory rubric: "Once upon a time, in a world that never was . . ."

That first exchange gets us to the heart of the matter, by establishing two fundamentals. One of these is that the essence of any doctrine of *personal* survival (or *personal* immortality) must be that it should assert that *we ourselves* shall in some fashion do things and suffer things after *our own* deaths (forever). It is this, and this alone, that warrants, or rather constitutes, what John Wisdom so correctly characterized as "the logically unique expectation."[4] It is important to emphasize that this is indeed of the essence: both because some doctrines employing the word immortality have from the beginning not been of this kind—Aristotle on the alleged immortality of the intellect, for instance—and because others, which started as genuine doctrines of personal immortality, have been so interpreted and reinterpreted that they have surreptitiously ceased to be anything of the such. (These latter have thus suffered "the death by a thousand qualifications."[5]) It is also, it seems, sometimes necessary to point out that personal survival is presupposed by, and is no sort of alternative to, personal immortality.[6] For, as was famously said with regard to another remarkable claim to survival: "It is the first step which counts."

The second fundamental is this. Any doctrine of personal survival or personal immortality has got to find some way around or over an enormous initial obstacle. In the ordinary, everyday understandings of the words involved, to say that someone survived death is to contradict yourself, while to assert that we all of us live forever is to assert a manifest falsehood, the flat contrary of a universally known universal truth: namely, the truth, hallowed in the traditional formal logic, that "All men are mortal."

2. POSSIBLE ROUTES AROUND OR OVER THAT OBSTACLE

We may distinguish three sorts of ways in which we might attempt to circumvent or to overcome this formidable barrier, although the route-finding image becomes awkward when we notice that most living faiths have incorporated elements of more than one. Let us label these three ways "Reconstitutionist," "Astral Body," and "Platonic-Cartesian."

(i) The first of these cannot be better explained than by unrolling a pair of quotations. One is an epitaph composed for himself by Benjamin Franklin. I copied it from a plaque erected not on but beside his grave in Christ Church cemetery, Philadelphia: "The body of B. Franklin, Printer, Like the Cover of an old Book, Its Contents torn out, And stript of its Lettering and Gilding, Lies Here, Food for Worms. But the work shall not be lost; for it will, as he believ'd, appear once more in a new and more elegant Edition Corrected and improved By the Author."

The other comes from chapter 12 "The Night Journey" in the Koran. As usual, it is Allah speaking: "Thus shall they be rewarded: because they disbelieved our revelations and said, 'When we are turned to bones and dust shall we be raised to life?' Do they not see that Allah, who has created the heavens and the earth, has power to create their like? Their fate is preordained beyond all doubt. Yet the wrongdoers persist in unbelief."[7]

This direct Reconstitutionist Way is blocked by the Replica Objection. This is that the "new and more elegant edition" would not be the original Founding Father, Signer of the American Declaration of Independence, but only a replica, and that Allah spoke more truly than his Prophet realized when he claimed, not the ability to reconstitute the same persons, but only the "power to create their like." The force of the Replica Objection is all the greater, and all the more decisive, in as much as the "new . . . edition" and "their like" are both to be the creations of a quasipersonal, rewarding and punishing Creator, not just things that occur unintended.[8]

It is clear that Aquinas, unlike some of our contemporaries who think to follow him, appreciated all this. But his Reconstitutionism incorporated an element of our third kind. For he believed that a soul, which is a substance, in the sense of something that can significantly be said to exist separately yet is most emphatically not in such separate existence a whole person, survives what would normally be called death and dissolution. This soul will eventually be—shall we say?—incorporated into what, had provision not been made for this element of partly personal continuity, might otherwise have had to be dismissed as merely a replica of the original person.[9]

About this Thomist response the only thing we need to say at this stage is that this sort of semisoul, which is not by itself a whole person, must be exposed to all the objections that can be brought against a full Platonic soul, which is, or could be. Also, to the extent that the Thomist soul is not a whole person, its claim to constitute the essential but sufficient link maintaining personal identity is bound to weaken.

(ii) To explain the Astral Body approach it is best to think of cinematic representations—for example, in the movie version of Noël Coward's *Blithe Spirit*—in which a shadow person, visible only sometimes and only to some of the characters, detaches itself from a person shown as dead, and thereafter continues to participate in the developing action, at one time discernably and at another time not. This elusive entity is taken to be itself the real, the essential, person.

It is not, however, essential for our present purposes that an astral body be of human shape, much less that, even after the traumatic detachment of death, it should remain—as in those decent old days it did—neatly and conventionally clad. The crux is that it should possess the corporeal characteristics of size, shape, and position, and that—although eluding crude, untutored observation—it should nevertheless be in principle detectable. If it were not both in this minimum sense corporeal and in principle detectable, it would not be relevantly different from the Platonic-Cartesian soul. If it were not in practice excessively difficult to detect, no one could with any plausibility suggest that such a thing might slip away unnoticed from the deathbed.

The vulgar, materialist notion of souls—a notion Plato derides in the *Phaedo* (77D)—satisfies the present, studiously undemanding specification for astral bodies; that notion of souls surely was, as near as makes no matter, that of Epicurus and Lucretius. There seems reason to believe that many of the early Christian Fathers thought of souls as something less than totally and perfectly incorporeal.[10] So their souls also must for present purposes be classified as astral bodies.

The Way of the Astral Body runs between a rock and a hard place.

For the more we make astral bodies like the ordinary flesh and blood persons from which they are supposedly detachable—in order to make sure that each person's astral body can be identified as the real and essential person—the more difficult it becomes to make out that it is not already known that no such astral bodies do in fact detach themselves at death. If, on the other hand, we take care so to specify the nature of our hypothesized astral bodies that the falsification of the hypothesis that such there be, while still possible in principle, is in practice indefinitely deferred, then we find that we have made it impossibly difficult to identify creatures of too, too solid flesh and blood with any such perennially elusive hypothetical entities. Under these and other pressures those who have started to attempt the Way of the Astral Body tend so to refine away the corporeal characteristics of these putative bodies that they become indiscernible from Platonic-Cartesian souls.

(iii) The third, Platonic-Cartesian Way is, of course, the most familiar. It is based upon, or consists in, two assumptions. The first is that what is ordinarily thought of as a person is in fact composed of two utterly disparate elements: the one, the body, earthy, corporeal and perishable; the other, the soul, incorporeal, invisible, intangible, and perhaps imperishable. The second assumption, and equally essential, is that the second of these elements is the real person, the agent, the rational being, the me or the you.

Traditionally these assumptions have been taken absolutely for granted; in discussions of survival and immortality, they still are. They are rarely even stated and distinguished. Still more rarely do we find anyone attempting justification. The founders of the British Society for Psychical Research hoped that its work might serve to verify what they feared that the advance of all the other sciences was falsifying: a Platonic-Cartesian view of the nature of man. In the middle decades of the present century J. B. Rhine cherished the same hope, and believed that the parapsychological work done in his laboratories at Durham, North Carolina, had indeed supplied the hoped-for verification. This is neither the place nor the occasion for yet another demonstration that these desired findings were in fact presupposed in prejudicial misdescriptions of that work, rather than supported by it.[11]

But it is perhaps just worth mentioning that when people construe out-of-body experiences as evidence for a Platonic-Cartesian view they make exactly the same mistake. If a patient claims to have "seen" something "when out of the body," something that she could not have seen with her eyes and from her bed, then the more economical as well as the more intelligible thing to say is that she "saw" that something clairvoyantly from her bed, rather than that it was "seen," equally clairvoyantly, by her temporarily detached soul.

3. WHAT BUTLER SAW AS "STRANGE PERPLEXITIES"

Whether or not the two assumptions that together define the Platonic-Cartesian Way can in the end be justified, it most certainly will not do, notwithstanding that this is what usually is done, to take them as from the beginning given, as if they either required no proof or had been proved already. The truth is that it is very far from obvious that disembodied personal survival is conceivable, that is, that talk of persons as substantial incorporeal souls is coherent. For in their ordinary, everyday understanding of person words—the personal pronouns, personal names, words for persons playing particular roles (such as "spokesperson," "official," "Premier," "aviator," etc.), and so on—all these are words employed to name or otherwise refer to members of a very special class of creatures of flesh and blood.

In this ordinary, everyday understanding—what other do we have? —incorporeal persons are no more a sort of persons than are imaginary, fictitious, or otherwise nonexistent persons. "Incorporeal" is here, like those others, an alienans adjective.[12] To put the point less technically but more harshly: to assert, in that ordinary, everyday understanding, that somebody survived death, but disembodied, is to contradict yourself. Hence the incorrigible Thomas Hobbes was so rude as to say that, "If a man talks to me of 'a round quadrangle'; or 'accidents of bread in cheese'; or 'immaterial substances'; . . . I should not say that he was in error, but that his words were without meaning: that is to say, absurd."[13]

(i) This absurdity is very rarely recognized and admitted as such. Even Richard Swinburne, whose theological trilogy constitutes the most formidable of all contemporary defenses of theism, is sometimes inclined to take these two Platonic-Cartesian assumptions as given. Thus the second sentence of *The Coherence of Theism* reads: "By a 'God' he [the theist] understands something like a person without a body (i.e., a spirit) . . ." Later we are told that "Human persons have bodies: he [God] does not."[14] Again, in the course of a discussion of "What it is for a body to be mine," Swinburne, having first listed various peculiarly personal characteristics, tells us that "we learn to apply the term 'person' to various individuals around us in virtue of their possession of the characteristics which I have outlined."

This, surely, is all wrong. If persons really were creatures *possessing* bodies, rather than, as in fact we are, creatures that just essentially *are* members of one special sort of creatures of flesh and blood, then it would make sense to speak of a whole body amputation. Who is it, too, who is presupposed to be able sensibly to ask which of various bodies is his, or hers? How is such a puzzled person to be identified, or to self-identify, save by reference to the living organism he or she actually is?

As for Swinburne's suggestion that we could, and even do, learn to apply the word "person" to "various individuals around us" by first learning how to pick out certain peculiarly personal characteristics, and then identifying persons as creatures of the kind that possess these characteristics, this constitutes a perfect paradigm of the literally preposterous. For the manifest truth is that our only experience of any peculiarly personal characteristics is, and indeed has to be, of these as characteristics peculiar to that particular kind of creatures we have first learnt to identify as mature and normal human beings. The identification of such peculiarly personal characteristics therefore is and must be posterior rather than prior to the identification of members of the particular kind of creatures to which alone these characteristics can be and are attributed.

Swinburne thought to deflect the ferocity of such critical onslaughts by making the emollient point that no one has any business to argue, just because all the so-and-sos with which they happen themselves to have been acquainted with were such-and-such, that therefore such-and-suchness must be an essential characteristic of anything that is to be properly rated a so-and-so.[15] This is, of course, correct. Certainly it would be preposterous, and worse, to argue that because all the human beings with whom you had so far become acquainted had had black skins that therefore anyone with any other skin pigmentation must be disqualified as a human being.

Incorporeality, however, is a very different kettle of fish, or, more like, no kettle and no fish. For to characterize something as incorporeal is to make an assertion that is at one and the same time both extremely comprehensive and wholly negative. Those proposing to do this surely owe it both to themselves and to others not only to indicate what positive characteristics might significantly be attributed to their putative incorporeal entities but also to specify how such entities could, if only in principle, be identified and reidentified. It is not exclusively, or even primarily, a question of what predicates these putative spiritual subjects might take, but of how they themselves might be identified in the first place, and only after that reidentified as numerically the same through an effluxion of time.

(ii) The main reason the need to attempt answers to these questions is so rarely recognized must be, surely, the easy and widespread assumption that common knowledge of the untechnical vernacular equips us with a concept of incorporeal persons, and hence that what ought to be meant by talk of the identity of such entities is already determined. It is this assumption that supports and is in turn supported by those reckless claims to be able to image (to form a private mental image of) personal survival in a disembodied state. The assumption itself is sustained by the familiarity both of talk about minds or souls and of talk about survival or immortality. Since both sorts of talk are without doubt intelligible, does it not follow that we do have concepts of soul and of mind, as well as of disembodied personal existence? No, or rather, yes and no.

Just because we can indeed understand hopes or fears of survival or immortality it does not follow that we can conceive, much less image, existence as persons, but disembodied. No one has ever emphasized and commended incorporeality more strongly than Plato. Yet when in the myth of Er he labors to describe the future life awaiting his supposedly disembodied souls, everything even that master craftsman of the pen has to say about them presupposes that they will still be just such creatures of flesh and blood as we are now and he was then.

On the other hand, the familiarity and intelligibility of talk about minds and about souls does entitle us to infer that we possess both a concept of mind and a concept of soul. But these particular semantic possessions are precisely not what is needed if doctrines of the survival and perhaps the immortality of souls or of minds are to be viable. The crux is that, in their everyday understandings, the words "minds" and "souls" are not words for sorts of substances, not words, that is, for what could significantly be said to survive the deaths and dissolutions of those flesh and blood persons whose minds or souls they are. To construe the question whether she has a mind of her own, or the assertion that he is a mean-souled man, as a question, or an assertion, about some hypothesized incorporeal substances is like taking the loss of the Red Queen's dog's temper as if this was on all fours with his loss of his bone, or like looking for the grin remaining after the Cheshire Cat has vanished.[16]

This distinction is crucial to my argument. Certainly the fact that we can say so many sensible and intelligible things about minds or souls does show that we have concepts of minds or souls, just as the facts that we can talk sensibly about grins or tempers shows that we have concepts both of a grin and of a temper. But none of this shows, what is not the case, that we can sensibly talk of grins and tempers existing separately from the faces of which they are configurations or of the people who sometimes lose them or—and this is vital—that we can talk sensibly about the mind or soul surviving the dissolution of the flesh and blood person whose mind or soul it was.

(iii) Earlier I mentioned, and described as reckless, claims that we can not merely conceive but also image—form mental pictures of—disembodied survival. In the twentieth-century literature this claim was, I believe, first made by Moritz Schlick:

> In fact I can easily imagine, e.g. witnessing the funeral of my own body and continuing to exist without a body, for nothing is easier than to describe a world which differs from our ordinary world only in the complete absence of all data which I would call parts of my own body. We must conclude that immortality, in the sense defined, should . . . be regarded . . . as an empirical hypothesis, because it possesses logical verifiability. It could be verified by following the prescription "Wait until you die!"[17]

A more puckishly picturesque version was later provided by John Wisdom: "I know indeed what it would be like to witness my own funeral—the men in tall silk hats, the flowers, and the face beneath the glass-topped coffin."[18]

This is a thesis that was, so far as I know, first challenged by me, in a paper first published twenty years after that of Schlick.[19] In the subsequent thirty-seven years there has, again so far as I know, been no counter-challenge, although my paper has been reprinted at least five times. My point, which I now repeat, was that Schlick's thesis can and should be challenged, and the challenge can be pressed home without presuming to draw limits to Wisdom's no doubt extremely extensive powers of private mental picturing. The crux is that there is a world of difference between, on the one hand, imagining what it would be like to witness my own funeral, and, on the other hand, imagining what it would be like for *me* to witness my own funeral. What Schlick and Wisdom and everyone else can certainly do is the former. What would be needed to warrant Schlick's conclusions is the latter. The question at issue is a question about possible pictures and possible captions. Everyone knows what picture fits the first caption. What picture fits, and justifies, the second?

If it is really I who witness, then it is not my funeral but only "my funeral" (between disclaiming quotes). If it really is my funeral, then I cannot be a witness, since I shall be dead and in the coffin. Of course I can imagine (image) what might be described as my "watching my own funeral." For I can remember Harry Lime in the film *The Third Man* watching "his own funeral," and of course I can imagine being in the same situation as Harry Lime. But it was not really Lime's funeral. The crucial question remains: "Was the flesh and blood creature Flew really there, alive, or was there only his corpse in the coffin?"

What Schlick and Wisdom really were doing when they engaged in these misdescribed exercises of imagination was causing themselves to have the kind of nonperceptual visual experience that might conceivably be suffered by an incorporeal subject of consciousness, if indeed such an entity could conceivably be said to exist. Precisely because it would be by the hypothesis incorporeal such a hypothetical subject of consciousness could not be identified with Schlick or Wisdom or anyone else. So the kind of conscious experience under discussion would not be an experience had by a person, in any ordinary understanding of that crucial term, but one had by a hypothetical we know not what, for which no means of identification has yet been provided. In consequence this hypothetical we know not what has not been provided with any means of reidentification through time as one and the same individual we know not what.

That second and consequential point is surely much the more important of the two. For in most of our exercises of imaging we are not ourselves among the objects of that imaging. So we might easily be tempted to think that we were on these occasions imagining what it would be like for us to survive, but disembodied. But a long series of great and less great philosophers, working on the false assumption that persons, or at any rate, their "selves," are essentially incorporeal, have tried but failed to suggest any criterion for the identity of such postulated incorporeal entities.

NOTES

1. Joseph Butler, "A Dissertation of Personal Identity," in *Butler's Works,* ed. by W. E. Gladstone, vol. 1 (Oxford: Clarendon, 1896), p. 387.

2. Lucretius, *De Rerum Natura* [On the Nature of Things], translated by W. H. D. Rowse (London, and Cambridge, Mass.: Heinemann, and Harvard University Press), 3.862–69.

3. Plato, *The Republic,* 10.614B–621D.

4. *Philosophy and Psychoanalysis* (Oxford: Blackwell, 1953), p. 150.

5. "Theology and Falsification," in Antony Flew and Alasdair MacIntyre, eds., *New Essays in Philosophical Theology* (London: SCM Press, 1955), p. 97; also, in various languages, in at least thirty other places later.

6. Contrast Roy Holland, reviewing C. B. Martin, *Religious Belief* (Ithaca, N.Y.: Cornell University Press, 1959), in *Mind* (1961): 572.

7. The Koran, translated by W. J. Dawood (Harmondsworth: Penguin}, p. 234.

8. Does anyone really believe that posthumous justice could be done to Hitler or Stalin or any of the other multimillion murderers of our tormented century if only we had the technology to create such replicas?

9. See the Reply to Object 4 in Article 2 under Question 79 of Book III of the *Summa Theologica.* We have here another example of the great synthesizer trying to have it both ways.

10. See, for instance, Tertullian's *De Anima* [Concerning the Soul]. In chapter 7 he finds "in the Gospel itself . . . the clearest evidence for the corporeal nature of the soul. . . . For an incorporeal thing suffers nothing, not having that which makes it capable of suffering; else, if it had such a capacity, it must be a bodily substance." In chapter 9 Tertullian then tells a tale of "a sister whose lot it has been to be favored with sundry gifts of revelation." She is said to have testified, "A spirit has been in the habit of appearing to me; not, however, a

void and empty illusion, but such as would offer itself to be even grasped by the hand, soft and transparent and of an etherial colour, and in form resembling a human being in every respect."

11. For extensive discussion of these and other related questions, compare Antony Flew, ed., *Readings in the Philosophical Problems of Parapsychology* (Amherst, N.Y.: Prometheus Books, 1987).

12. "Alienans adjective" is a medieval, Scholastic technicality. Whereas, for example, the ordinary adjectival expression "red book" is used to imply that something is both red and a book, such alienans adjectives as imaginary, fictitious, or nonexistent are not similarly employed in order to pick out a subset for some more extensive set: imaginary books, unlike red books, are not species of the genus books!

13. *Leviathan*, chapter 5.

14. Richard Swinburne, *The Coherence of Theism* (Oxford: Clarendon, 1977), p. 51.

15. Ibid., p. 54.

16. In this crucial sense of "substance"—which is by no means the only sense in which that word has been employed—a substantial soul or life could significantly, even if not truly, be said not only to preexist but to survive whatever it had "animated" or "ensouled." Perhaps the most effective way of fixing this concept firmly in mind is by appealing to examples from Lewis Carroll's *Alice in Wonderland* and *Through the Looking Glass,* examples in which the absurdities are produced by treating words that everyone realizes are not words for sorts of substances as if they were. Remember, for instance, the subtraction sum the Red Queen set for Alice: "Take a bone from a dog, what would remain?" The answer that nothing would remain is rejected. For the dog losing its temper would depart, while the lost temper would remain. Or, again, what of the grinning Cheshire Cat, which progressively vanished, leaving only the grin behind?

17. See his "Meaning and Verification," in the *Philosophical Review* (1937), later reprinted in H. Feigl and W. Sellars, eds., *Readings in Philosophical Analysis* (New York: Appleton-Century-Crofts, 1949).

18. John Wisdom, *Other Minds* (Oxford: Blackwell, 1952), p. 36.

19. "Can a man witness his own funeral?" in the *Hibbert Journal* (1956) and later reprinted in J. Feinberg, *Reason and Responsibility* (Belmont, Calif.: Dickenson, 1971); in W. J. Blackstone, ed., *Meaning and Existence* (New York: Holt, Rinehart and Winston, 1972); in F. A. Westphal, ed., *The Art of Philosophy* (Englewood Cliffs, N.J.: Prentice-Hall, 1972); and in P. A. French, ed., *Exploring Philosophy* (Morristown, N.J.: General Learning Press, 1975). There is also a retitled and very much revised version in Antony Flew, *God, Freedom, and Immortality* (Amherst, N.Y.: Prometheus Books, 1984).

PART 4

THE NATURE OF RELIGIOUS BELIEF

If we think that this search for God is a vain search, and that there is no reality to be discovered, . . . then the history of religion becomes a study of the aberrations of the human mind.

—Cyril Bailey
The Greek Atomists and Epicurus (1928)

12

THE NATURAL HISTORY OF RELIGION
(1757)

David Hume

David Hume (1711–1776) was born in Edinburgh and studied law at Edinburgh University, but left to become a philosopher. His Treatise of Human Nature *(1739–40), although poorly received in its day, has become a philosophical landmark, as has his* Philosophical Essays Concerning Human Understanding *(1748; revised as* An Enquiry Concerning Human Understanding, *1758).* Hume espoused a skeptical empiricism, asserting that knowledge of the real world can only be a matter of probabilities based on sense-perception and inferences therefrom. In several later works—especially "The Natural History of Religion" *(part of* Four Dissertations, *1757) and* Dialogues Concerning Natural Religion *(published posthumously in 1779)—Hume pioneered the anthropological approach to religion, claiming that religious belief emerged in primitive peoples' hopes and fears about the world around them, especially the fear of death. Hume also refuted the "argument from design," maintaining that the appearance of design in the world could have come about from numerous causes aside from an "intelligent creator." In the following extract, Hume deprecates the ill effects of religion, produced chiefly by ignorance and superstition.*

From David Hume, *The Natural History of Religion* (1757; reprint, Stanford: Stanford University Press, 1957), pp. 65–66, 67–73.

IMPIOUS CONCEPTIONS OF THE DIVINE NATURE IN POPULAR RELIGIONS OF BOTH KINDS

T**HE PRIMARY RELIGION OF MANKIND** arises chiefly from an anxious fear of future events; and what ideas will naturally be entertained of invisible, unknown powers, while men lie under dismal apprehensions of any kind, may easily be conceived. Every image of vengeance, severity, cruelty, and malice must occur, and must augment the ghastliness and horror, which oppresses the amazed religionist. A panic having once seized the mind, the active fancy still farther multiplies the objects of terror; while that profound darkness, or, what is worse, that glimmering light, with which we are environed, represents the spectres of divinity under the most dreadful appearances imaginable. And no idea of perverse wickedness can be framed, which those terrified devotees do not readily, without scruple, apply to their deity.

This appears the natural state of religion, when surveyed in one light. But if we consider, on the other hand, that spirit of praise and eulogy, which necessarily has place in all religions, and which is the consequence of these very terrors, we must expect a quite contrary system of theology to prevail. Every virtue, every excellence, must be ascribed to the divinity, and no exaggeration will be deemed sufficient to reach those perfections, with which he is endowed. Whatever strains of panegyric can be invented, are immediately embraced, without consulting any arguments of phænomena: It is esteemed a sufficient confirmation of them, that they give us more magnificent ideas of the divine objects of our worship and adoration.

Here therefore is a kind of contradiction between the different principles of human nature, which enter into religion. Our natural terrors present the notion of a devilish and malicious deity: Our propensity to adulation leads us to acknowledge an excellent and divine. And the influence of these opposite principles are various, according to the different situation of the human understanding. . . .

But as men farther exalt their idea of their divinity; it is their notion of his power and knowledge only, not of his goodness, which is improved. On the contrary, in proportion to the supposed extent of his science and authority, their terrors naturally augment; while they believe, that no secrecy can conceal them from his scrutiny, and that even the inmost recesses of their breast lie open before him. They must then be careful not to form expressly any sentiment of blame and disapprobation. All must be applause, ravishment, extacy. And while their gloomy apprehensions make them ascribe to him measures of conduct, which, in human creatures, would be highly blamed, they must still affect to praise and admire that conduct in the object of their devotional addresses. Thus it may safely be affirmed, that popular religions are really, in the conception of their more vulgar votaries, a species of dæmonism; and the higher the deity is exalted in power and knowledge, the lower of course is he depressed in goodness and benevolence; whatever epithets of praise may be bestowed on him by his amazed adorers. Among idolaters, the words may be false, and belie the secret opinion: But among more exalted religionists, the opinion itself contracts a kind of falsehood, and belies the inward sentiment. The heart secretly detests such measures of cruel and implacable vengeance; but the judgment dares not but pronounce them perfect and adorable. And the additional misery of this inward struggle aggravates all the other terrors, by which these unhappy victims to superstition are for ever haunted.

Lucian[1] observes that a young man, who reads the history of the gods in Homer or Hesiod, and finds their factions, wars, injustice, incest, adultery, and other immoralities so highly celebrated, is much surprised afterwards, when he comes into the world, to observe that punishments are by law inflicted on the same actions, which he had been taught to ascribe to superior beings. The contradiction is still perhaps stronger between the representations given us by some later religions and our natural ideas of generosity, lenity, impartiality, and justice; and in proportion to the multiplied terrors of these religions, the barbarous conceptions of the divinity are multiplied upon us. Nothing can preserve untainted the genuine principles of morals in our judgment of human conduct, but the absolute necessity of these principles to the existence of society. If common conception can indulge princes in a system of ethics, somewhat different from that which should regulate private persons; how much more those superior beings, whose attributes, views, and nature are so totally unknown to us? *Sunt superis sua jura.*[2] The gods have maxims of justice peculiar to themselves.

BAD INFLUENCE OF POPULAR RELIGIONS ON MORALITY

Here I cannot forbear observing a fact, which may be worth the attention of such as make human nature the object of their enquiry. It is certain, that, in every religion, however sublime the verbal definition which it gives of its divinity, many of the votaries, perhaps the greatest number, will still seek the divine favor, not by virtue and good morals, which alone can be acceptable to a perfect being, but either by frivolous observances, by intemperate zeal, by rapturous extasies, or by the belief of mysterious and absurd opinions. The least part of the *Sadder*, as well as of the *Pentateuch*,[3] consists in precepts of morality; and we may also be assured, that that part was always the least observed and regarded. When the old Romans were attacked with a pestilence, they never ascribed their sufferings to their vices, or dreamed of repentance and amendment. They never thought, that they were the general robbers of the world, whose ambition and avarice made desolate the earth, and reduced opulent nations to want and beggary. They only created a dictator, in order to drive a nail into a door; and by that means, they thought that they had sufficiently appeased their incensed deity.

In Ægina, one faction forming a conspiracy, barbarously and treacherously assassinated seven hundred of their fellow-citizens; and carried their fury so far, that, one miserable fugitive having fled to the temple, they cut off his hands, by which he clung to the gates, and carrying him out of holy ground, immediately murdered him. *By this impiety*, says Herodotus, (not by the other many cruel assassinations) *they offended the gods, and contracted an inexpiable guilt.*

Nay, if we should suppose, what never happens, that a popular religion were found, in which it was expressly declared, that nothing but morality could gain the divine favor; if an order of priests were instituted to inculcate this opinion, in daily sermons, and with all the arts of persuasion; yet so inveterate are the people's prejudices, that, for want of some other superstition, they would make the very attendance on these sermons the essentials of religion, rather than place them in virtue and good morals. The sublime prologue of Zaleucus's[4] laws inspired not the Locrians, so far as we can learn, with any sounder notions of the measures of acceptance with the deity, than were familiar to the other Greeks.

This observation, then, holds universally: But still one may be at some loss to account for it. It is not sufficient to observe, that the people, every where, degrade their deities into a similitude with themselves, and consider them merely as a species of human creatures, somewhat more potent and intelligent. This will not remove the difficulty. For there is no *man* so stupid, as that, judging by his natural reason, he would not esteem virtue and honesty the most valuable qualities, which any person could possess. Why not ascribe the same sentiment to his deity? Why not make all religion, or the chief part of it, to consist in these attainments?

Nor is it satisfactory to say, that the practice of morality is more difficult than that of superstition; and is therefore rejected. For, not to mention the excessive penances of the *Brachmans* and *Talapoins*;[5] it is certain, that the *Rhamadan*[6] of the Turks, during which the poor wretches, for many days, often in the hottest months of the year, and in some of the hottest climates of the world, remain without eating or drinking from the rising to the setting sun; this *Rhamadan*, I say, must be more severe than the practice of any moral duty, even to the most vicious and depraved of mankind. The four lents of the Muscovites, and the austerities of some *Roman Catholics*, appear more disagreeable than meekness and benevolence. In short, all virtue, when men are reconciled to it by ever so little practice, is agreeable: All superstition is for ever odious and burthensome.

Perhaps, the following account may be received as a true solution of the difficulty. The duties, which a man performs as a friend or parent, seem merely owing to his benefactor or children; nor can he be wanting to these duties, without breaking through all the ties of nature and morality. A strong inclination may prompt him to the performance: A sentiment of order and moral obligation joins its force to these natural ties: And the whole man, if truly virtuous, is drawn to his duty, without any effort or endeavour. Even with regard to the virtues, which are more austere, and more founded on reflection, such as public spirit, filial duty, temperance, or integrity; the moral obligation, in our apprehension, removes all pretension to religious merit; and the virtuous conduct is deemed no more than what we owe to society and to ourselves. In all this, a superstitious man finds nothing, which he has properly performed for the sake of his deity, or which can peculiarly recommend him to the divine favor and protection. He considers not, that the most genuine method of serving the divinity is by promoting the happiness of his creatures. He still looks out for some more immediate service of the supreme Being, in order to allay those terrors, with which he is haunted. And any practice, recommended to him, which either serves to no purpose in life, or offers the strongest violence to his natural inclinations; that practice he will the more readily embrace, on account of those very circumstances, which should make him absolutely reject it. It seems the more purely religious, because it proceeds from no mixture of any other motive or consideration. And if, for its sake, he sacrifices much of his ease and quiet, his claim of merit appears still to rise upon him, in proportion to the zeal and devotion which he discovers. In restoring a loan, or paying a debt, his divinity is nowise beholden to him; because these acts of justice are what he was bound to perform, and what many would have performed, were there no god in the universe. But if he fast a day, or give himself a sound whipping; this has a direct reference, in his opinion, to the service of God. No other motive could engage him to such austerities. By these distinguished marks of devotion, he has now acquired the divine favor; and may expect, in recompense, protection and safety in this world, and eternal happiness in the next.

Hence the greatest crimes have been found, in many instances, compatible with a superstitious piety and devotion; Hence, it is justly regarded as unsafe to draw any certain inference in favor of a man's morals, from the fervour or strictness of his religious exercises, even though he himself believe them sincere. Nay, it has been observed, that enormities of the blackest dye have been rather apt to produce superstitious terrors, and encrease the religious passion. Bomilcar, having formed a conspiracy for assassinating at once the whole senate of Carthage, and invading the liberties of his country, lost the opportunity, from a continual regard to omens and prophecies.[7] *Those who undertake the most criminal and most dangerous enterprizes are commonly the most superstitious;* as an ancient historian remarks on this occasion. Their devotion and spiritual faith rise with their fears. Catiline was not contented with the established deities and received rites of the national religion: His anxious terrors made him seek new inventions of this kind; which he never probably had dreamed of, had he remained a good citizen, and obedient to the laws of his country.[8]

To which we may add, that, after the commission of crimes, there arise remorses and secret horrors, which give no rest to the mind, but make it have recourse to religious rites and ceremonies, as expiations of its offences. Whatever weakens or disorders the internal frame promotes the interests of superstition: And nothing is more destructive to them than a manly, steady virtue, which either preserves us from disastrous, melancholy accidents, or teaches us to bear them. During such calm sunshine of the mind, these spectres of false divinity never make their appearance. On the other hand, while we abandon ourselves to the natural undisciplined suggestions of our timid and anxious hearts, every kind of barbarity is ascribed to the supreme Being, from the terrors with which we are agitated; and every kind of caprice, from the methods which we embrace in order to appease him. *Barbarity, caprice;* these qualities, however nominally disguised, we may universally observe, form the ruling character of the deity in popular religions. Even priests, instead of correcting these depraved ideas of mankind, have often been found ready to foster and encourage them. The more tremendous the divinity is represented, the more tame and submissive do men become his ministers: And the more unaccountable the measures of acceptance required by him, the more necessary does it become to abandon our natural reason, and yield to their ghostly guidance and direction. Thus it may be allowed, that the artifices of men aggravate our natural infirmities and follies of this kind, but never originally beget them. Their root strikes deeper into the mind, and springs from the essential and universal properties of human nature.

NOTES

1. *Necyomantia,* 3. [Lucian of Samosata (120?–180?), Syrian-born Greek satirist. The work referred to by Hume is more commonly known as *Menippus or The Descent into Hades.*]

2. ["The gods have their own laws." Ovid, *Metamorphoses* 9.499.]

3. [*Sadder* refers to the *Seder Eliyyahu,* a Jewish book of homilies written between the third and tenth centuries C.E. The Pentateuch is the first five books of the Old Testament.]

4. [Zaleucus (fl. 550 B.C.E.), lawgiver of the Locrians and disciple of Pythagoras.]

5. [Brahmans or Brahmins are the priestly caste among the Hindus. Talapoins are Buddhist monks.]

6. [The ninth month of the lunar calendar, during which Muslims are to abstain from eating and drinking between sunrise and sunset.]

7. [Bomilcar or Bormilcar was a Carthaginian general (fl. 310 B.C.E.) who unsuccessfully sought to become tyrant in Carthage.]

8. [L. Sergius Catilina (108–62 B.C.E.), Roman patrician who attempted to lead a revolt against the government. Cicero delivered four celebrated orations condemning him.]

13

EVANGELICAL TEACHING
(1855)

George Eliot

George Eliot (the pseudonym of Mary Ann Evans, 1819–1890) read the-
ology diligently in her youth, but was encouraged in freethinking by the
philosophers and philanthropists Charles and Cara Bray. She was asked
to translate David Friedrich Strauss's controversial Das Leben Jesu
(1835), which asserted that the miracles in the New Testament
(including the resurrection of Jesus) are merely the results of primitive
myth-making. Her translation appeared in 1846 as The Life of Jesus
Critically Examined. *In 1851 she was appointed assistant editor of the*
Westminster Review *and wrote many articles for it. The next year she*
became acquainted with the freethinking philosopher George Henry
Lewes; they decided to live together, since Lewes was already married to
another woman, but separated from her. The couple suffered social
ostracism for years but remained devoted to each other. Eliot became one
of the leading novelists of her time with such works as Adam Bede
(1859), The Mill on the Floss *(1860),* Silas Marner *(1861),* Romola
(1863), Middlemarch *(1871–72),* Daniel Deronda *(1876), and*
others. In the following essay—published in the Westminster Review *for*
October 1855—Eliot attacks the writings of an evangelical preacher of
the day whose narrow, dogmatic, and uncharitable views are strikingly
similar to those of many contemporary fundamentalists.

From George Eliot, "Evangelical Teaching: Dr. Cumming" (1855), in *The Writings of
George Eliot*, vol. 21 (Boston: Houghton Mifflin, 1908), pp. 125–29, 133–36,
139–57, 160–69.

GIVEN, A MAN WITH MODERATE intellect, a moral standard not higher than the average, some rhetorical affluence and great glibness of speech, what is the career in which, without the aid of birth or money, he may most easily attain power and reputation in English society? Where is that Goshen of mediocrity in which a smattering of science and learning will pass for profound instruction, where platitudes will be accepted as wisdom, bigoted narrowness as holy zeal, unctuous egoism as God-given piety? Let such a man become an evangelical preacher; he will then find it possible to reconcile small ability with great ambition, superficial knowledge with the prestige of erudition, a middling morale with a high reputation for sanctity. Let him shun practical extremes and be ultra only in what is purely theoretic: let him be stringent on predestination, but latitudinarian on fasting; unflinching in insisting on the eternity of punishment, but diffident of curtailing the substantial comforts of time; ardent and imaginative on the premillennial advent of Christ, but cold and cautious towards every other infringement of the *status quo*. Let him fish for souls not with the bait of inconvenient singularity, but with the drag-net of comfortable conformity. Let him be hard and literal in his interpretation only when he wants to hurl texts at the heads of unbelievers and adversaries, but when the letter of the Scriptures presses too closely on the genteel Christianity of the nineteenth century, let him use his spiritualizing alembic and disperse it into impalpable ether. Let him preach less of Christ than of Antichrist; let him be less definite in showing what sin is than in showing who is the Man of Sin, less expansive on the blessedness of faith than on the accursedness of infidelity. Above all, let him set up as an interpreter of prophecy, and rival Moore's Almanack in the prediction of political events, tickling the interest of hearers who are but moderately spiritual by showing how the Holy Spirit has dictated problems and charades for their benefit, and how, if they are ingenious enough to solve these, they may have their Christian graces nourished by learning precisely to whom they may point as the "horn that had eyes," "the lying prophet," and the "unclean spirits." In this way he will draw men to him by the strong cords of their passions, made reason-proof by being baptized with the name of piety. In this way he may gain a metropolitan pulpit; the avenues to his church will be as crowded as the passages to the opera; he has but to print his prophetic sermons and bind them in lilac and gold, and they will adorn the drawing-room table of all evangelical ladies, who will regard as a sort of pious "light reading" the demonstration that the prophecy of the locusts, whose sting is in their tail, is fulfilled in the fact of the Turkish commander's having taken a horse's tail for his standard, and that the French are the very frogs predicted in the Revelation.

Pleasant to the clerical flesh under such circumstances is the arrival of Sunday! Somewhat at a disadvantage during the week, in the presence of working-day interests and lay splendours, on Sunday the preacher becomes the cynosure of a thousand eyes, and predominates at once over the Amphitryon with whom he dines, and the most captious member of his church or vestry. He has an immense advantage over all other public speakers. The platform orator is subject to the criticism of hisses and groans. Counsel for the plaintiff expects the retort of counsel for the defendant. The honorable gentleman on one side of the House is liable to have his facts and figures shown up by his honourable friend on the opposite side. Even the scientific or literary lecturer, if he is dull or incompetent, may see the best part of his audience slip quietly out one by one. But the preacher is completely master of the situation: no one may hiss, no one may depart. Like the writer of imaginary conversations, he may put what imbecilities he pleases into the mouths of his antagonists, and swell with triumph when he has refuted them. He may riot in gratuitous assertions, confident that no man will contradict him; he may exercise perfect free-will in logic, and invent illustrative experience; he may give an evangelical edition of history with the inconvenient facts omitted;—all this he may do with impunity, certain that those of his hearers who are not sympathizing are not listening. For the Press has no band of critics who go the round of the churches and chapels, and are on the watch for a slip or defect in the preacher, to make a "feature" in their article: the clergy are practically, the most irresponsible of all talkers. For this reason, at least, it is well that they do not always allow their discourses to be merely fugitive, but are often induced to fix them in that black and white in which they are open to the criticism of any man who has the courage and patience to treat them with thorough freedom of speech and pen.

It is because we think this criticism of clerical teaching desirable for the public good that we devote some pages to Dr. Cumming.[1] He is, as every one knows, a preacher of immense popularity, and of the numerous publications in which he perpetuates his pulpit labours, all circulate widely, and some, according to their title-page, have reached the sixteenth thousand. Now our opinion of these publications is the very opposite of that given by a newspaper eulogist: we do *not* "believe that the repeated issues of Dr. Cumming's thoughts are having a beneficial effect on society," but the reverse; and hence, little inclined as we are to dwell on his pages, we think it worth while to do so, for the sake of pointing out in them what we believe to be profoundly mistaken and pernicious. Of Dr. Cumming personally we know absolutely nothing: our acquaintance with him is confined to a perusal of his works; our judgement of him is founded solely on the manner in which he has written himself down on his pages. We know neither how he looks nor how he lives. We are ignorant whether, like Saint Paul, he has a bodily presence that is weak and contemptible, or whether his person is as florid and as prone to amplification as his style. For aught we know, he may not only have the gift of prophecy but may bestow the profits of all his works to feed the poor, and be ready to give his own body to be burned with as much alacrity as he infers the everlasting burning of Roman Catholics and Puseyites.[2] Out of the pulpit he may be a model of justice, truthfulness, and the love that thinketh no evil; but we are obliged to judge of his charity by the spirit we find in his sermons, and shall only be glad to learn that his practice is, in many respects, an amiable *non sequitur* from his teaching. . . .

One of the most striking characteristics of Dr. Cumming's writings is *unscrupulosity of statement*. His motto apparently is, *Christianitatem, quocunque modo, Christianitatem;*[3] and the only system he includes under the term Christianity is Calvinistic Protestantism. Experience has so long shown that the human brain is a congenial nidus for inconsistent beliefs that we do not pause to inquire how Dr. Cumming, who attributes the conversion of the unbelieving to the Divine Spirit, can think it necessary to co-operate with that Spirit by argumentative white lies. Nor do we for a moment impugn the genuineness of his zeal for Christianity, or the sincerity of his conviction that the doctrines he preaches are necessary to salvation; on the contrary, we regard the flagrant unveracity found on his pages as an indirect result of that conviction—as a result, namely, of the intellectual and moral distortion of view which is inevitably produced by assigning to dogmas, based on a very complex structure of evidence, the place and authority of first truths. A distinct appreciation of the value of evidence—in other words, the intellectual perception of truth—is more closely allied to truthfulness of statement, or the moral quality of veracity, than is generally admitted. That highest moral habit, the constant preference of truth, both theoretically and practically, pre-eminently demands the co-operation of the intellect with the impulses—as is indicated by the fact that it is only found in anything like completeness in the highest class of minds. And it is commonly seen that, in proportion as religious sects believe themselves to be guided by direct inspiration rather than by a spontaneous exertion of their faculties, their sense of truthfulness is misty and confused. No one can have talked to the more enthusiastic Methodists and listened to their stories of miracles without perceiving that they require no other passport to a statement than that it accords with their wishes and their general conception of God's dealings; nay, they regard as a symptom of sinful scepticism an inquiry into the evidence for a story which they think unquestionably tends to the glory of God, and in retailing such stories, new particulars, further tending to His glory, are "borne in" upon their minds. Now, Dr. Cumming, as we have said, is no enthusiastic pietist: within a certain circle—within the mill of evangelical orthodoxy—his intellect is perpetually at work; but that principle of sophistication which our friends the Methodists derive from the predominance of their pietistic feelings is involved for him in the doctrine of verbal inspiration; what is for them a state of emotion submerging the intellect is with him a formula imprisoning the intellect, depriving it of its proper function—the free search for truth—and making it the mere servant-of-all-work to a foregone conclusion. Minds fettered by this doctrine no longer inquire concerning a proposition whether it is attested by sufficient evidence, but whether it accords with Scripture; they do not search for facts, as such, but for facts that will bear out their doctrine. They become accustomed to reject the more direct evidence in favour of the less direct, and where adverse evidence reaches demonstration they must resort to devices and expedients in order to explain away contradiction. It is easy to see that this mental habit blunts not only the perception of truth, but the sense of truthfulness, and that the man whose faith drives him into fallacies treads close upon the precipice of falsehood.

We have entered into this digression for the sake of mitigating the inference that is likely to be drawn from that characteristic of Dr. Cumming's works to which we have pointed. He is much in the same intellectual condition as that professor of Padua, who, in order to disprove Galileo's discovery of Jupiter's satellites, urged that as there were only seven metals there could not be more than seven planets—a mental condition scarcely compatible with candour. And we may well suppose that if the professor had held the belief in seven planets, and no more, to be a necessary condition of salvation, his mental vision would have been so dazed that even if he had consented to look through Galileo's telescope, his eyes would have reported in accordance with his inward alarms rather than with the external fact. So long as a belief in propositions is regarded as indispensable to salvation, the pursuit of truth *as such* is not possible, any more than it is possible for a man who is swimming for his life to make meteorological observations on the storm which threatens to overwhelm him. The sense of alarm and haste, the anxiety for personal safety, which Dr. Cumming insists upon as the proper religious attitude, unmans the nature, and allows no thorough, calm thinking, no truly noble, disinterested feeling. Hence, we by no means suspect that the unscrupulosity of statement with which we charge Dr. Cumming extends beyond the sphere of his theological prejudices: religion apart, he probably appreciates and practices veracity. . . .

In marshalling the evidences of Christianity, Dr. Cumming directs most of his arguments against opinions that are either totally imaginary, or that belong to the past rather than to the present; while he entirely fails to meet the difficulties actually felt and urged by those who are unable to accept Revelation. There can hardly be a stronger proof of misconception as to the character of free-thinking in the present day than the recommendation of Leland's *Short and Easy Method with the Deists*,[4]—a method which is unquestionably short and easy for preachers disinclined to consider their stereotyped modes of thinking and arguing, but which has quite ceased to realize those epithets in the conversion of Deists. Yet Dr. Cumming not only recommends this book, but takes the trouble himself to write a feebler version of its arguments. For example, on the question of the genuineness and authenticity of the New Testament writings, he says:—

"If, therefore, at a period long subsequent to the death of Christ, a number of men had appeared in the world, drawn up a book which they christened by the name of Holy Scripture, and recorded these things which appear in it as facts when they were only the fancies of their own imagination, surely the *Jews* would have instantly reclaimed that no such events transpired, that no such person as Jesus Christ appeared in their capital, and that *their* crucifixion of Him, and their alleged evil treatment of His apostles, were mere fictions."[5]

It is scarcely necessary to say that, in such argument as this, Dr. Cumming is beating the air. He is meeting a hypothesis which no one holds, and totally missing the real question. The only type of "infidel" whose existence Dr. Cumming recognizes is that fossil personage who "calls the Bible a lie and a forgery." He seems to be ignorant—or he chooses to ignore the fact—that there is a large body of eminently instructed and earnest men who regard the Hebrew and Christian Scriptures as a series of historical documents, to be dealt with according to the rules of historical criticism; and that an equally large number of men, who are not historical critics, find the dogmatic scheme built on the letter of the Scriptures opposed to their profoundest moral convictions. Dr. Cumming's infidel is a man who, because his life is vicious, tries to convince himself that there is no God, and that Christianity is an imposture, but who is all the while secretly conscious that he is opposing the truth, and cannot help "letting out" admissions "that the Bible is the Book of God." We are favoured with the following "Creed of the Infidel":—

"I believe that there is no God, but that matter is God, and God is matter; and that it is no matter whether there is any God or not. I believe also that the world was not made, but that the world made itself, or that it had no beginning, and that it will last for ever. I believe that man is a beast; that the soul is the body, and that the body is the soul; and that after death there is neither body nor soul. I believe that there is no religion, that *natural religion is the only religion, and all religion unnatural.* I believe not in Moses; I believe in the first philosophers. I believe not in the evangelists; I believe in Chubb, Collins, Toland, Tindal, and Hobbes. I believe in Lord Bolingbroke, and I believe not in Saint Paul. I believe not in revelation; *I believe in tradition; I believe in the Talmud; I believe in the Koran;* I believe not in the Bible. I believe in Socrates; I believe in Confucius; I believe in Mahomet; I believe not in Christ. And lastly, *I believe* in all unbelief."

The intellectual and moral monster whose creed is this complex web of contradictions is, moreover, according to Dr. Cumming, a being who unites much simplicity and imbecility with his Satanic hardihood,—much tenderness of conscience with his obdurate vice. Hear the "proof":—

"I once met with an acute and enlightened infidel, with whom I reasoned day after day, and for hours together; I submitted to him the internal, the external, and the experimental evidences, but made no impression on his scorn and unbelief. At length I entertained a suspicion that there was something morally, rather than intellectually wrong, and that the bias was not in the intellect, but in the heart; one day therefore I said to him—'I must now state my conviction, and you may call me uncharitable, but duty compels me: you are living in some known and gross sin.' *The man's countenance became pale; he bowed and left me.*"[6]

Here we have the remarkable psychological phenomenon of an "acute and enlightened" man who, deliberately purposing to indulge in a favourite sin, and regarding the Gospel with scorn and unbelief, is nevertheless so much more scrupulous than the majority of Christians that he cannot "embrace sin and the Gospel simultaneously"; who is so alarmed at the Gospel in which he does not believe that he cannot be easy without trying to crush it; whose acuteness and enlightenment suggest to him, as a means of crushing the Gospel, to argue from day to day with Dr. Cumming; and who is withal so naive that he is taken by surprise when Dr. Cumming, failing in argument, resorts to accusation, and so tender in conscience that, at the mention of his sin, he turns pale and leaves the spot. If there be any human mind in existence capable of holding Dr. Cumming's "Creed of the Infidel," of at the same time believing in tradition and "believing in all unbelief," it must be the mind of the infidel just described, for whose existence we have Dr. Cumming's *ex officio* word as a theologian; and to theologians we may apply what Sancho Panza says of the bachelors of Salamanca, that they never tell lies—except when it suits their purpose.

The total absence from Dr. Cumming's theological mind of any demarcation between fact and rhetoric is exhibited in another passage, where he adopts the dramatic form:—

"Ask the peasant on the hills—*and I have asked amid the mountains of Braemar and Deeside*—'How do you know that this book is divine, and that the religion you profess is true? You never read Paley?' 'No, I never heard of him.' 'You have never read Butler?' 'No, I have never heard of him.' 'Nor Chalmers?'[7] 'No, I do not know him.' 'You have never read any books on evidence?' 'No, I have read no such books.'

'Then, how do you know this book is true?' 'Know it! Tell me that the Dee, the Clunie, and the Garrawalt, the streams at my feet, do not run; that the winds do not sigh amid the gorges of these blue hills; that the sun does not kindle the peaks of Loch-na-Gar,—tell me my heart does not beat, and I will believe you; but do not tell me the Bible is not divine. I have found its truth illuminating my footsteps; its consolations sustaining my heart. May my tongue cleave to my mouth's roof, and my right hand forget its cunning, if I ever deny what is my deepest inner experience, that this blessed book is the Book of God."[8]

Dr. Cumming is so slippery and lax in his mode of presentation that we find it impossible to gather whether he means to assert that this is what a peasant on the mountains of Braemar *did* say, or that it is what such a peasant *would* say: in the one case, the passage may be taken as a measure of his truthfulness; in the other, of his judgement.

His own faith, apparently, has not been altogether intuitive, like that of his rhetorical peasant, for he tells us[9] that he has himself experienced what it is to have religious doubts. "I was tainted while at the University by this spirit of scepticism. I thought Christianity might not be true. The very possibility of its being true was the thought I felt I must meet and settle. Conscience could give me no peace till I had settled it. I read, and I have read from that day, for fourteen or fifteen years, till this, and now I am as convinced, upon the clearest evidence, that this book is the Book of God, as that I now address you." This experience, however, instead of impressing on him the fact that doubt may be the stamp of a truth-loving mind—that *sunt quibus non credidisse honor est, et fidei futurae pignus*[10]—seems to have produced precisely the contrary effect. It has not enabled him even to conceive the condition of a mind "perplext in faith but pure in deed," craving light, yearning for a faith that will harmonize and cherish its highest powers and aspirations, but unable to find that faith in dogmatic Christianity. His own doubts apparently were of a different kind. Nowhere in his pages have we found a humble, candid, sympathetic attempt to meet the difficulties that may be felt by an ingenuous mind. Everywhere he supposes that the doubter is hardened, conceited, consciously shutting his eyes to the light—a fool who is to be answered according to his folly—that is, with ready replies made up of reckless assertions, of apocryphal anecdotes, and, where other resources fail, of vituperative imputations. As to the reading which he has prosecuted for fifteen years—*either* it has left him totally ignorant of the relation which his own religious creed bears to the criticism and philosophy of the nineteenth century, *or* he systematically blinks that criticism and that philosophy; and instead of honestly and seriously endeavouring to meet and solve what he knows to be the real difficulties, contents himself with setting up popinjays to shoot at, for the sake of confirming the ignorance and winning the cheap admiration of his evangelical hearers and readers. Like the Catholic preacher who, after throwing down his cap and apostrophizing it as Luther, turned to his audience and said, "You see this heretical fellow has not a word to say for himself," Dr. Cumming, having drawn his ugly portrait of the infidel, and put arguments of a convenient quality into his mouth, finds a "short and easy method" of confounding this "croaking frog."

In his treatment of infidels, we imagine he is guided by a mental process which may be expressed in the following syllogism: Whatever tends to the glory of God is true; it is for the glory of God that infidels should be as bad as possible; therefore, whatever tends to show that infidels are as bad as possible is true. All infidels, he tells us, have been men of "gross and licentious lives." Is there not some well-known unbeliever—David Hume, for example—of whom even Dr. Cumming's readers may have heard as an exception? No matter. Some one suspected that he was *not* an exception; and as that suspicion tends to the glory of God, it is one for a Christian to entertain.[11] If we were unable to imagine this kind of self-sophistication, we should be obliged to suppose that, relying on the ignorance of his evangelical disciples, he fed them with direct and conscious falsehoods. "Voltaire," he informs them, "declares there is no God"; he was "an antitheist—that is, one who deliberately and avowedly opposed and hated God; who swore in his blasphemy that he would dethrone Him"; and "advocated the very depths of the lowest sensuality." With regard to many statements of a similar kind, equally at variance with truth, in Dr. Cumming's volumes, we presume that he has been misled by hearsay or by the second-hand character of his acquaintance with free-thinking literature. An evangelical preacher is not obliged to be well read. Here, however, is a case which the extremist supposition of educated ignorance will not reach. Even books of "evidences" quote from Voltaire the line—

"Si Dieu n'existait pas, il faudrait l'inventer";[12]

even persons fed on the mere whey and buttermilk of literature must know that in philosophy Voltaire was nothing if not a theist—must know that he wrote not against God, but against Jehovah, the God of the Jews, whom he believed to be a false God—must know that to say Voltaire was an atheist on this ground is as absurd as to say that a Jacobite opposed hereditary monarchy because he declared the Brunswick family had no title to the throne. That Dr. Cumming should repeat the vulgar fables about Voltaire's death[13] is merely what we might expect from the specimens we have seen of his illustrative stories. A man whose accounts of his own experience are apocryphal is not likely to put borrowed narratives to any severe test.

The alliance between intellectual and moral perversion is strikingly typified by the way in which he alternates from the unveracious to the absurd, from misrepresentation to contradiction. Side by side with the adduction of "facts" such as those we have quoted, we find him arguing on one page that the doctrine of the Trinity was too grand to have been conceived by man, and was *therefore* Divine; and on another page, that the Incarnation *had* been preconceived by man, and is *therefore* to be accepted as Divine. But we are less concerned with the fallacy of his "ready replies" than with their falsity; and even of this we can only afford space for a very few specimens. Here is one: "There is a *thousand times* more proof that the Gospel of John was written by him than there is that the 'Anabasis' was written by Xenophon, or the 'Ars Poetica' by Horace." If Dr. Cumming had chosen Plato's Epistles or Anacreon's Poems,[14] instead of the "Anabasis" or the "Ars Poetica," he would have reduced the extent of the falsehood, and would have furnished a ready reply, which would have been equally effective with his Sunday-school teachers and their disputants. Hence we conclude this prodigality of misstatement, this exuberance of mendacity, is an effervescence of zeal *in majorem gloriam Dei*.[15] Elsewhere he tells us that "the idea of the author of the 'Vestiges' is that man is the development of a monkey, that the monkey is the embryo man; so that *if you keep a baboon long enough, it will develop itself into a man*."[16] How well Dr. Cumming has qualified himself to judge of the ideas in "that very unphilosophical book," as he pronounces it, may be inferred from the fact that he implies the author of the "Vestiges" to have *originated* the nebular hypothesis.

In the volume from which the last extract is taken, even the hardihood of assertion is surpassed by the suicidal character of the argument.

It is called *The Church before the Flood*, and is devoted chiefly to the adjustment of the question between the Bible and Geology. Keeping within the limits we have prescribed to ourselves, we do not enter into the matter of this discussion; we merely pause a little over the volume in order to point out Dr. Cumming's mode of treating the question. He first tells us that "the Bible has not a single scientific error in it"; that "*its slightest intimations of scientific principles or natural phenomena have in every instance been demonstrated to be exactly and strictly true*"; and he asks:—

"How is it that Moses, with no greater education than the Hindoo or the ancient philosopher, has written his book, touching science at a thousand points, so accurately that scientific research has discovered no flaws in it; and yet in those investigations which have taken place in more recent centuries, it has not been shown that he has committed one single error, or made one solitary assertion which can be proved by the maturest science, or by the most eagle-eyed philosopher, to be incorrect, scientifically or historically?"

According to this, the relation of the Bible to science should be one of the strong points of apologists for revelation: the scientific accuracy of Moses should stand at the head of their evidences; and they might urge with some cogency that, since Aristotle, who devoted himself to science, and lived many ages after Moses, does little else than err ingeniously, this fact, that the Jewish lawgiver, though touching science at a thousand points, has written nothing that has not been "demonstrated to be exactly and strictly true," is an irrefragable proof of his having derived his knowledge from a supernatural source. How does it happen, then, that Dr. Cumming forsakes this strong position? How is it that we find him, some pages further on, engaged in reconciling Genesis with the discoveries of science, by means of imaginative hypotheses and feats of "interpretation"? Surely that which has been demonstrated to be exactly and strictly true does not require hypothesis and critical argument, in order to show that it may *possibly* agree with those very discoveries by means of which its exact and strict truth has been demonstrated. And why should Dr. Cumming suppose, as we shall presently find him supposing, that men of science hesitate to accept the Bible because it appears to contradict their discoveries? By his own statement, that appearance of contradiction does not exist; on the contrary, it has been demonstrated that the Bible precisely agrees with their discoveries. Perhaps, however, in saying of the Bible that its "slightest intimations of scientific principles or natural phenomena have in every instance been demonstrated to be exactly and strictly true," Dr. Cumming merely means to imply that theologians have found out a way of explaining the Biblical text so that it no longer, in their opinion, appears to be in contradiction with the discoveries of science. One of two things, therefore: either, he uses language without the slightest appreciation of its real meaning; or, the assertions he makes on one page are directly contradicted by the arguments he urges on another.

Dr. Cumming's principles—or, we should rather say, confused notions—of Biblical interpretation, as exhibited in this volume, are particularly significant of his mental calibre. He says:—[17]

"Men of science, who are full of scientific investigation, and enamoured of scientific discovery, will hesitate before they accept a book which, they think, contradicts the plainest and the most unequivocal disclosures they have made in the bowels of the earth, or among the stars of the sky. To all these we answer, as we have already indicated, there is not the least dissonance between God's written book and the most mature discoveries of geological science. One thing, however, there may be: *there may be a contradiction between the discoveries of geology and our preconceived interpretations of the Bible*. But this is not because the Bible is wrong, but because our interpretation is wrong." (The italics in all cases are our own.)

Elsewhere he says:—

"It seems to me plainly evident that the record of Genesis, when read fairly, and not in the light of our prejudices,—*and mind you, the essence of Popery is to read the Bible in the light of our opinions, instead of viewing our opinions in the light of the Bible, in its plain and obvious sense,*—falls in perfectly with the assertion of geologists."

On comparing these two passages, we gather that when Dr. Cumming, under stress of geological discovery, assigns to the Biblical text a meaning entirely different from that which, on his own showing, was universally ascribed to it for more than three thousand years, he regards himself as "viewing his opinions in the light of the Bible in its plain and obvious sense"! Now he is reduced to one of two alternatives: either, he must hold that the "plain and obvious meaning" lies in the sum of knowledge possessed by each successive age—the Bible being an elastic garment for the growing thought of mankind; or, he must hold that some portions are amenable to this criterion, and others not so. In the former case, he accepts the principle of interpretation adopted by the early German rationalists; in the latter case, he has to show a further criterion by which we can judge what parts of the Bible are elastic and what rigid. If he says that the interpretation of the text is rigid wherever it treats of doctrines necessary to salvation, we answer, that for doctrines to be necessary to salvation they must first be true; and in order to be true, according to his own principle, they must be founded on a correct interpretation of the Biblical text. Thus he makes the necessity of doctrines to salvation the criterion of infallible interpretation, and infallible interpretation the criterion of doctrines being necessary to salvation. He is whirled round in a circle, having, by admitting the principle of novelty in interpretation, completely deprived himself of a basis. That he should seize the very moment in which he is most palpably betraying that he has no test of Biblical truth beyond his own opinion, as an appropriate occasion for flinging the rather novel reproach against Popery that its essence is to "read the Bible in the light of our opinions," would be an almost pathetic self-exposure, if it were not disgusting. Imbecility that is not even meek, ceases to be pitiable, and becomes simply odious.

Parenthetic lashes of this kind against Popery are very frequent with Dr. Cumming, and occur even in his more devout passages, where their introduction must surely disturb the spiritual exercises of his hearers. Indeed, Roman Catholics fare worse with him even than infidels. Infidels are the small vermin—the mice to be bagged *en passant*. The main object of his chase—the rats which are to be nailed up as trophies—are the Roman Catholics. Romanism is the masterpiece of Satan. But reassure yourselves! Dr. Cumming has been created. Antichrist is enthroned in the Vatican; but he is stoutly withstood by the Boanerges of Crown Court. The personality of Satan, as might be expected, is a very prominent tenet in Dr. Cumming's discourses; those who doubt it are, he thinks, "generally specimens of the victims of Satan as a triumphant seducer"; and it is through the medium of this doctrine that he habitually contemplates Roman Catholics. They are the puppets of which the Devil holds the strings. It is only exceptionally that he speaks of them as fellow men, acted on by the same desires, fears, and hopes as himself; his rule is to hold them up to his hearers as foredoomed instruments of Satan, and vessels of wrath. If he is obliged to admit that they are "no shams," that they are "thoroughly in earnest"—that is because they are inspired by hell, because they are under an "infranatural" influence. If their missionaries are found wherever Protestant missionaries go, this zeal in propagating their faith is not in them a consistent virtue, as it is in Protestants, but a "melancholy fact," affording additional evidence that they are instigated and assisted by the Devil. And Dr. Cumming is inclined to think that they work miracles, because that is no more than might be expected from the known ability of Satan who inspires them.[18] He admits, indeed, that "there is a fragment of the Church of Christ in the very bosom of that awful apostasy,"[19] and that there are members of the Church of Rome in glory; but this admission is rare and episodical—is a declaration, *pro forma*, about as influential on the general disposition and habits as an aristocrat's profession of democracy.

This leads us to mention another conspicuous characteristic of Dr. Cumming's teaching—the *absence of genuine charity*. It is true that he makes large profession of tolerance and liberality within a certain circle; he exhorts Christians to Unity; he would have Churchmen fraternize with Dissenters, and exhorts these two branches of God's family to defer the settlement of their differences till the millennium. But the love thus taught is the love of the *clan*, which is the correlative of antagonism to the rest of mankind. It is not sympathy and helpfulness towards men as men, but towards men as Christians, and as Christians in the sense of a small minority. Dr. Cumming's religion may demand a tribute of love, but it gives a charter to hatred; it may enjoin charity, but it fosters all uncharitableness. If I believe that God tells me to love my enemies, but at the same time hates His own enemies and requires me to have one will with Him, which has the larger scope, love or hatred? And we refer to those pages of Dr. Cumming's in which he opposes Roman Catholics, Puseyites, and infidels—pages which form the larger proportion of what he has published—for proof that the idea of God which both the logic and spirit of his discourses keep present to his hearers is that of a God who hates His enemies, a God who teaches love by fierce denunciations of wrath—a God who encourages obedience to His precepts by elaborately revealing to us that His own government is in precise opposition to those precepts. We know the usual evasions on this subject. We know Dr. Cumming would say that even Roman Catholics are to be loved and succored as men; that he would help even that "unclean spirit," Cardinal Wiseman, out of a ditch. But who that is in the slightest degree acquainted with the action of the human mind will believe that any genuine and large charity can grow out of an exercise of love which is always to have an *arrière-pensée*[20] of hatred? Of what quality would be the conjugal love of a husband who loved his spouse as a wife, but hated her as a woman? It is reserved for the regenerate mind, according to Dr. Cumming's conception of it, to be "wise, amazed, temperate and furious, loyal and neutral, in a moment." Precepts of charity uttered with faint breath at the end of a sermon are perfectly futile, when all the force of the lungs has been spent in keeping the hearer's mind fixed on the conception of his fellow men, not as fellow sinners and fellow sufferers, but as agents of hell, as automata through whom Satan plays his game upon earth,—not on objects which call forth their reverence, their love, their hope of good even in the most strayed and perverted, but on a minute identification of human things with such symbols as the scarlet whore, the beast out of the abyss, scorpions whose sting is in their tails, men who have the mark of the beast, and unclean spirits like frogs. You might as well attempt to educate a child's sense of beauty by hanging its nursery with the horrible and grotesque pictures in which the early painters represented the Last Judgement, as expect Christian graces to flourish on that prophetic interpretation which Dr. Cumming offers as the principal nutriment of his flock. Quite apart from the critical basis of that interpretation, quite apart from the degree of truth there may be in Dr. Cumming's prognostications—questions into which we do not choose to enter—his use of prophecy must be *a priori* condemned, in the judgement of right-minded persons, by its results as testified in the net moral effect of his sermons. The best minds that accept Christianity as a divinely inspired system believe that the great end of the Gospel is not merely the saving but the educating of men's souls, the creating within them of holy dispositions, the subduing of egoistical pretensions, and the perpetual enhancing of the desire that the will of God—a will synonymous with goodness and truth—may be done on earth. But what relation to all this has a system of interpretation which keeps the mind of the Christian in the position of a spectator at a gladiatorial show, of which Satan is the wild beast in the shape of the great red dragon, the two thirds of mankind the victims—the whole provided and got up by God for the edification of the saints? The demonstration that the Second Advent is at hand, if true, can have no really holy, spiritual effect; the highest state of mind inculcated by the Gospel is resignation to the disposal of God's providence—"Whether we live, we live unto the Lord; whether we die, we die unto the Lord"—not an eagerness to see a temporal manifestation which shall confound the enemies of God and give exaltation to the saints; it is to dwell in Christ by spiritual communion with His nature, not to fix the date when He shall appear in the sky. Dr. Cumming's delight in shadowing forth the downfall of the Man of Sin, in prognosticating the battle of Gog and Magog, and in advertising the premillennial Advent, is simply the transportation of political passions on to a so-called religious platform; it is the anticipation of the triumph of "our party," accomplished by our principal men being "sent for" into the clouds. Let us be understood to speak in all seriousness. If we were in search of amusement, we should not seek for it by examining Dr. Cumming's works in order to ridicule them. We are simply discharging a disagreeable duty in delivering our opinion that, judged by the highest standard even of orthodox Christianity, they are little calculated to produce

"A closer walk with God,
A calm and heavenly frame";[21]

but are more likely to nourish egoistic complacency and pretension, a hard and condemnatory spirit towards one's fellow men, and a busy occupation with the minutiæ of events, instead of a reverent contemplation of great facts and a wise application of great principles. It would be idle to consider Dr. Cumming's theory of prophecy in any other light,—as a philosophy of history or a specimen of Biblical interpretation; it bears about the same relation to the extension of genuine knowledge as the astrological "house" in the heavens bears to the true structure and relations of the universe. . . .

One more characteristic of Dr. Cumming's writings, and we have done. This is the *perverted moral judgement* that everywhere reigns in them. Not that this perversion is peculiar to Dr. Cumming; it belongs to the dogmatic system which he shares with all evangelical believers. But the abstract tendencies of systems are represented in very different degrees, according to the different characters of those who embrace them; just as the same food tells differently on different constitutions: and there are certain qualities in Dr. Cumming that cause the perversion of which we speak to exhibit itself with peculiar prominence in his teaching. A single extract will enable us to explain what we mean:—

"The 'thoughts' are evil. If it were possible for human eye to discern and to detect the thoughts that flutter round the heart of an unregenerate man—to mark their hue and their multitude—it would be found that they are indeed 'evil.' We speak not of the thief, and the murderer, and the adulterer, and such-like, whose crimes draw down the cognizance of earthly tribunals, and whose unenviable character it is to take the lead in the paths of sin; but we refer to the men who are marked out by their practice of many of the seemliest moralities of life—by the exercise of the kindliest affections, and the interchange of the sweetest reciprocities—and of these men, if unrenewed and unchanged, we pronounce that their thoughts are evil. To ascertain this, we must refer to the object around which our thoughts ought continually to circulate. The Scriptures assert that this object is *the glory of God;* that for this we ought to think, to act, and to speak; and that in thus thinking, acting, and speaking, there is involved the purest and most endearing bliss. Now it will be found true of the most amiable men that with all their good society and kindliness of heart, and all their strict and unbending integrity, they never or rarely think of the glory of God. The question never occurs to them—Will this redound to the glory of God? Will this make His name more known, His being more loved, His praise more sung? And just inasmuch as their every thought comes short of this lofty aim, in so much does it come short of good, and entitle itself to the character of evil. If the glory of God is not the absorbing and the influential aim of their thoughts, then they are evil; but God's glory never enters into their minds. They are amiable, because it chances to be one of the constitutional tendencies of their individual character, left uneffaced by the Fall; and *they are just and upright, because they have perhaps no occasion to be otherwise, or find it subservient to their interests to maintain such a character.*"[22]

Again we read:—[23]

"There are traits in the Christian character which the mere worldly man cannot understand. He can understand the outward morality, but he cannot understand the inner spring of it; he can understand Dorcas's liberality to the poor, but he cannot penetrate the ground of Dorcas's liberality. *Some men give to the poor because they are ostentatious, or because they think the poor will ultimately avenge their neglect; but the Christian gives to the poor, not only because he has sensibilities like other men,* but because inasmuch as ye did it to the least of these my brethren, ye did it unto me."

Before entering on the more general question involved in these quotations, we must point to the clauses we have marked with italics, where Dr. Cumming appears to express sentiments which, we are happy to think, are not shared by the majority of his brethren in the faith. Dr. Cumming, it seems, is unable to conceive that the natural man can have any other motive for being just and upright than that it is useless to be otherwise, or that a character for honesty is profitable; according to his experience, between the feelings of ostentation and selfish alarm and the feeling of love to Christ, there lie no sensibilities which can lead a man to relieve want. Granting, as we should prefer to think, that it is Dr. Cumming's exposition of his sentiments which is deficient rather than his sentiments themselves, still, the fact that the deficiency lies precisely here, and that he can overlook it not only in the haste of oral delivery but in the examination of proof-sheets is strongly significant of his mental bias—of the faint degree in which he sympathizes with the disinterested elements of human feeling, and of the fact, which we are about to dwell upon, that those feelings are totally absent from his religious theory. Now, Dr. Cumming invariably assumes that, in fulminating against those who differ from him, he is standing on a moral elevation to which they are compelled reluctantly to look up; that his theory of motives and conduct is in its loftiness and purity a perpetual rebuke to their low and vicious desires and practice. It is time he should be told that the reverse is the fact; that there are men who do not merely cast a superficial glance at his doctrine, and fail to see its beauty or justice, but who, after a close consideration of that doctrine, pronounce it to be subversive of true moral development, and therefore positively noxious. Dr. Cumming is fond of showing-up the teaching of Romanism, and accusing it of undermining true morality: it is time he should be told that there is a large body, both of thinkers and practical men, who hold precisely the same opinion of his own teaching—with this difference, that they do not regard it as the inspiration of Satan, but as the natural crop of a human mind where the soil is chiefly made up of egoistic passions and dogmatic beliefs.

Dr. Cumming's theory, as we have seen, is that actions are good or evil according as they are prompted or not prompted by an exclusive reference to the "glory of God." God, then, in Dr. Cumming's conception, is a Being who has no pleasure in the exercise of love and truthfulness and justice, considered as affecting the well-being of His creatures; He has satisfaction in us only in so far as we exhaust our motives and dispositions of all relation to our fellow beings, and replace sympathy with men by anxiety for the "glory of God." The deed of Grace Darling, when she took a boat in the storm to rescue drowning men and women, was not good if it was only compassion that nerved her arm and impelled her to brave death for the chance of saving others; it was only good if she asked herself—Will this redound to the glory of God? The man who endures tortures rather than betray a trust, the man who spends years in toil in order to discharge an obligation from which the law declares him free, must be animated not by the spirit of fidelity to his fellow man, but by a desire to make "the name of God more known." The sweet charities of domestic life—the ready hand and the soothing word in sickness, the forbearance towards frailties, the prompt helpfulness in all efforts and sympathy in all joys—are simply evil if they result from a "constitutional tendency," or from dispositions disciplined by the experience of suffering and the perception of moral loveliness. A wife is not to devote herself to her husband out of love to him and a sense of the duties implied by a close relation—she is to be a faithful wife for the glory of God; if she feels her natural affections welling up too strongly, she is to repress them; it would not do to act from natural affection—she must think of the glory of God. A man is to guide his affairs with energy and discretion, not from an honest desire to fulfil his responsibilities as a member of society and a father, but— that "God's praise may be sung." Dr. Cumming's Christian pays his debts for the glory of God: were it not for the coercion of that supreme motive, it would be evil to pay them. A man is not to be just from a feeling of justice; he is not to help his fellow men out of good will to his fellow men; he is not to be a tender husband and father out of affection: all his natural muscles and fibres are to be torn away and replaced by a patent steel-spring—anxiety for the "glory of God."

Happily, the constitution of human nature forbids the complete prevalence of such a theory. Fatally powerful as religious systems have been, human nature is stronger and wider than religious systems, and though dogmas may hamper, they cannot absolutely repress its growth: build walls round the living tree as you will, the bricks and mortar have by and by to give way before the slow and sure operation of the sap. But next to that hatred of the enemies of God which is the principle of persecution, there perhaps has been no perversion more obstructive of true moral development than this substitution of a reference to the glory of God for the direct promptings of the sympathetic feelings. Benevolence and justice are strong only in proportion as they are directly and inevitably called into activity by their proper objects: pity is strong only because we are strongly impressed by suffering; and only in proportion as it is compassion that speaks through the eyes when we soothe, and moves the arm when we succour, is a deed strictly benevolent. If the soothing or the succour be given because another being wishes or approves it, the deed ceases to be one of benevolence, and becomes one of deference, of obedience, of self-interest, or vanity. Accessory motives may aid in producing an *action*, but they presuppose the weakness of the direct motive; and conversely, when the direct motive is strong, the action of accessory motives will be excluded. If then, as Dr. Cumming inculcates, the glory of God is to be "the absorbing and the influential aim" in our thoughts and actions, this must tend to neutralize the human sympathies; the stream of feeling will be diverted from its natural current in order to feed an artificial canal. The idea of God is really moral in its influence—it really cherishes all that is best and loveliest in man—only when God is contemplated as sympathizing with the pure elements of human feeling, as possessing infinitely all those attributes which we recognize to be moral in humanity. In this light, the idea of God and the sense of His presence intensify all noble feeling, and encourage all noble effort, on the same principle that human sympathy is found a source of strength: the brave man feels braver when he knows that another stout heart is beating time with his; the devoted woman who is wearing out her years in patient effort to alleviate suffering or save vice from the last stages of degradation finds aid in the pressure of a friendly hand which tells her that there is one who understands her deeds, and in her place would do the like. The idea of a God who not only sympathizes with all we feel and endure for our fellow men, but who will pour new life into our too languid love, and give firmness to our vacillating purpose, is an extension and multiplication of the effects produced by human sympathy; and it has been intensified for the better spirits who have been under the influence of orthodox Christianity, by the contemplation of Jesus as "God manifest in the flesh." But Dr. Cumming's God is the very opposite of all this: He is a God who, instead of sharing and aiding our human sympathies, is directly in collision with them; who, instead of strengthening the bond between man and man, by encouraging the sense that they are both alike the objects of His love and care, thrusts Himself between them and forbids them to feel for each other except as they have relation to Him. He is a God who, instead of adding His solar force to swell the tide of those impulses that tend to give humanity a common life in which the good of one is the good of all, commands us to check those impulses, lest they should prevent us from thinking of His glory. It is in vain for Dr. Cumming to say that we are to love man for God's sake: with the conception of God which his teaching presents, the love of man for God's sake involves, as his writings abundantly show, a strong principle of hatred. We can only love one being for the sake of another when there is an habitual delight in associating the idea of those two beings—that is, when the object of our indirect love is a source of joy and honour to the object of our direct love. But, according to Dr. Cumming's theory, the majority of mankind—the majority of his neighbours—are in precisely the opposite relation to God. His soul has no pleasure in them: they belong more to Satan than to Him; and if they contribute to His glory, it is against their will. Dr. Cumming, then, can only love *some* men for God's sake; the rest he must in consistency *hate* for God's sake.

There must be many, even in the circle of Dr. Cumming's admirers, who would be revolted by the doctrine we have just exposed, if their natural good sense and healthy feeling were not early stifled by dogmatic beliefs, and their reverence misled by pious phrases. But as it is, many a rational question, many a generous instinct, is repelled as the suggestion of a supernatural enemy, or as the ebullition of human pride and corruption. This state of inward contradiction can be put an end to only by the conviction that the free and diligent exertion of the intellect, instead of being a sin, is a part of their responsibility—that Right and Reason are synonymous. The fundamental faith for man is faith in the result of a brave, honest, and steady use of all his faculties:—

> Let knowledge grow from more to more,
> But more of reverence in us dwell;
> That mind and soul according well
> May make one music as before,
> But vaster.[24]

Before taking leave of Dr. Cumming, let us express a hope that we have in no case exaggerated the unfavourable character of the inferences to be drawn from his pages. His creed often obliges him to hope the worst of men, and to exert himself in proving that the worst is true; but thus far we are happier than he. We have no theory which requires us to attribute unworthy motives to Dr. Cumming, no opinions, religious or irreligious, which can make it a gratification to us to detect him in delinquencies. On the contrary, the better we are able to think of him as a man, while we are obliged to disapprove him as a theologian, the stronger will be the evidence for our conviction, that the tendency towards good in human nature has a force which no creed can utterly counteract, and which ensures the ultimate triumph of that tendency over all dogmatic perversions.

NOTES

1. [John Cumming (1807–1881), Scottish Presbyterian clergyman. The works to which Eliot refers in this article are *Is Christianity from God: A Manual of Christian Evidences* (1847), *Apocalyptic Sketches* (1848–50), *Occasional Discourses* (1852), *The Church Before the Flood* (1853), and *Signs of the Times* (1854).]

2. [Followers of Edward Pusey (1800–1882), a leader of the Oxford Movement, which sought to bring Anglican belief and practice closer to Roman Catholicism.]

3. ["Christianity, in whatever manner, Christianity."]

4. [Eliot's error for Charles Leslie (1650–1722), *A Short and Easy Method with the Deists* (1698), an attack on Deism from the standpoint of orthodox Christianity.]

5. *Manual of Christian Evidences*, p. 81.

6. *Manual of Christian Evidences*, p. 254.

7. [The references are to William Paley (1743–1805), author of *A View of the Evidences of Christianity* (1794); Joseph Butler (see n. 13 to chapter 2); and Thomas Chalmers (1780–1847), Scottish theologian.]

8. *Church Before the Flood*, p. 35.

9. *Apocalyptic Sketches*, p. 405.

10. ["There are those for whom it is an honor to have once been an unbeliever, and a pledge for future faith."]

11. See See *Manual of Christian Evidences*, p. 73.

12. [See A. J. Ayer, p. 102 n. 3.]

13. [It was frequently asserted by theists that Voltaire experienced a deathbed conversion to Catholicism.]

14. [Eliot refers to two ancient works whose authorship is in doubt.]

15. ["For the greater glory of God."]

16. [The reference is to Robert Chambers (1802–1871), a Scottish author whose *Vestiges of the Natural History of Creation* (1844) broached a theory of evolution dimly anticipating Darwin's.]

17. *Christ Before the Flood*, p. 93.

18. *Signs of the Times*, p. 38.

19. *Apocalyptic Sketches*, p. 243.

20. ["Hidden motive."]

21. [William Cowper, *Olney Hymns* (1779), no. 1.]

22. *Occasional Discourses*, vol. i, p. 8.

23. Ibid., p. 236.

24. [Alfred, Lord Tennyson, *In Memoriam: A. H. H.* (1850), Prologue, stanza 7.]

14

HUMANITY'S GAIN FROM UNBELIEF
(1889)

Charles Bradlaugh

Englishman Charles Bradlaugh (1833–1891) was one of the most con-
troversial freethinkers and political figures of the later nineteenth cen-
tury. Having developed doubts about religion at an early age, Bradlaugh
began lecturing on freethought and republicanism in open-air meetings
in the 1850s. In 1880, after several defeats, he was elected to Parlia-
ment; but a controversy raged for years afterward over his refusal to take
the oath of office on a Bible, and he was excluded from holding his seat
until 1886; he remained in Parliament for the rest of his life. Bradlaugh
was involved in several lawsuits relating to the freedom of the press to
criticize religion, especially in his long-running weekly, the National
Reformer. *A prolific writer, Bradlaugh wrote such treatises as* Half-
Hours with the Freethinkers *(1856–57),* Genesis: It Authorship
and Authenticity *(1882), and* Political Essays *(1887–89). His*
Autobiography *was published in 1873. In the trenchant essay*
"Humanity's Gain from Unbelief" (first published in the North American Review *for March 1889), Bradlaugh argues that religious toler-*
ance was largely brought about by increasing skepticism, and that other
advances in humanitarianism, such as that abolition of slavery, were led
by figures not because, but in spite, of their religious beliefs.

A S AN UNBELIEVER, I ASK leave to plead that humanity has been a
real gainer from scepticism, and that the gradual and growing

---

From Charles Bradlaugh, "Humanity's Gain from Unbelief," *North American Review*
148, no. 3 (March 1889): 294–306.

rejection of Christianity—like the rejection of the faiths which preceded it—has, in fact, added, and will add, to man's happiness and well-being. I maintain that, in physics, science is the outcome of scepticism, and that general progress is impossible without scepticism on matters of religion. I mean by religion, every form of belief which accepts or asserts the super-natural. I write as a Monist, and use the word "nature" as meaning all phenomena, every phenomenon, all that is necessary for the happening of any and every phenomenon. Every religion is constantly changing, and at any given time is the measure of the civilization attained by what Guizot[1] described as the *juste milieu* of those who profess it. Each religion is slowly, but certainly, modified in its dogma and practice by the gradual development of the peoples amongst whom it is professed. Each discovery destroys in whole or part some theretofore-cherished belief. No religion is suddenly rejected by any people; it is, rather, gradually outgrown. None see a religion die; dead religions are like dead languages and obsolete customs; the decay is long, and, like the glacier-march, is only perceptible to the careful watcher by comparisons extending over long periods. A superseded religion may often be traced in the festivals, ceremonies, and dogmas of the religion which has replaced it. Traces of obsolete religions may often be found in popular customs, in old-wives' stories, and in children's tales.

It is necessary, in order that my plea should be understood, that I should explain what I mean by Christianity; and in the very attempt at this explanation there will, I think, be found strong illustration of the value of unbelief. Christianity in practice may be gathered from its more ancient forms represented by the Roman Catholic and the Greek churches, or from the various churches which have grown up in the last few centuries. Each of these churches calls itself Christian. Some of them deny the right of the others to use the word Christian. Some Christian churches treat, or have treated, other Christian churches as heretics or unbelievers. The Roman Catholics and the Protestants in Great Britain and Ireland have, in turn, been terribly cruel one to the other, and the ferocious laws of the seventeenth and eighteenth centuries enacted by the English Protestants against English and Irish Papists are a disgrace to civilization. These penal laws, enduring longest in Ireland, still bear fruit in much of the political mischief and agrarian crime of to-day. It is only the tolerant indifference of scepticism that has repealed, one after the other, most of the laws directed by the Established Christian Church against Papists and Dissenters, and also against Jews and heretics. Church-of-England clergymen have in the past gone to great lengths in denouncing non-conformity; and even in the present day an effective sample of such denunciatory bigotry may be found in a sort of orthodox catechism written by the Rev. F. A. Grace, of Great Barling, Essex, the popularity of which is vouched for by the fact that it has gone through ten editions. This catechism for little children teaches that "dissent is a great sin" and that Dissenters "worship God according to their own evil and corrupt imaginations, and not according to his revealed will, and therefore their worship is idolatrous." Church-of-England Christians and dissenting Christians, when fraternizing amongst themselves, often publicly draw the line at Unitarians, and positively deny that these have any sort of right to call themselves Christians.

In the first half of the seventeenth century, Quakers were flogged and imprisoned in England as blasphemers, and the early Christian settlers in New England, escaping from the persecution of Old-World Christians, showed scant mercy to the followers of Fox and Penn. It is customary, in controversy, for those advocating the claims of Christianity to include all good done by men in nominally Christian countries, as if such good were the result of Christianity, while they contend that the evil which exists prevails in spite of Christianity. I shall try to make out that the ameliorating march of the last few centuries has been initiated by the heretics of each age, though I quite concede that the men and women denounced and persecuted as infidels by the pious of one century are frequently classed as saints by the pious of a later generation.

What, then, is Christianity? As a system or scheme of doctrine, Christianity may, I submit, not unfairly be gathered from the Old and New Testaments. It is true that some Christians to-day desire to escape from submission to part, at any rate, of the Old Testament; but this very tendency seems to me to be part of the result of the beneficial heresy for which I am pleading. Man's humanity has revolted against Old-Testament barbarism, and, therefore, he has attempted to dissociate the Old Testament from Christianity. Unless Old and New Testaments are accepted as God's revelation to man, Christianity has no higher claim than any other of the world's many religions—if no such claim can be made out for it apart from the Bible. And though it is quite true that some who deem themselves Christians put the Old Testament completely in the background, this is, I allege, because they are outgrowing their Christianity. Without the doctrine of the atoning sacrifice of Jesus, Christianity, as a religion, is naught; but unless the story of Adam's fall is accepted, the redemption from the consequences of that fall cannot be believed. Both in Great Britain and in the United States the Old and New Testaments are forced on the people as part of Christianity, for it is blasphemy at common law to deny the scriptures of the Old and New Testaments to be of divine authority, and such denial is punishable with fine and imprisonment, or even worse. The rejection of Christianity intended throughout this paper is, therefore, the rejection of the Old and New Testaments as being of divine revelation. It is the rejection alike of the authorized teachings of the Church of Rome and of the Church of England, as these may be found in the Bible; the creeds, the encyclicals, the prayer-book, the canons, and the homilies of either or both of these churches. It is the rejection of the Christianity of Luther, of Calvin, and of Wesley.

A ground frequently taken by Christian theologians is that the progress and civilization of the world are due to Christianity, and the discussion is complicated by the fact that many eminent servants of humanity have been nominal Christians of one or other of the sects. My allegation will be that the special service rendered to human progress by these exceptional men has not been in consequence of their adhesion to Christianity, but in spite of it; and that the specific points of advantage to human kind have been in ratio of their direct opposition to precise Biblical enactments. Take one clear gain to humanity consequent on unbelief—i.e., the abolition of slavery in some countries, the abolition of the slave-trade in most civilized countries, and the tendency to its total abolition. I am unaware of any religion in the world which in the past forbade slavery. The professors of Christianity for ages supported it; the Old Testament repeatedly sanctioned it by special laws; the New Testament has no repealing declaration. Though we are at the close of the nineteenth century of the Christian era, it is only during the past three-quarters of a century that the battle for freedom has been gradually won. It is scarcely a quarter of a century since the famous emancipation amendment was carried to the United States Constitution; and it is impossible for any well-informed Christian to deny that the abolition movement in North America was most steadily and bitterly opposed by the religious bodies in the various States. Henry Wilson, in his *Rise and Fall of the Slave-Power in America*; Samuel J. May, in his *Recollections of the Anti-Slavery Conflict*, and J. Greenleaf Whittier, in his poems, alike are witnesses that the Bible and pulpit, the church and its great influence, were used against abolition and in favor of the slaveowner. I know that Christians in the present day often declare that Christianity had a large share in bringing about the abolition of slavery, and this because men professing Christianity were Abolitionists. I plead that those so-called Christian Abolitionists were men and women whose humanity—recognizing freedom for all—was, in this, in direct conflict with Christianity. It is not yet fifty years since the European Christian Powers jointly agreed to abolish the slave trade. What of the effect of Christianity on these Powers in the centuries which had preceded? The heretic Condorcet pleaded powerfully for freedom, whilst Christian France was still slave-holding. For many centuries Christian Spain and Christian Portugal held slaves. Porto Rico freedom is not of long date, and Cuban emancipation is even yet newer. It was a Christian king, Charles V., and a Christian friar, who founded in Spanish America the slave-trade between the Old World and the New. For some 1,800 years almost all Christians kept slaves, bought slaves, sold slaves, bred slaves, stole slaves. Pious Bristol and godly Liverpool, less than one hundred years ago, openly grow rich on the traffic. During the ninth century Greek Christians sold slaves to the Saracens. In the eleventh century prostitutes were publicly sold in Rome as slaves, and the profit went to the church.

It is said that William Wilberforce[2] was a Christian, but, at any rate, his Christianity was strongly diluted with unbelief. As an Abolitionist, he did not believe Leviticus, c. 25, v. 44–46; he must have rejected Exodus, c. 21, v. 2–6;[3] he could not have accepted the many permissions and injunctions by the Bible Deity to his chosen people to capture and hold slaves. In the House of Commons on the 18th of February, 1796, Wilberforce reminded that Christian assembly that infidel and anarchic France had given liberty to the Africans, whilst Christian and monarchic England was "obstinately continuing a system of cruelty and injustice." Wilberforce, whilst advocating the abolition of slavery, found the whole influence of the English court and the great weight of the Episcopal bench against him. George III., a most Christian king, regarded abolition theories with abhorrence, and the Christian House of Lords was utterly opposed to granting freedom to the slave. When Christian missionaries, some sixty-two years ago, preached to Demerara negroes under the rule of Christian England, they were treated by Christian judges, holding commission from Christian England, as criminals for so preaching. A Christian commissioned officer, member of the Established Church of England, signed the auction notices for the sale of slaves as late as the year 1824. In the evidence before a Christian court-martial a missionary is charged with having tended to make the negroes dissatisfied with their condition as slaves, and with having promoted discontent and dissatisfaction amongst the slaves against their lawful masters. For this the Christian judges sentenced the Demerara Abolitionist missionary to be hanged by the neck till he was dead. The judges belonged to the Established Church; the missionary was a Methodist. In this the Church-of-England Christians in Demerara were no worse than Christians of other sects. Their Roman Catholic Christian brethren in St. Domingo fiercely attacked the Jesuits as criminals, because they treated the negroes as though they were men and women, in encouraging "two slaves to separate their interest and safety from that of the gang," whilst orthodox Christians let them couple promiscuously and breed for the benefit of the owners, like any other of their plantation cattle. In 1823 the *Royal Gazette* (Christian) of Demerara said: "We shall not suffer you to enlighten our slaves, who are by law our property, till you can demonstrate that, when they are made religious and knowing, they will continue to be our slaves."

When William Lloyd Garrison, the pure-minded and most earnest Abolitionist, delivered his first anti-slavery address in Boston, Massachusetts, the only building he could obtain in which to speak was the infidel hall owned by Abner Kneeland, the "infidel" editor of the *Boston Investigator*, who had been sent to jail for blasphemy. All the Christian sects had, in turn, refused Mr. Lloyd Garrison the use of the buildings they severally controlled. Lloyd Garrison told me, himself, how honored deacons of a Christian church joined in an actual attempt to hang him. When abolition was advocated in the United States in 1790, the representative from South Carolina was able to plead that the Southern clergy "did not condemn either slavery or the slave-trade," and Mr. Jackson, the representative from Georgia, pleaded that "from Genesis to Revelation" the current was favorable to slavery. Elias Hicks, the brave Abolitionist Quaker, was denounced as an atheist, and less than twenty years ago a Hicksite Quaker was expelled from one of the Southern American legislatures because of the reputed irreligion of these Abolitionist "Friends." When the Fugitive-Slave Law was under discussion in North America, large numbers of clergymen, of nearly every denomination, were found ready to defend this infamous act. Samuel James May, the famous Abolitionist, was driven from the pulpit as irreligious, solely because of his attacks on slave-holding. Northern clergymen tried to induce "silver-tongued" Wendell Phillips to abandon his advocacy of abolition. Southern pulpits rang with praises for the murderous attack on Charles Sumner. The slayers of Elijah Lovejoy were highly-reputed Christian men.

Guizot, notwithstanding that he tries to claim that the Church exerted its influence to restrain slavery, says (*European Civilization*, Vol. I., p. 110):

> It has often been repeated that the abolition of slavery among modern people is entirely due to Christians. That, I think, is saying too much. Slavery existed for a long period in the heart of Christian society, without its being particularly astonished or irritated. A multitude of causes, and a great development in other ideas and principles of civilization, were necessary for the abolition of this iniquity of all iniquities.

And my contention is that this "development in other ideas and principles of civilization" was long retarded by governments in which the Christian Church was dominant. The men who advocated liberty were imprisoned, racked, and burned, so long as the church was strong enough to be merciless. The Rev. Francis Minton, Rector of Middlewich, in his recent earnest volume[4] on the struggles of labor, admits that "a few centuries ago slavery was acknowledged throughout Christendom to have the divine sanction. . . . Neither the exact cause nor the precise time of the decline of the belief in the righteousness of slavery can be defined. It was, doubtless, due to a combination of causes, one probably being as indirect as the recognition of the greater economy of free labor. With the decline of the belief, the abolition of slavery took place." The institution of slavery was actually existent in Christian Scotland in the seventeenth century, where the white coal-workers and salt-workers of East Lothian were chattels, as were their negro brethren in the Southern States thirty years since, and "went to those who succeeded to the property of the works, and they could be sold, bartered, or pawned."[5] There is, says J. M. Robertson, "no trace that the Protestant clergy of Scotland ever raised a voice against the slavery which grew up before their eyes. And it was not until 1799, after Republican and irreligious France had set the example, that it was legally abolished."

Take the further gain to humanity consequent on the unbelief, or rather disbelief, in witchcraft and wizardry. Apart from the brutality by Christians towards those suspected of witchcraft, the hindrance to scientific initiative or experiment was incalculably great so long as belief in magic obtained. The inventions of the past two centuries, and especially those of this nineteenth century, might have benefited mankind much earlier and much more largely but for the foolish belief in witchcraft and the shocking ferocity exhibited towards those suspected of necromancy. After quoting a large number of cases of trial and punishment for witchcraft from official records in Scotland, J. M. Robertson says: "The people seem to have passed from cruelty to cruelty, precisely as they became more and more fanatical, more and more devoted to their church, till, after many generations, the slow spread of human science began to counteract the ravages of superstition, the clergy resisting reason and humanity to the last."

The Rev. Mr. Minton[6] concedes that it is "the advance of knowledge which has rendered the idea of Satanic agency, through the medium of witchcraft, grotesquely ridiculous." He admits that "for more than fifteen hundred years the belief in witchcraft was universal in Christendom," and that "the public mind was saturated with the idea of Satanic agency in the economy of nature." He adds: "If we ask why the world now rejects what was once so unquestioningly believed, we can only reply that advancing knowledge has gradually undermined the belief."

In a letter recently sent to the *Pall Mall Gazette* against modern Spiritualism, Professor Huxley declares "that the older form of the same fundamental delusion—the belief in possession and in witchcraft—gave rise, in the fifteenth, sixteenth, and seventeenth centuries, to persecutions by Christians of innocent men, women, and children, more extensive, more cruel, and more murderous than any to which the Christians of the first three centuries were subjected by the authorities of pagan Rome." And Professor Huxley adds:

> No one deserves much blame for being deceived in these matters. We are all intellectually handicapped in youth by the incessant repetition of the stories about possession and witchcraft in both the Old and the New

Testament. The majority of us are taught nothing which will help us to observe accurately, and to interpret observations with due caution.

The English statute-book under Elizabeth and under James was disfigured by enactments against witchcraft passed under pressure from the Christian churches, which acts have only been repealed in consequence of the disbelief in the Christian precept, "Thou shalt not suffer a witch to live." The statute 1 James I., c. 12, condemned to death "all persons invoking any evil spirits, or consulting, covenanting with, entertaining, employing, feeding, or rewarding any evil spirit," or generally practising any "infernal arts." This was not repealed until the eighteenth century was far advanced. Edison's phonograph would, two hundred and eighty years ago, have insured martyrdom for the inventor; the utilization of electric force to transmit messages around the world would have been clearly the practice of an infernal art. At least, we may plead that unbelief has healed the bleeding feet of science and made the road free for her upward march.

Is it not also fair to urge the gain to humanity which has been apparent in the wiser treatment of the insane consequent on the unbelief in the Christian doctrine that these unfortunates were either examples of demoniacal possession or of special visitation of Deity? For centuries, under Christianity, mental disease was most ignorantly treated. Exorcism, shackles, and the whip were the penalties, rather than the curatives, for mental maladies. From the heretical departure of Pinel, at the close of the last century, to the position of Maudsley to-day, every step illustrates the march of unbelief.[7] Take the gain to humanity in the unbelief, not yet complete, but now largely preponderant, in the dogma that sickness, pestilence, and famine were manifestations of divine anger, the results of which could neither be avoided nor prevented. The Christian churches have done little or nothing to dispel this superstition. The official and authorized prayers of the principal denominations even to-day reaffirm it. Modern study of the laws of health, experiments in sanitary improvements, more careful application of medical knowledge, have proved more efficacious in preventing or diminishing plagues and pestilence than have the intervention of the priest or the practice of prayer. Those in England who hold the old faith that prayer will suffice to cure disease are to-day termed "peculiar people," and are occasionally indicted for manslaughter, when their sick children die, because the parents have trusted to God instead of appealing to the resources of science.

It is certainly clear gain to astronomical science that the church which tried to compel Galileo to unsay the truth, has been overborne by the growing unbelief of the age, even though our little children are yet taught that Joshua made the sun and moon stand still, and that for Hezekiah the sun-dial reversed its record. As Buckle, arguing for the morality of scepticism, says:[8]

> As long as men refer the movements of the comets to the immediate finger of God, and as long as they believe that an eclipse is one of the modes by which the Deity expresses his anger, they will never be guilty of the blasphemous presumption of attempting to predict such supernatural appearances. Before they could dare to investigate the causes of the mysterious phenomena, it is necessary that they should believe, or, at all events, that they should suspect, that the phenomena themselves were capable of being explained by the human mind.

As in astronomy, so in geology, the gain of the knowledge to humanity has been almost solely in measure of the rejection of the Christian theory, a century since almost universally held, that the world was created six thousand years ago, or, at any rate, that by the sin of the first man, Adam, death commenced about that period. Ethnology and anthropology have only been possible in so far as, adopting the regretful words of Sir W. Jones,[9] "intelligent and virtuous persons are inclined to doubt the authenticity of the documents delivered by Moses concerning the primitive world."

Surely it is clear gain to humanity that unbelief has sprung up against the divine right of kings; that men no longer believe that the monarch is "God's anointed," or that "the powers that be are ordained of God." In the struggles for political freedom, the weight of the church was mostly thrown on the side of the tyrant. The homilies of the Church of England declare that "even the wicked rulers have their power and authority from God," that "such subjects as are disobedient or rebellious against their princes, disobey God and procure their own damnation." It can scarcely be necessary to argue to the citizens of the United States of America that the origin of their liberties was in the rejection of this faith in the divine right of George III. Will any one, save the most bigoted, contend that it is not certain gain to humanity to spread unbelief in the terrible doctrine that eternal torment is the probable fate of the great majority of the human family? Is it not gain to have diminished the faith that it was the duty of the wretched and the miserable to be content with the lot in life which Providence had awarded them?

If it stood alone, it would be almost sufficient to plead, as justification for heresy, the approach towards equality and liberty for the utterance of all opinions achieved because of growing unbelief. At one period in Christendom each government acted as though only one religious faith could be true, and as though the holding, or, at any rate, the making known, of any other opinion was a criminal act deserving punishment. Under the one word, "infidel," even as late as Lord Coke,[10] were classed together all who were not Christians, even though they were Mohommedans, Brahmans, or Jews. All who did not accept the Christian faith were sweepingly denounced as infidels and, therefore, *hors de la loi*.[11] One hundred and forty-five years since, the Attorney General, pleading in our highest court, said:[12] "What is the definition of an infidel? Why, one who does not believe in the Christian religion. Then a Jew is an infidel." And English history for several centuries prior to the Commonwealth shows how, habitually and most atrociously, Christian kings, Christian courts, and Christian churches persecuted and harassed these infidel Jews. There was a time in England when Jews were such infidels that they were not even allowed to be sworn as witnesses. In 1740, a legacy left for establishing an assembly for the reading of the Jewish Scriptures was held to be void[13] because it was "for the propagation of the Jewish law in contradiction to the Christian religion." It is only in very modern times that municipal rights have been accorded in England to Jews. It is barely thirty years since they have been allowed to sit in Parliament. In 1801, the late Mr. Newdegate, in debate,[14] objected "that they should have sitting in that House an individual who regarded our Redeemer as an impostor." Lord Chief Justice Raymond has shown[15] how it was that Christian intolerance was gradually broken down: "A Jew may sue at this day, but heretofore he could not; for then they were looked upon as enemies, but now commerce has taught the world more humanity." Lord Coke treated the infidel as one who, in law, had no right of any kind, with whom no contract need be kept, to whom no debt was payable. The plea of "alien infidel," as answer to a claim, was actually pleaded in court as late as 1737.[16] In a solemn judgment Lord Coke says:[17] "All infidels are, in law, *perpetui inimici*,[18] for between them, as with the devils whose subjects they be, and the Christians, there is perpetual hostility." Twenty years ago the law of England required the writer of any periodical, publication, or pamphlet under sixpence in price to give sureties for eight hundred pounds against the publication of blasphemy. I was the last person prosecuted, in 1868, for non-compliance with that law, which was repealed by Mr. Gladstone in 1869. Up till the 23d of December, 1888, an infidel in Scotland was only allowed to enforce any legal claim in court on condition that, if challenged, he denied his infidelity. If he lied and said that he was a Christian, he was accepted, despite his lying. If he told the truth and said that he was an unbeliever, then he was practically an outlaw, incompetent to give evidence for himself or for any other. Fortunately, all this was changed by the royal assent to the Oaths Act on the 24th of December. Has not humanity clearly gained a little in this struggle through unbelief?

For more than a century and a half the Roman Catholic had, in practice, harsher measure dealt out to him by the English Protestant Christian than was, even during that period, the fate of the Jew or the unbeliever. If the Roman Catholic would not take the oath of abjuration, which, to a sincere Romanist, was impossible, he was, in effect, an outlaw, and the "jury-packing," so much complained of to-day in Ireland, is one of the survivals of the old, bad time when Roman Catholics were thus, by law, excluded from the jury-box.

The *Scotsman* of January 5, 1889, notes that, in 1860, the Rev. Dr. Robert Lee, of Greyfriars, gave a course of Sunday evening lectures on Biblical Criticism, in which he showed the absurdity and untenableness of regarding every word in the Bible as inspired, and adds:

> We well remember the awful indignation such opinions inspired, and it is refreshing to contrast them with the calmness with which they are now received. Not only from the pulpits of the city, but from the press (misnamed religious) were his doctrines denounced. And one eminent U.P. minister went the length of publicly praying for him, and for the students under his care. It speaks volumes for the progress made since then, when we think that, in all probability, Dr. Charteris, Dr. Lee's successor in the chair, differs, in his teaching, from the Confession of Faith much more widely than Dr. Lee ever did, and yet he is

considered supremely orthodox, whereas the stigma of heresy was attached to the other all his life.

And this change and gain to humanity are due to the gradual progress of unbelief alike inside and outside the churches. Take, from differing churches, two recent illustrations. The late Principal, Dr. Lindsay Alexander, a strict Calvinist, in his important work on *Biblical Theology*, claims that "all the statements of Scripture are alike to be deferred to, as presenting to us the mind of God." Yet the Reverend Doctor of Divinity also says: "We find in their writings [i.e., in the writings of the sacred authors] statements which no ingenuity can reconcile with what modern research has shown to be the scientific truth." At the last Southwell Diocesan Church-of-England Conference, at Derby, the Bishop of the Diocese presiding, the Rev. J. G. Richardson said of the Old Testament that "it was no longer honest, or even safe, to deny that this noble literature, rich in all the elements of moral or spiritual grandeur, given—so the Church had always taught and would always teach—under the inspiration of Almighty God, was sometimes mistaken in its science, was sometimes inaccurate in its history, and sometimes relative and accommodatory in its morality. It resumed theories of the physical world which science has abandoned and could never resume; it contained passages of narrative which devout and temperate men pronounced discredited both by external and internal evidence; it praised, or justified, or approved, or condoned, or tolerated conduct which the teaching of Christ and the conscience of the Christian alike condemned." Or—as I should urge—the gain to humanity by unbelief is that the "teaching of Christ" has been modified, enlarged, widened, and humanized, and that "the conscience of the Christian" is, in quantity and quality, made fitter for the ever-increasing additions of knowledge of these later and more heretical days.

NOTES

1. [François-Pierre-Guillaume Guizot (1787–1874), French politician and highly regarded historian. He wrote *Histoire de la civilization en Europe* (1828; *General History of Civilization in Europe*), *Histoire de la civilization en France* (1829–32; *History of Civilization in France*), and other works. As minister

of education (1832–37) Guizot established the right of primary secular education for all French citizens.]

2. [William Wilberforce (1759–1833), British politician who, purportedly under the influence of evangelical Christianity, led the movement for the abolition of slavery in England.]

3. [Bradlaugh refers to two notorious passages in the Bible dealing with slavery. The former recommends the keeping of slaves from "the heathen that are round about you" and from "the children of the strangers that do sojourn among you," and states that these shall be "your bondmen for ever" (Leviticus 25:44–46); the latter cites laws governing the buying of "a Hebrew servant."]

4. *Capital and Wages,* p. 19.

5. *Perversion of Scotland,* p. 197.

6. *Capital and Wages,* pp. 15, 16.

7. [Philippe Pinel (1745–1826), French physician who initiated the humane treatment of mentally ill patients by abandoning the belief that they were possessed by demons. Henry Maudsley (1835–1918), a British alienist and avowed atheist who, influenced by Darwin and Spencer, advocated the physical basis of mental disease.]

8. *History of Civilization,* Vol. I., p. 345. [Henry Thomas Buckle (1821–1862), British historian best known for *History of Civilization in England* (1857–61), which downplayed the role of religion in human affairs.]

9. [Sir William Jones (1746–1794), British Orientalist and authority in the Persian language.]

10. [Sir Edward Coke (1552–1634), attorney general of Great Britain (1594–1606) and chief justice of the Court of Common Pleas (1606–16), known for his ruthless prosecutions for libel and treason.]

11. ["Outside of the law."]

12. Omychund vs. Barker, 1 Atkyns, 29.

13. D'Costa vs. D'Pays, Amb., 228.

14. 3 Hansard, cxvi., 381.

15. 1 Lord Raymond's Reports, 282, Wells vs. Williams.

16. Ramkijsenseat vs. Barker, 1 Atkyns, 51.

17. Coke's reports, Calvin's case.

18. ["Perpetual enemies."]

15

MIRACLE
(1895)

Anatole France

Anatole France was the pseudonym of Jacques-Anatole-François Thibault (1844–1924). He began writing in the 1860s and—in addition to numerous essays on literature, politics, and society—produced a succession of daring and controversial novels that established him as among the leading French writers of his time. These include Le Crime de Sylvestre Bonnard *(1881),* Thaïs *(1891),* Le Lys rouge *(1894; The Red Lily),* L'Ile des pingouins *(1908; Penguin Island),* Les Dieux ont soif *(1912; The Gods Are Athirst), and* Le Révolte des anges *(1914; The Revolt of the Angels), a pungent satire on Christianity. France exhibited a lifelong anticlericalism and disrespect for authority, but this did not prevent him from winning the Nobel Prize for literature in 1921. In the following essay from* Le Jardin d'Epicure *(1895; The Garden of Epicurus), France interprets religious "miracles" as natural occurrences of whose scientific explanation we are as yet ignorant.*

WE SHOULD NOT SAY: THERE are no miracles, because none has ever been proved. This always leaves it open to the Orthodox to appeal to a more complete state of knowledge. The truth is, no miracle can, from the nature of things, be stated as an established fact; to do so will always involve drawing a premature conclusion. A deeply

From Anatole France, "Miracle," in *Le Jardin d'Epicure* (1895), trans. Alfred Allison as *The Garden of Epicurus* (London: John Lane, The Bodley Head; New York: John Lane Co., 1908), pp. 175–81.

rooted instinct tells us that whatever Nature embraces in her bosom is conformable to her laws, either known or occult. But, even supposing he could silence this presentiment of his, a man will never be in a position to say: "Such and such a fact is outside the limits of Nature." Our researches will never carry us as far as that. Moreover, if it is of the essence of miracle to elude scientific investigation, every dogma attesting it invokes an intangible witness that is bound to evade our grasp to the end of time.

This notion of miracles belongs to the infancy of the mind, and cannot continue when once the human intellect has begun to frame a systematic picture of the universe. The wise Greeks could not tolerate the idea. Hippocrates said, speaking of epilepsy: "This malady is called divine; but all diseases are divine, and all alike come from the gods." There he spoke as a natural philosopher. Human reason is less assured of itself nowadays. What annoys me above all is when people say: "We do not believe in miracles, because no miracle is proved."

Happening to be at Lourdes, in August, I paid a visit to the grotto where innumerable crutches were hung up in token of a cure. My companion pointed to these trophies of the sick-room and hospital ward, and whispered in my ear:

"One wooden leg would be more to the point."

It was the word of a man of sense; but speaking philosophically, the wooden leg would be no whit more convincing than a crutch. If an observer of a genuinely scientific spirit were called upon to verify that a man's leg, after amputation, had suddenly grown again as before, whether in a miraculous pool or anywhere else, he would not cry: "Lo! a miracle." He would say this: "An observation, so far unique, points us to a presumption that under conditions still undetermined, the tissues of a human leg have the property of reorganizing themselves like a crab's or lobster's claws and a lizard's tail, but much more rapidly. Here we have a fact of nature in apparent contradiction with several other facts of the like sort. The contradiction arises from our ignorance, and clearly shows that the science of animal physiology must be reconstituted, or to speak more accurately, that it has never yet been properly constituted. It is little more than two hundred years since we first had any true conception of the circulation of the blood. It is barely a century since we learned what is implied in the act of breathing." I admit it would need some boldness to speak in this strain. But the man of science should be above surprise. At the same time, let us hasten to add, none of them have ever been put to such a proof, and nothing leads us to apprehend any such prodigy. Such miraculous cures as the doctors have been able to verify to their satisfaction are all quite in accordance with physiology. So far the tombs of the Saints, the magic springs and sacred grottoes, have never proved efficient except in the case of patients suffering from complaints either curable or susceptible of instantaneous relief. But were a dead man revived before our eyes, no miracle would be proved, unless we knew what life is and death is, and that we shall never know.

What is the definition of a miracle? We are told: a breach of the laws of nature. But we do not know the laws of nature; how, then, are we to know whether a particular fact is a breach of these laws or no?

"But surely we know some of these laws?"

"True, we have arrived at some idea of the correlation of things. But failing as we do to grasp all the natural laws, we can be sure of none, seeing they are mutually interdependent."

"Still, we might verify our miracle in those series of correlations we *have* arrived at."

"No, not with anything like philosophical certainty. Besides, it is precisely those series we regard as the most stable and best determined which suffer least interruption from the miraculous. Miracles never, for instance, try to interfere with the mechanism of the heavens. They never disturb the course of the celestial bodies, and never advance or retard the calculated date of an eclipse. On the contrary, their favourite field is the obscure domain of pathology as concerned with the internal organs, and above all nervous diseases. However, we must not confound a question of fact with one of principle. In principle the man of science is ill-qualified to verify a supernatural occurrence. Such verification presupposes a complete and final knowledge of nature, which he does not possess, and will never possess, and which no one ever did possess in this world. It is just because I would not believe our most skilful oculists as to the miraculous healing of a blind man that *a fortiori* I do not believe Matthew or Mark either, who were not oculists. A miracle is by definition unidentifiable and unknowable."

The savants cannot in any case certify that a fact is in contradiction with the universal order, that is with the unknown ordinance of the Divinity. Even God could do this only by formulating a pettifogging distinction between the general manifestations and the particular manifestations of His activity, acknowledging that from time to time He gives little timid finishing touches to His work and condescending to the humiliating admission that the cumbersome machine He has set agoing needs every hour or so, to get it to jog along indifferently well, a push from its contriver's hand.

Science is well fitted, on the other hand, to bring back under the data of positive knowledge facts which seemed to be outside its limits. It often succeeds very happily in accounting by physical causes for phenomena that had for centuries been regarded as supernatural. Cures of spinal affections were confidently believed to have taken place at the tomb of the Deacon Paris at Saint-Médard and in other holy places. These cures have ceased to surprise since it has become known that hysteria occasionally simulates the symptoms associated with lesions of the spinal marrow.

The appearance of a new star to the mysterious personages whom the Gospels call the "Wise Men of the East" (I assume the incident to be authentic historically) was undoubtedly a miracle to the Astrologers of the Middle Ages, who believed that the firmament, in which the stars were stuck like nails, was subject to no change whatever. But, whether real or supposed, the star of the Magi has lost its miraculous character for us, who know that the heavens are incessantly perturbed by the birth and death of worlds, and who in 1866 saw a star suddenly blaze forth in the Corona Borealis, shine for a month, and then go out.

It did not proclaim the Messiah; all it announced was that, at an infinitely remote distance from our earth, an appalling conflagration was burning up a world in a few days,—or rather had burnt it up long ago, for the ray that brought us the news of this disaster in the heavens had been on the road for five hundred years and possibly longer.

The miracle of Bolsena is familiar to everybody, immortalized as it is in one of Raphael's *Stanze* at the Vatican. A sceptical priest was celebrating Mass; the host, when he broke it for Communion, appeared bespattered with blood. It is only within the last ten years that the Academies of Science would not have been sorely puzzled to explain so strange a phenomenon. Now no one thinks of denying it, since the discovery of a microscopic fungus, the spores of which, having germinated in the meal or dough, offer the appearance of clotted blood. The naturalist who first found it, rightly thinking that here were the red blotches on the wafer in the Bolsena miracle, named the fungus *micrococcus prodigiosus*.

There will always be a fungus, a star, or a disease that human science does not know of; and for this reason it must always behove the philosopher, in the name of the undying ignorance of man, to deny every miracle and say of the most startling wonders,—the host of Bolsena, the star in the East, the cure of the paralytic and the like: Either it is not, or it is; and if it is, it is part of nature and therefore natural.

PART 5

RELIGION
AND SCIENCE

And if thou slay Him, shall the ghost not rise?
Yea! if thou conquer Him thine enemy,
His specter from the dark shall visit thee—
Invincible, necessitous and wise.
The tyrant and mirage of human eyes,
Exhaled upon the spirit's darkened sea,
Shares He thy moment of eternity,
Thy truth confronted ever with His lies.

Thy banners gleam a little, and are furled;
Against thy turrets surge His phantom tow'rs;
Drugged with his Opiates the nations nod,
Refusing still the beauty of thine hours;
And fragile is thy tenure of this world
Still haunted by the monstrous ghost of God.

—George Sterling
"To Science" (1919)

16

AUTOBIOGRAPHY
(1876)

Charles Darwin

Few figures in Western history evoked, and continue to evoke, such controversy in religious and secular circles as Charles Darwin (1809–1882), although he himself was an exceptionally mild-mannered individual. Darwin attended the University of Edinburgh and Cambridge, where he was urged to study science by a professor, J. T. Henslow, who secured for him a non-paying post on board the H.M.S. Beagle. *Darwin's extensive observations of natural phenomena during the* Beagle's *voyage to South America established his reputation. His reports were published as* Journal of Researches into the Geology and Natural History of the Various Countries Visited by H.M.S. Beagle *(1839; later known as* The Voyage of the Beagle*). On this trip, his noticing of differences within animal species on the Galapagos Islands and in South America led him to begin developing the theory of evolution by means of natural selection; he had evolved the theory in its essentials as early as 1842, but did not publish his results until 1859, when* On the Origin of Species *appeared. That volume and its successor,* The Descent of Man *(1871), revolutionized scientific thought. Darwin himself, however, was reluctant to become involved in the theological controversies arising out of his theory, leaving that task to his more aggressive colleague Thomas Henry Huxley. In the last chapter of the* Origin *Darwin actually refers to laws of nature having been "impressed on matter by the Creator," but in the end he realized that evolution had both destroyed the "argument from design" and rendered*

From Charles Darwin, *Autobiography* (1876), in *The Life and Letters of Charles Darwin*, ed. Francis Darwin, vol. 1 (London: John Murray, 1888), pp. 307–13.

belief in God doubtful. In his autobiography—published in abridged
form in his son Francis Darwin's edition of his Life and Letters
(1888), and in complete form in 1958—Darwin speaks of the devel-
opment of his agnostic views.

URING THESE TWO YEARS [OCTOBER 1936 to January 1839] I
was led to think much about religion. Whilst on board the
Beagle I was quite orthodox, and I remember being heartily laughed at
by several of the officers (though themselves orthodox) for quoting the
Bible as an unanswerable authority on some point of morality. I suppose it was the novelty of the argument that amused them. But I had
gradually come by this time, i.e., 1836 to 1839, to see that the Old Testament was no more to be trusted than the sacred books of the Hindoos. The question then continually rose before my mind and would
not be banished,—is it credible that if God were now to make a revelation to the Hindoos, he would permit it to be connected with the belief
in Vishnu, Siva, &c., as Christianity is connected with the Old Testament? This appeared to me utterly incredible.

By further reflecting that the clearest evidence would be requisite to
make any sane man believe in the miracles by which Christianity is supported,—and that the more we know of the fixed laws of nature the
more incredible do miracles become,—that the men at that time were
ignorant and credulous to a degree almost incomprehensible by us,—
that the Gospels cannot be proved to have been written simultaneously
with the events,—that they differ in many important details, far too
important, as it seemed to me, to be admitted as the usual inaccuracies
of eye-witnesses;—by such reflections as these, which I give not as
having the least novelty or value, but as they influenced me, I gradually
came to disbelieve in Christianity as a divine revelation. The fact that
many false religions have spread over large portions of the earth like
wild-fire had some weight with me.

But I was very unwilling to give up my belief; I feel sure of this, for I
can well remember often and often inventing day-dreams of old letters
between distinguished Romans, and manuscripts being discovered at
Pompeii or elsewhere, which confirmed in the most striking manner all
that was written in the Gospels. But I found it more and more difficult,
with free scope given to my imagination, to invent evidence which

would suffice to convince me. Thus disbelief crept over me at a very slow rate, but was at last complete. The rate was so slow that I felt no distress.

Although I did not think much about the existence of a personal God until a considerably later period of my life, I will here give the vague conclusions to which I have been driven. The old argument from design in Nature, as given by Paley, which formerly seemed to me so conclusive, fails, now that the law of natural selection has been discovered. We can no longer argue that, for instance, the beautiful hinge of a bivalve shell must have been made by an intelligent being, like the hinge of a door by man. There seems to be no more design in the variability of organic beings, and in the action of natural selection, than in the course which the wind blows. But I have discussed this subject at the end of my book on the *Variation of Domesticated Animals and Plants*, and the argument there given has never, as far as I can see, been answered.

But passing over the endless beautiful adaptations which we everywhere meet with, it may be asked how can the generally beneficent arrangement of the world be accounted for? Some writers indeed are so much impressed with the amount of suffering in the world, that they doubt, if we look to all sentient beings, whether there is more of misery or of happiness; whether the world as a whole is a good or bad one. According to my judgment happiness decidedly prevails, though this would be very difficult to prove. If the truth of this conclusion be granted, it harmonizes well with the effects which we might expect from natural selection. If all the individuals of any species were habitually to suffer to an extreme degree, they would neglect to propagate their kind; but we have no reason to believe that this has ever, or at least often occurred. Some other considerations, moreover, lead to the belief that all sentient beings have been formed so as to enjoy, as a general rule, happiness.

Every one who believes, as I do, that all the corporeal and mental organs (excepting those which are neither advantageous nor disadvantageous to the possessor) of all beings have been developed through natural selection, or the survival of the fittest, together with use or habit, will admit that these organs have been formed so that their possessors may compete successfully with other beings, and thus increase in number. Now an animal may be led to pursue that course of action which is most beneficial to the species by suffering, such as pain, hunger, thirst, and fear; or by pleasure, as in eating and drinking, and in the propagation of the species, &c.; or by both means combined, as in the search for food. But pain or suffering of any kind, if long continued, causes depression and lessens the power of action, yet is well adapted to make a creature guard itself against any great or sudden evil. Pleasurable sensations, on the other hand, may be long continued without any depressing effect; on the contrary, they stimulate the whole system to increased action. Hence it has come to pass that most or all sentient beings have been developed in such a manner, through natural selection, that pleasurable sensations serve as their habitual guides. We see this in the pleasure from exertion, even occasionally from great exertion of the body or mind,—in the pleasure of our daily meals, and especially in the pleasure derived from sociability, and from loving our families. The sum of such pleasures as these, which are habitual or frequently recurrent, give, as I can hardly doubt, to most sentient beings an excess of happiness over misery, although many occasionally suffer much. Such suffering is quite compatible with the belief in Natural Selection, which is not perfect in its action, but tends only to render each species as successful as possible in the battle for life with other species, in wonderfully complex and changing circumstances.

That there is much suffering in the world no one disputes. Some have attempted to explain this with reference to man by imagining that it serves for his moral improvement. But the number of men in the world is as nothing compared with that of all other sentient beings, and they often suffer greatly without any moral improvement. This very old argument from the existence of suffering against the existence of an intelligent First Cause seems to me a strong one; whereas, as just remarked, the presence of much suffering agrees well with the view that all organic beings have been developed through variation and natural selection.

At the present day the most usual argument for the existence of an intelligent God is drawn from the deep inward conviction and feelings which are experienced by most persons.

Formerly I was led by feelings such as those just referred to (although I do not think that the religious sentiment was ever strongly developed in me), to the firm conviction of the existence of God, and of the immortality of the soul. In my Journal I wrote that whilst standing in the midst of the grandeur of a Brazilian forest, "it is not possible to give an adequate idea of the higher feelings of wonder, admiration, and devotion, which fill and elevate the mind." I well remember my conviction that there is more in man than the mere breath of his body. But now the grandest scenes would not cause any such convictions and feelings to rise in my mind. It may be truly said that I am like a man who has become colour-blind, and the universal belief by men of the existence of redness makes my present loss of perception of not the least value as evidence. This argument would be a valid one if all men of all races had the same inward conviction of the existence of one God; but we know that this is very far from being the case. Therefore I cannot see that such inward convictions and feelings are of any weight as evidence of what really exists. The state of mind which grand scenes formerly excited in me, and which was intimately connected with a belief in God, did not essentially differ from that which is often called the sense of sublimity; and however difficult it may be to explain the genesis of this sense, it can hardly be advanced as an argument for the existence of God, any more than the powerful though vague and similar feelings excited by music.

With respect to immortality, nothing shows me [so clearly] how strong and almost instinctive a belief it is, as the consideration of the view now held by most physicists, namely, that the sun with all the planets will in time grow too cold for life, unless indeed some great body dashes into the sun, and thus gives it fresh life. Believing as I do that man in the distant future will be a far more perfect creature than he now is, it is an intolerable thought that he and all other sentient beings are doomed to complete annihilation after such long-continued slow progress. To those who fully admit the immortality of the human soul, the destruction of our world will not appear so dreadful.

Another source of conviction in the existence of God, connected with the reason, and not with the feelings, impresses me as having much more weight. This follows from the extreme difficulty or rather impossibility of conceiving this immense and wonderful universe, including man with his capacity of looking far backwards and far into futurity, as the result of blind chance or necessity. When thus reflecting I feel compelled to look to a First Cause having an intelligent mind in some degree analogous to that of man; and I deserve to be called a Theist. This conclusion was strong in my mind about the time, as far as I can remember, when I wrote the *Origin of Species*; and it is since that time that it has very gradually, with many fluctuations, become weaker. But then arises the doubt, can the mind of man, which has, as I fully believe, been developed from a mind as low as that possessed by the lowest animals, be trusted when it draws such grand conclusions?

I cannot pretend to throw the least light on such abstruse problems. The mystery of the beginning of all things is insoluble by us; and I for one must be content to remain an Agnostic.

17

THE ANTICHRIST
(1888)

Friedrich Nietzsche

Much of the work of German philosopher Friedrich Nietzsche (1844–1900) is antireligious, since Nietzsche saw in many religions (particularly the Christian religion) a negation of his life-affirming "will to power," which sought to actualize the potentialities of the mind and body. Among Nietzsche's most significant works are Thus Spake Zarathustra *(1883–92),* Beyond Good and Evil *(1886), and* On the Genealogy of Morals *(1887). The* Antichrist *(written 1888; published 1895) is, with* The Twilight of the Idols *(written 1888; published 1889), his most unrestrained attack on religion. In the extracts printed below (in the 1920 translation by H. L. Mencken), Nietzsche, in his typically exuberant style, focuses on the myth of Adam and Eve's expulsion from Eden for eating from the tree of knowledge to excoriate Christianity for its hostility to science and the advancement of learning.*

47.

THE THING THAT SETS US apart is not that we are unable to find God, either in history, or in nature, or behind nature—but that we regard what has been honoured as God, not as "divine," but as pitiable, as absurd, as injurious; not as a mere error, but as a *crime against life*. . . . We deny that God is God. . . . If any one were to *show* us this Christian

From Friedrich Nietzsche, *The Antichrist*, trans. H. L. Mencken (New York: Knopf, 1920), pp. 135–50, 180–82.

God, we'd be still less inclined to believe in him.—In a formula: *deus, qualem Paulus creavit, dei negatio.*[1] Such a religion as Christianity, which does not touch reality at a single point and which goes to pieces the moment reality asserts its rights at any point, must be inevitably the deadly enemy of the "wisdom of this world," which is to say, of *science*—and it will give the name of good to whatever means serve to poison, calumniate and *cry down* all intellectual discipline, all lucidity and strictness in matters of intellectual conscience, and all noble coolness and freedom of the mind. "Faith," as an imperative, vetoes science—*in praxi*, lying at any price. . . . Paul *well knew* that lying—that "faith"—was necessary; later on the church borrowed the fact from Paul.—The God that Paul invented for himself, a God who "reduced to absurdity" "the wisdom of this world" (especially the two great enemies of superstition, philology and medicine), is in truth only an indication of Paul's resolute *determination* to accomplish that very thing himself: to give one's own will the name of God, *thora*[2]—that is essentially Jewish. Paul *wants* to dispose of the "wisdom of this world": his enemies are the *good* philologians and physicians of the Alexandrine school—on them he makes his war. As a matter of fact no man can be a *philologian* or a physician without being also *Antichrist*. That is to say, as a philologian a man sees *behind* the "holy books," and as a physician he sees *behind* the physiological degeneration of the typical Christian. The physician says "incurable"; the philologian says "fraud." . . .

48.

—Has any one ever clearly understood the celebrated story at the beginning of the Bible—of God's mortal terror of *science*? . . . No one, in fact, has understood it. This priest-book *par excellence* opens, as is fitting, with the great inner difficulty of the priest: *he* faces only one great danger; *ergo*, "God" faces only one great danger.—

The old God, wholly "spirit," wholly the high-priest, wholly perfect, is promenading his garden: he is bored and trying to kill time. Against boredom even gods struggle in vain.[3] What does he do? He creates man—man is entertaining. . . . But then he notices that man is also bored. God's pity for the only form of distress that invades all paradises knows no bounds: so he forthwith creates other animals. God's first mistake: to man these other animals were not entertaining—he sought dominion over them; he did not want to be an "animal" himself.—So God created woman. In the act he brought boredom to an end—and also many other things! Woman was the *second* mistake of God.— "Woman, at bottom, is a serpent, Heva"—every priest knows that; "from woman comes every evil in the world"—every priest knows that, too. *Ergo*, she is also to blame for *science*. . . . It was through woman that man learned to taste of the tree of knowledge.—What happened? The old God was seized by mortal terror. Man himself had been his *greatest* blunder; he had created a rival to himself; science makes men *godlike*— it is all up with priests and gods when man becomes scientific!—Moral: science is the forbidden *per se*; it alone is forbidden. Science is the *first* of sins, the germ of all sins, the *original* sin. *This is all there is of morality.*—"Thou shalt *not* know":—the rest follows from that.—God's mortal terror, however, did not hinder him from being shrewd. How is one to *protect* one's self against science? For a long while this was the capital problem. Answer: Out of paradise with man! Happiness, leisure, foster thought—and all thoughts are bad thoughts!—Man *must* not think.—And so the priest invents distress, death, the mortal dangers of childbirth, all sorts of misery, old age, decrepitude, above all, *sickness*— nothing but devices for making war on science! The troubles of man don't *allow* him to think. . . . Nevertheless—how terrible!—, the edifice of knowledge begins to tower aloft, invading heaven, shadowing the gods—what is to be done?—The old God invents *war*; he separates the peoples; he makes men destroy one another (—the priests have always had need of war. . . .). War—among other things, a great disturber of science!—Incredible! Knowledge, *deliverance from the priests*, prospers in spite of war.—So the old God comes to his final resolution: "Man has become scientific—*there is no help for it: he must be drowned!*" . . .

49.

—I have been understood. At the opening of the Bible there is the *whole* psychology of the priest.—The priest knows of only one great danger: that is science—the sound comprehension of cause and effect. But science flourishes, on the whole, only under favourable conditions—a man must have time, he must have an *overflowing* intellect, in order to "know." . . . "*Therefore*, man must be made unhappy,"—this been, in all ages, the logic of the priest.—It is easy to see just *what*, by this logic, was the first thing to come into the world:—"*sin*." . . . The concept of guilt and punishment, the whole "moral order of the world," was set up *against* science— *against* the deliverance of man from priests. . . . Man must *not* look outward; he must look inward. He must *not* look at things shrewdly and cautiously, to learn about them; he must not look at all; he must *suffer*. . . . And he must suffer so much that he is always in need of the priest.—Away with physicians! *What is needed is a Saviour.*—The concept of guilt and punishment, including the doctrines of "grace," of "salvation," of "forgiveness"—*lies* through and through, and absolutely without psychological reality—were devised to destroy man's *sense of causality*: they are an attack upon the concept of cause and effect!—And *not* an attack with the fist, with the knife, with honesty in hate and love! On the contrary, one inspired by the most cowardly, the most crafty, the most ignoble of instincts! An attack of *priests*! An attack of *parasites*! The vampirism of pale, subterranean leeches! . . . When the natural consequences of an act are no longer "natural," but are regarded as produced by the ghostly creations of superstition—by "God," by "spirits," by "souls"—and reckoned as merely "moral" consequences, as rewards, as punishments, as hints, as lessons, then the whole groundwork of knowledge is destroyed—*then the greatest of crimes against humanity has been perpetrated*.—I repeat that sin, man's self-desecration *par excellence*, was invented in order to make science, culture, and every elevation and ennobling of man impossible; the priest *rules* through the invention of sin.—

50.

—In this place I can't permit myself to omit a psychology of "belief," of the "believer," for the special benefit of "believers." If there remain any today who do not yet know how *indecent* it is to be "believing"—*or* how much a sign of *décadence*, of a broken will to live—then they will know it well enough tomorrow. My voice reaches even the deaf.—It appears, unless I have been incorrectly informed, that there prevails among Christians a sort of criterion of truth that is called "proof by power." "Faith makes blessed: *therefore* it is true."—It might be objected right here that blessedness is not demonstrated, it is merely *promised*: it hangs upon "faith" as a condition—one *shall* be blessed *because* one believes. . . . But what of the thing that the priest promises to the believer, the wholly transcendental "beyond"—how is *that* to be demonstrated?— The "proof by power," thus assumed, is actually no more at bottom than a belief that the effects which faith promises will not fail to appear. In a formula: "I believe that faith makes for blessedness—*therefore*, it is true." . . . But this is as far as we may go. This "therefore" would be *absurdum* itself as a criterion of truth.—But let us admit, for the sake of politeness, that blessedness by faith may be demonstrated (—*not* merely hoped for, and *not* merely promised by the suspicious lips of a priest): even so, *could* blessedness—in a technical term, *pleasure*—ever be a proof of truth? So little is this true that it is almost a proof against truth when sensations of pleasure influence the answer to the question "What is true?" or, at all events, it is enough to make that "truth" highly suspicious. The proof by "pleasure" is a proof *of* "pleasure"—nothing more; why in the world should it be assumed that *true* judgments give more pleasure than false ones, and that, in conformity to some pre-established harmony, they necessarily bring agreeable feelings in their train?—The experience of all disciplined and profound minds teaches *the contrary*. Man has had to fight for every atom of the truth, and has had to pay for it almost everything that the heart, that human love, that human trust cling to. Greatness of soul is needed for this business: the service of truth is the hardest of all services.—What, then, is the meaning of *integrity* in things intellectual? It means that a man must be severe with his own heart, that he must scorn "beautiful feelings," and that he makes every Yea and Nay a matter of conscience!—Faith makes blessed: *therefore*, it lies. . . .

51.

The fact that faith, under certain circumstances, may work for blessedness, but that this blessedness produced by an *idée fixe* by no means makes the idea itself true, and the fact that faith actually moves no mountains, but instead *raises them up* where there were none before: all this is made sufficiently clear by a walk through a *lunatic asylum*. *Not*, of course, to a priest: for his instincts prompt him to the lie that sickness is not sickness and lunatic asylums not lunatic asylums. Christianity finds sickness *necessary*, just as the Greek spirit had need of a super-abundance of health—the actual ulterior purpose of the whole system of salvation of the church is to *make* people ill. And the church itself—doesn't it set up a Catholic lunatic asylum as the ultimate ideal?—The whole earth as a madhouse?—The sort of religious man that the church *wants* is a typical *décadent*; the moment at which a religious crisis dominates a people is always marked by epidemics of nervous disorder; the "inner world" of the religious man is so much like the "inner world" of the overstrung and exhausted that it is difficult to distinguish between them; the "highest" states of mind, held up before mankind by Christianity as of supreme worth, are actually epileptoid in form—the church has granted the name of holy only to lunatics or to gigantic frauds *in majorem dei honorem*. . . .[4] Once I ventured to designate the whole Christian system of *training*[5] in penance and salvation (now best studied in England) as a method of producing a *folie circulaire*[6] upon a soil already prepared for it, which is to say, a soil thoroughly unhealthy. Not every one may be a Christian: one is not "converted" to Christianity—one must first be sick enough for it. . . . We others, who have the *courage* for health *and* likewise for contempt,—we may well despise a religion that teaches misunderstanding of the body! that refuses to rid itself of the superstition about the soul! that makes a "virtue" of insufficient nourishment! that combats health as a sort of enemy, devil, temptation! that persuades itself that it is possible to carry about a "perfect soul" in a cadaver of a body, and that, to this end, had to devise for itself a new concept of "perfection," a pale, sickly, idiotically ecstatic state of existence, so-called "holiness"—a holiness that is itself merely a series of symptoms of an impoverished, enervated and incurably disordered body! . . . The Christian movement, as a European movement, was from the start no more than a general uprising of all sorts of outcast and refuse elements (—who now, under cover of Christianity, aspire to power). It does *not* represent the decay of a race; it represents, on the contrary, a conglomeration of *décadence* products from all directions, crowding together and seeking one another out. It was *not*, as has been thought, the corruption of antiquity, of *noble* antiquity, which made Christianity possible; one cannot too sharply challenge the learned imbecility which today maintains that theory. At the time when the sick and rotten Chandala[7] classes in the whole *imperium* were Christianized, the *contrary type*, the nobility, reached its finest and ripest development. The majority became master; democracy, with its Christian instincts, *triumphed*. . . . Christianity was not "national," it was not based on race—it appealed to all the varieties of men disinherited by life, it had its allies everywhere. Christianity has the rancour of the sick at its very core—the instinct against the *healthy*, against *health*. Everything that is well-constituted, proud, gallant and, above all, beautiful gives offence to its ears and eyes. Again I remind you of Paul's priceless saying: "And God hath chosen the *weak* things of the world, the *foolish* things of the world, the *base* things of the world, and things which are *despised*:"[8] *this* was the formula; *in hoc signo* the *décadence* triumphed— *God on the cross*—is man always to miss the frightful inner significance of this symbol?—Everything that suffers, everything that hangs on the cross, is *divine*. . . . We all hang on the cross, consequently *we* are divine. . . . We alone are divine. . . . Christianity was thus a victory: a nobler attitude of mind was destroyed by it—Christianity remains to this day the greatest misfortune of humanity.—

52.

Christianity also stands in opposition to all *intellectual* well-being,— sick reasoning is the only sort that it *can* use as Christian reasoning; it takes the side of everything that is idiotic; it pronounces a curse upon "intellect," upon the *superbia*[9] of the healthy intellect. Since sickness is inherent in Christianity, it follows that the typically Christian state of "faith" *must* be a form of sickness too, and that all straight, straightforward and scientific paths to knowledge *must* be banned by the church as *forbidden* ways. Doubt is thus a sin from the start. . . . The complete lack of psychological cleanliness in the priest—revealed by a glance at him—is a phenomenon resulting from *décadence*,—one may observe in hysterical women and in rachitic children how regularly the falsification of instincts, delight in lying for the mere sake of lying, and incapacity for looking straight and walking straight are symptoms of *décadence*. "Faith" means the will to avoid knowing what is true. The pietist, the priest of either sex, is a fraud *because* he is sick: his instinct *demands* that the truth shall never be allowed its rights on any point. "Whatever makes for illness is *good*; whatever issues from abundance, from super-abundance, from power, is *evil*": so argues the believer. The *impulse to lie*—it is by this that I recognize every foreordained theologian.— Another characteristic of the theologian is his *unfitness for philology*. What I here mean by philology is, in a general sense, the art of reading with profit—the capacity for absorbing facts *without* interpreting them falsely, and *without* losing caution, patience and subtlety in the effort to understand them. Philology as *ephexis*[10] in interpretation: whether one be dealing with books, with newspaper reports, with the most fateful events or with weather statistics—not to mention the "salvation of the soul.". . . The way in which a theologian, whether in Berlin or in Rome, is ready to explain, say, a "passage of Scripture," or an experience, or a victory by the national army, by turning upon it the high illumination of the Psalms of David, is always so *daring* that it is enough to make a philologian run up a wall. But what shall he do when pietists and other such cows from Suabia[11] use the "finger of God" to convert their miserably commonplace and huggermugger existence into a miracle of "grace," a "providence" and an "experience of salvation"? The most modest exercise of the intellect, not to say of decency, should certainly be enough to convince these interpreters of the perfect childishness and unworthiness of such a misuse of the divine digital dexterity. However small our piety, if we ever encountered a god who always cured us of a cold in the head at just the right time, or got us into our carriage at the very instant heavy rain began to fall, he would seem so absurd a god that he'd have to be abolished even if he existed. God as a domestic servant, as a letter carrier, as an almanac-man—at bottom, he is a mere name for the stupidest sort of chance. . . . "Divine Providence," which every third man in "educated Germany" still believes in, is so strong an argument against God that it would be impossible to think of a stronger. And in any case it is an argument against Germans! . . .

62.

—With this I come to a conclusion and pronounce my judgment. I *condemn* Christianity; I bring against the Christian church the most terrible of all the accusations that an accuser has ever had in his mouth. It is, to me, the greatest of all imaginable corruptions; it seeks to work the ultimate corruption, the worst possible corruption. The Christian church has left nothing untouched by its depravity; it has turned every value into worthlessness, and every truth into a lie, and every integrity into baseness of soul. Let any one dare to speak to me of its "humanitarian" blessings! Its deepest necessities range it against any effort to abolish distress; it lives by distress; it *creates* distress to make *itself* immortal. . . . For example, the worm of sin: it was the church that first enriched mankind with this misery!—The "equality of souls before God"—this fraud, this pretext for the *rancune*[12] of all the base-minded—this explosive concept, ending in revolution, the modern idea, and the notion of overthrowing the whole social order—this is *Christian* dynamite. . . . The "humanitarian" blessings of Christianity forsooth! To breed out of *humanitas* a self-contradiction, an art of self-pollution, a will to lie at any price, an aversion and contempt for all good and honest instincts! All this, to me, is the "humanitarianism" of Christianity!—Parasitism as the *only* practice of the church; with its anæmic and "holy" ideals, sucking all the blood, all the love, all the hope out of life; the beyond as the will to deny all reality; the cross as the distinguishing mark of the most subterranean conspiracy ever heard of,—against health, beauty, well-being, intellect, *kindness* of soul—*against life itself.* . . .

This eternal accusation against Christianity I shall write upon all walls, wherever walls are to be found—I have letters that even the blind will be able to see. . . . I call Christianity the one great curse, the one great intrinsic depravity, the one great instinct of revenge, for which no means are venomous enough, or secret, subterranean and *small* enough, —I call it the one immortal blemish upon the human race. . . .

And mankind reckons *time* from the *dies nefastus*[13] when this fatality befell—from the *first* day of Christianity!—*Why not rather from its last?—From today?*—The transvaluation of all values! . . .

NOTES

1. ["A God such as Paul created is the negation of God."]

2. [Or Torah, primarily a reference to the Pentateuch but more generally the Written and Oral Law embodied in it.]

3. A paraphrase of Schiller's "Against stupidity even gods struggle in vain." [Mencken's note]

4. ["For the greater honor of God."]

5. The word *training* is in English in the text. [Mencken's note]

6. [Alternating or cyclic madness; extreme mood swings from euphoria to depression.]

7. [The Chandala are the lowest ("untouchable") caste of Hindu society; here the term is used figuratively.]

8. I Corinthians i, 27, 28. [Mencken's note]

9. ["Pride."]

10. That is to say, scepticism. Among the Greeks scepticism was also occasionally called ephecticism. [Mencken's note]

11. A reference to the University of Tübingen and its famous school of Biblical criticism. The leader of this school was F. C. Baur, and one of the men greatly influenced by it was Nietzsche's pet abomination, David F. Strauss, himself a Suabian. [Mencken's note]

12. ["Spite."]

13. ["Cursed day."]

18

ON THE SCOPES TRIAL
(1925)

H. L. Mencken

Henry Louis Mencken (1880–1956) gained a foothold in journalism as a teenager and continued in the profession for the next fifty years. A longtime columnist for the Baltimore Evening Sun, *Mencken also edited the* Smart Set *(1914–23) and founded and edited the* American Mercury *(1924–33). His incisive essays and reviews—collected in the six-volume series,* Prejudices *(1919–27)—made him the most influential American critic of the 1920s. Early in his career Mencken wrote a pioneering study,* The Philosophy of Friedrich Nietzsche *(1908), and he later translated Nietzsche's* The Antichrist *(1920). His longtime hostility to organized religion was most exhaustively expressed in* Treatise on the Gods *(1930). His coverage of the Scopes "monkey trial" in 1925 gained him both celebrity and notoriety. In the first of the three extracts presented below, Mencken points out the inability of the average person to understand scientific explanations of phenomena; in the second, he directs his attention to the aging, embittered William Jennings Bryan's reaction to a speech by a defense attorney, Dudley Malone; and in the third, he offers concluding reflections on the significance of the trial.*

HOMO NEANDERTALENSIS

THE SO-CALLED RELIGIOUS ORGANIZATIONS WHICH now lead the war against the teaching of evolution are nothing more, at bottom, than conspiracies of the inferior man against his betters. They mirror very accurately his congenital hatred of knowledge, his bitter enmity to the man who knows more than he does, and so gets more out of life. Certainly it cannot have gone unnoticed that their membership is recruited, in the overwhelming main, from the lower orders—that no man of any education or other human dignity belongs to them. What they propose to do, at bottom and in brief, is to make the superior man infamous—by mere abuse if it is sufficient, and if it is not, then by law.

Such organizations, of course, must have leaders; there must be men in them whose ignorance and imbecility are measurably less abject than the ignorance and imbecility of the average. These super-Chandala often attain to a considerable power, especially in democratic states. Their followers trust them and look up to them; sometimes, when the pack is on the loose, it is necessary to conciliate them. But their puissance cannot conceal their incurable inferiority. They belong to the mob as surely as their dupes, and the thing that animates them is precisely the mob's hatred of superiority. Whatever lies above the level of their comprehension is of the devil. A glass of wine delights civilized men; they themselves, drinking it, would get drunk. *Ergo*, wine must be prohibited. The hypothesis of evolution is credited by all men of education; they themselves can't understand it. *Ergo*, its teaching must be put down.

This simple fact explains such phenomena as the Tennessee buffoonery. Nothing else can. We must think of human progress, not as of something going on in the race in general, but as of something going on in a small minority, perpetually beleaguered in a few walled towns. Now and then the horde of barbarians outside breaks through, and we have an armed effort to halt the process. That is, we have a Reformation, a French Revolution, a war for democracy, a Great Awakening. The minority is decimated and driven to cover. But a few survive—and a few are enough to carry on.

The inferior man's reasons for hating knowledge are not hard to discern. He hates it because it is complex—because it puts an unbearable burden upon his meager capacity for taking in ideas. Thus his search is always for short cuts. All superstitions are such short cuts. Their aim is to make the unintelligible simple, and even obvious. So on what seem to be higher levels. No man who has not had a long and arduous education can understand even the most elementary concepts of modern pathology. But even a hind at the plow can grasp the theory of chiropractic in two lessons. Hence the vast popularity of chiropractic among the submerged—and of osteopathy, Christian Science and other such quackeries with it. They are idiotic, but they are simple—and every man prefers what he can understand to what puzzles and dismays him.

The popularity of Fundamentalism among the inferior orders of men is explicable in exactly the same way. The cosmogonies that educated men toy with are all inordinately complex. To comprehend their veriest outlines requires an immense stock of knowledge, and a habit of thought. It would be as vain to try to teach to peasants or to the city proletariat as it would be to try to teach them to streptococci. But the cosmogony of Genesis is so simple that even a yokel can grasp it. It is set forth in a few phrases. It offers, to an ignorant man, the irresistible reasonableness of the nonsensical. So he accepts it with loud hosannas, and has one more excuse for hating his betters. . . .

MALONE THE VICTOR, EVEN THOUGH COURT SIDES WITH OPPONENTS, SAYS MENCKEN

. . . Bryan . . . sat through [Malone's speech] in his usual posture, with his palm-leaf fan flapping energetically and his hard, cruel mouth shut tight. The old boy grows more and more pathetic. He has aged greatly during the past few years and begins to look elderly and enfeebled. All that remains of his old fire is now in his black eyes. They glitter like dark gems, and in their glitter there is immense and yet futile malignancy. That is all that is left of the Peerless Leader of thirty years ago. Once he had one leg in the White House and the nation trembled under his roars.[1] Now he is a tinpot pope in the coca-cola belt and a brother to the forlorn pastors who belabor half-wits in galvanized iron tabernacles behind the railroad yards. His own speech was a grotesque performance and downright touching in its imbecility. Its climax came when he launched into a furious denunciation of the doctrine that man is a mammal. It seemed a sheer impossibility that any literate man should stand up in public and discharge any such nonsense. Yet the poor old fellow did it. Darrow stared incredulous. Malone sat with his mouth wide open. Hays indulged himself one of his sardonic chuckles. Stewart and Bryan *fils* looked extremely uneasy, but the old mountebank ranted on.[2] To call a man a mammal, it appeared, was to flout the revelation of God. The certain effect of the doctrine would be to destroy morality and promote infidelity. The defense let it pass. The lily needed no gilding.

There followed some ranting about the Leopold-Loeb case,[3] culminating in the argument that learning was corrupting—that the colleges by setting science above Genesis were turning their students into murderers. Bryan alleged that Darrow had admitted the fact in his closing speech at the Leopold-Loeb trial, and stopped to search for the passage in a printed copy of the speech. Darrow denied making any such statement, and presently began reading what he actually had said on the subject. Bryan then proceeded to denounce Nietzsche, whom he described as an admirer and follower of Darwin. Darrow challenged the fact and offered to expound what Nietzsche really taught. Bryan waved him off.

The effect of the whole harangue was extremely depressing. It quickly ceased to be an argument addressed to the court—Bryan, in fact, constantly said "My friends" instead of "Your Honor"—and became a sermon at the camp-meeting. All the familiar contentions of the Dayton divines appeared in it—that learning is dangerous, that nothing is true that is not in the Bible, that a yokel who goes to church regularly knows more than any scientist ever heard of. The thing went to fantastic lengths. It became a farrago of puerilities without coherence or sense. I don't think the old man did himself justice. He was in poor voice and his mind seemed to wander. There was far too much hatred in him for him to be persuasive.

The crowd, of course, was with him. It has been fed upon just such balderdash for years. Its pastors assault it twice a week with precisely the same nonsense. It is chronically in the position of a populace protected by an espionage act in time of war. That is to say, it is forbidden to laugh at the arguments of one side and forbidden to hear the case of the other side. Bryan has been roving around in the tall grass for years and he knows the bucolic mind. He knows how to reach and inflame its basic delusions and superstitions. He has taken them into his own stock and adorned them with fresh absurdities. Today he may well stand as the archetype of the American rustic. His theology is simply the elemental magic that is preached in a hundred thousand rural churches fifty-two times a year.

These Tennessee mountaineers are not more stupid than the city proletariat; they are only less informed. If Darrow, Malone and Hays could make a month's stumping tour in Rhea county I believe that fully a fourth of the population would repudiate fundamentalism, and that not a few of the clergy now in practice would be restored to their old jobs on the railroad. Malone's speech yesterday probably shook a great many true believers; another like it would fetch more than one of them. But the chances are heavily against them ever hearing a second. Once this trial is over, the darkness will close in again, and it will take long years of diligent and thankless effort to dispel it—if, indeed, it is ever dispelled at all. . . .

AFTERMATH

The Liberals, in their continuing discussion of the late trial of the infidel Scopes at Dayton, Tenn., run true to form. That is to say, they show all their habitual lack of humor and all their customary furtive weakness for the delusions of *Homo neandertalensis*. I point to two of their most enlightened organs: the eminent New York *World* and the gifted *New Republic*. The *World* is displeased with Mr. Darrow because, in his appalling cross-examination of the mountebank Bryan, he did some violence to the theological superstitions that millions of Americans cherish. The *New Republic* denounces him because he addressed himself, not to "the people of Tennessee" but to the whole country, and because he should have permitted "local lawyers" to assume "the most conspicuous position in the trial."

Once more, alas, I find myself unable to follow the best Liberal thought. What the *World*'s contention amounts to, at bottom, is simply the doctrine that a man engaged in combat with superstition should be very polite to superstition. This, I fear, is nonsense. The way to deal with superstition is not to be polite to it, but to tackle it with all arms, and so rout it, cripple it, and make it forever infamous and ridiculous. Is it, perchance, cherished by persons who should know better? Then their folly should be brought out into the light of day, and exhibited there in all its hideousness until they flee from it, hiding their heads in shame.

True enough, even a superstitious man has certain inalienable rights. He has a right to harbor and indulge his imbecilities as long as he pleases, provided only he does not try to inflict them upon other men by force. He has a right to argue for them as eloquently as he can, in season and out of season. He has a right to teach them to his children. But certainly he has no right to be protected against the free criticism of those who do not hold them. He has no right to demand that they be treated as sacred. He has no right to preach them without challenge. Did Darrow, in the course of his dreadful bombardment of Bryan, drop a few shells, incidentally, into measurably cleaner camps? Then let the garrisons of those camps look to their defenses. They are free to shoot back. But they can't disarm their enemy.

The meaning of religious freedom, I fear, is sometimes greatly misapprehended. It is taken to be a sort of immunity, not merely from governmental control but also from public opinion. A dunderhead gets himself a long-tailed coat, rises behind the sacred desk, and emits such bilge as would gag a Hottentot. Is it to pass unchallenged? If so, then what we have is not religious freedom at all, but the most intolerable and outrageous variety of religious despotism. Any fool, once he is admitted to holy orders, becomes infallible. Any half-wit, by the simple device of ascribing his delusions to revelation, takes on an authority that is denied to all the rest of us.

I do not know how many Americans entertain the ideas defended so ineptly by poor Bryan, but probably the number is very large. They are preached once a week in at least a hundred thousand rural churches, and they are heard too in the meaner quarters of the great cities. Nevertheless, though they are thus held to be sound by millions, these ideas remain mere rubbish. Not only are they not supported by the known facts; they are in direct contravention of the known facts. No man whose information is sound and whose mind functions normally can conceivably credit them. They are the products of ignorance and stupidity, either or both.

What should be a civilized man's attitude toward such superstitions? It seems to me that the only attitude possible to him is one of contempt. If he admits that they have any intellectual dignity whatever, he admits that he himself has none. If he pretends to a respect for those who believe in them, he pretends falsely, and sinks almost to their level. When he is challenged he must answer honestly, regardless of tender feelings. That is what Darrow did at Dayton, and the issue plainly justified the fact. Bryan went there in a hero's shining armor, bent deliberately upon a gross crime against sense. He came out a wrecked and preposterous charlatan, his tail between his legs. Few Americans have ever done so much for their country in a whole lifetime as Darrow did in two hours.

NOTES

1. [William Jennings Bryan (1860–1925), aside from running unsuccessfully for president in 1896, 1900, and 1908, was secretary of state under Woodrow Wilson (1913–15).]

2. [The references are to Arthur Garfield Hays, a defense attorney; A. T. Stewart, Circuit District Attorney; and Bryan's son, William Jennings Bryan Jr., who was assisting his father in the case.]

3. [In 1924 Darrow defended two young men, Richard Loeb and Nathan Leopold, seventeen and eighteen years of age, respectively, who were accused of murdering a fourteen-year-old boy, Robert Franks. Darrow's defense saved them from the death penalty, although they were sentenced to life imprisonment.]

19

THE DEMON-HAUNTED WORLD
(1995)

Carl Sagan

Carl Sagan (1934–1996) taught at Harvard before moving to Cornell University, where he became David Duncan Professor of Astronomy and Space Sciences and director of the Laboratory for Planetary Studies. One of the most renowned astronomers and popularizers of science in his time, Sagan wrote more than 600 papers and a dozen books, including The Dragons of Eden: Speculations on the Evolution of Human Intelligence *(1977), which won the Pulitzer Prize, and the novel* Contact *(1984). He gained his greatest celebrity for the thirteen-part television series,* Cosmos. *In the title essay of his final volume,* The Demon-Haunted World: Science as a Candle in the Dark *(1995), Sagan exhaustively treats the long history of belief in demons, much of it sanctioned by the church, leading to centuries-long persecution of so-called witches. In a later section of the essay (not reprinted here), Sagan likens this belief to modern theories of UFOs and alien abductions.*

There are demon-haunted worlds, regions of utter darkness.

—The Isa Upanishad
(India, ca. 600 B.C.)

Fear of things invisible is the natural seed of that which every one in himself calleth religion.

—Thomas Hobbes, *Leviathan* (1651)

T HE GODS WATCH OVER US and guide our destinies, many human cultures teach; other entities, more malevolent, are responsible for the existence of evil. Both classes of beings, whether considered natural or supernatural, real or imaginary, serve human needs. Even if they're wholly fanciful, people feel better believing in them. So in an age when traditional religions have been under withering fire from science, is it not natural to wrap up the old gods and demons in scientific raiment and call them aliens?

Belief in demons was widespread in the ancient world. They were thought of as natural rather than supernatural beings. Hesiod casually mentions them. Socrates described his philosophical inspiration as the work of a personal, benign demon. His teacher, Diotima of Mantineia, tells him (in Plato's *Symposium*) that "Everything demonic is intermediate between God and mortal. God has no contact with man," she continues; "only through the demonic is there intercourse and conversation between man and gods, whether in the waking state or during sleep."

Plato, Socrates' most celebrated student, assigned a high role to demons: "No human nature invested with supreme power is able to order human affairs," he said, "and not overflow with insolence and wrong. . . ."

> We do not appoint oxen to be the lords of oxen, or goats of goats, but we ourselves are a superior race and rule over them. In like manner God, in his love of mankind, placed over us the demons, who are a superior race, and they with great ease and pleasure to themselves, and no less to us, taking care of us and giving us peace and reverence and order and justice never failing, made the tribes of men happy and united.

He stoutly denied that demons were a source of evil, and represented Eros, the keeper of sexual passions, as a demon, not a god, "neither mortal nor immortal, neither good nor bad." But all later Platonists, including the Neo-Platonists who powerfully influenced Christian philosophy, held that some demons were good and others evil. The pendulum was swinging. Aristotle, Plato's famous student, seriously considered the contention that dreams are scripted by demons. Plutarch and Porphyry proposed that the demons, who filled the upper air, came from the Moon.

The early Church Fathers, despite having imbibed Neo-Platonism from the culture they swam in, were anxious to separate themselves from "pagan" belief-systems. They taught that all of pagan religion consisted of the worship of demons and men, both misconstrued as gods. When St. Paul complained (Ephesians 6:14) about wickedness in high places, he was referring not to government corruption, but to demons, who lived in high places:

> For we wrestle not against flesh and blood, but against principalities, against powers, against the rulers of the darkness of this world, against spiritual wickedness in high places.

From the beginning, much more was intended than demons as a mere poetic metaphor for evil in the hearts of men.

St. Augustine was much vexed with demons. He quotes the pagan thinking prevalent in his time: "The gods occupy the loftiest regions, men the lowest, the demons the middle region. . . . They have immortality of body, but passions of the mind in common with men." In Book VIII of *The City of God* (begun in 413), Augustine assimilates this ancient tradition, replaces gods by God, and demonizes the demons— arguing that they are, without exception, malign. They have no redeeming virtues. They are the fount of all spiritual and material evil. He calls them "aerial animals . . . most eager to inflict harm, utterly alien from righteousness, swollen with pride, pale with envy, subtle in deceit." They may profess to carry messages between God and man, disguising themselves as angels of the Lord, but this pose is a snare to lure us to our destruction. They can assume any form, and know many things—"demon" *means* "knowledge" in Greek[1]—especially about the material world. However intelligent, they are deficient in charity. They prey on "the captive and outwitted minds of men," wrote Tertullian. "They have their abode in the air, the stars are their neighbors, their commerce is with the clouds."

In the eleventh century, the influential Byzantine theologian, philosopher, and shady politician, Michael Psellus, described demons in these words:

> These animals exist in our own life, which is full of passions, for they are present abundantly in the passions, and their dwelling-place is that of matter, as is their rank and degree. For this reason they are also subject to passions and fettered to them.

One Richalmus, abbot of Schönthal, around 1270 penned an entire treatise on demons, rich in first-hand experience: He sees (but only when his eyes are shut) countless malevolent demons, like motes of dust, buzzing around his head—and everyone else's. Despite successive waves of rationalist, Persian, Jewish, Christian, and Moslem world views, despite revolutionary social, political, and philosophical ferment, the existence, much of the character, and even the name of demons remained unchanged from Hesiod through the Crusades.

Demons, the "powers of the air," come down from the skies and have unlawful sexual congress with women. Augustine believed that witches were the offspring of these forbidden unions. In the Middle Ages, as in classical antiquity, nearly everyone believed such stories. The demons were also called devils, or fallen angels. The demonic seducers of women were labeled incubi; of men, succubi. There are cases in which nuns reported, in some befuddlement, a striking resemblance between the incubus and the priest-confessor, or the bishop, and awoke the next morning, as one fifteenth-century chronicler put it, to "find themselves polluted just as if they had commingled with a man." There are similar accounts, but in harems not convents, in ancient China. So many women reported incubi, argued the Presbyterian religious writer Richard Baxter (in his *Certainty of the World of Spirits*, 1691), "that 'tis impudence to deny it."[2]

As they seduced, the incubi and succubi were perceived as a weight bearing down on the chest of the dreamer. *Mare*, despite its Latin meaning, is the Old English word for incubus, and *nightmare* meant originally the demon that sits on the chests of sleepers, tormenting them with dreams. In Athanasius' *Life of St. Anthony* (written around 360) demons are described as coming and going at will in locked rooms; 1400 years later, in his work *De Daemonialitate*, the Franciscan scholar Ludovico Sinistrari assures us that demons pass through walls.

The external reality of demons was almost entirely unquestioned from antiquity through late medieval times. Maimonides denied their reality, but the overwhelming majority of rabbis believed in *dybbuks*. One of the few cases I can find where it is even hinted that demons might be *internal*, generated in our minds, is when Abba Poemen—one of the desert fathers of the early Church—was asked,

"How do the demons fight against me?"

"The demons fight against you?" Father Poemen asked in turn. "Our own wills become the demons, and it is these which attack us."

The medieval attitudes on incubi and succubi were influenced by Macrobius' fourth-century *Commentary on the Dream of Scipio*, which went through dozens of editions before the European Enlightenment. Macrobius described phantoms (*phantasmata*) seen "in the moment between wakefulness and slumber." The dreamer "imagines" the phantoms as predatory. Macrobius had a skeptical side which his medieval readers tended to ignore.

Obsession with demons began to reach a crescendo when, in his famous Bull of 1484, Pope Innocent VIII declared,

> It has come to Our ears that members of both sexes do not avoid to have intercourse with evil angels, incubi, and succubi, and that by their sorceries, and by their incantations, charms, and conjurations, they suffocate, extinguish, and cause to perish the births of women

as well as generate numerous other calamities. With this Bull, Innocent initiated the systematic accusation, torture and execution of countless "witches" all over Europe. They were guilty of what Augustine had described as "a criminal tampering with the unseen world." Despite the evenhanded "members of both sexes" in the language of the Bull, unsurprisingly it was mainly girls and women who were so persecuted.

Many leading Protestants of the following centuries, their differences with the Catholic Church notwithstanding, adopted nearly identical views. Even humanists such as Desiderius Erasmus and Thomas More believed in witches. "The giving up of witchcraft," said John Wesley, the founder of Methodism, "is in effect the giving up of the Bible." William Blackstone, the celebrated jurist, in his *Commentaries on the Laws of England* (1765), asserted:

To deny the possibility, nay, actual existence of witchcraft and sorcery is at once flatly to contradict the revealed word of God in various passages of both the Old and New Testament.

Innocent commended "Our dear sons Henry Kramer and James Sprenger," who "have been by Letters Apostolic delegated as Inquisitors of these heretical [de]pravities." If "the abominations and enormities in question remain unpunished," the souls of multitudes face eternal damnation.

The pope appointed Kramer and Sprenger to write a comprehensive analysis, using the full academic armory of the late fifteenth century. With exhaustive citations of Scripture and of ancient and modern scholars, they produced the *Malleus Maleficarum*, the "Hammer of Witches"—aptly described as one of the most terrifying documents in human history. Thomas Ady, in *A Candle in the Dark*, condemned it as "villainous Doctrines & Inventions," "horrible lyes and impossibilities," serving to hide "their unparalleled cruelty from the ears of the world." What the *Malleus* comes down to, pretty much, is that if you're accused of witchcraft, you're a witch. Torture is an unfailing means to demonstrate the validity of the accusation. There are no rights of the defendant. There is no opportunity to confront the accusers. Little attention is given to the possibility that accusations might be made for impious purposes—jealousy, say, or revenge, or the greed of the inquisitors who routinely confiscated for their own private benefit the property of the accused. This technical manual for torturers also includes methods of punishment tailored to release demons from the victim's body before the process kills her. The *Malleus* in hand, the Pope's encouragement guaranteed, inquisitors began springing up all over Europe.

It quickly became an expense account scam. All costs of investigation, trial, and execution were borne by the accused or her relatives— down to per diems for the private detectives hired to spy on her, wine for her guards, banquets for her judges, the travel expenses of a messenger sent to fetch a more experienced torturer from another city, and the faggots, tar and hangman's rope. Then there was a bonus to the members of the tribunal for each witch burned. The convicted witch's remaining property, if any, was divided between Church and State. As this legally and morally sanctioned mass murder and theft became institutionalized, as a vast bureaucracy arose to serve it, attention was turned from poor hags and crones to the middle class and well-to-do of both sexes.

The more who, under torture, confessed to witchcraft, the harder it was to maintain that the whole business was mere fantasy. Since each "witch" was made to implicate others, the numbers grew exponentially. These constituted "frightful proofs that the Devil is still alive," as it was later put in America in the Salem witch trials. In a credulous age, the most fantastic testimony was soberly accepted—that tens of thousands of witches had gathered for a Sabbath in public squares in France, or that 12,000 of them darkened the skies as they flew to Newfoundland. The Bible had counseled, "Thou shalt not suffer a witch to live." Legions of women were burnt to death.[3] And the most horrendous tortures were routinely applied to every defendant, young or old, after the instruments of torture were first blessed by the priests. Innocent himself died in 1492, following unsuccessful attempts to keep him alive by transfusion (which resulted in the deaths of three boys) and by suckling at the breast of a nursing mother. He was mourned by his mistress and their children.

In Britain witch-finders, also called "prickers," were employed, receiving a handsome bounty for each girl or woman they turned over for execution. They had no incentive to be cautious in their accusations. Typically they looked for "devil's marks"—scars or birthmarks or nevi—that when pricked with a pin neither hurt nor bled. A simple sleight of hand often gave the appearance that the pin penetrated deep into the witch's flesh. When no visible marks were apparent, "invisible marks" sufficed. Upon the gallows, one mid-seventeenth-century pricker "confessed he had been the death of above 220 women in England and Scotland, for the gain of twenty shillings apiece."[4]

In the witch trials, mitigating evidence or defense witnesses were inadmissible. In any case, it was nearly impossible to provide compelling alibis for accused witches: The rules of evidence had a special character. For example, in more than one case a husband attested that his wife was asleep in his arms at the very moment she was accused of frolicking with the devil at a witch's Sabbath; but the archbishop patiently explained that a demon had taken the place of the wife. The husbands were not to imagine that their powers of perception could exceed Satan's powers of deception. The beautiful young women were perforce consigned to the flames.

There were strong erotic and misogynistic elements—as might be expected in a sexually repressed, male-dominated society with inquisitors drawn from the class of nominally celibate priests. The trials paid close attention to the quality and quantity of orgasm in the supposed copulations of defendants with demons or the Devil (although Augustine had been certain "we cannot call the Devil a fornicator"), and to the nature of the Devil's "member" (cold, by all reports). "Devil's marks" were found "generally on the breasts or private parts" according to Ludovico Sinistrari's 1700 book. As a result pubic hair was shaved, and the genitalia were carefully inspected by the exclusively male inquisitors. In the immolation of the 20-year-old Joan of Arc, after her dress had caught fire the Hangman of Rouen slaked the flames so onlookers could view "all the secrets which can or should be in a woman."

The chronicle of those who were consumed by fire in the single German city of Würzburg in the single year 1598 penetrates the statistics and lets us confront a little of the human reality:

> The steward of the senate named Gering; old Mrs. Kanzler; the tailor's fat wife; the woman cook of Mr. Mengerdorf; a stranger; a strange woman; Baunach, a senator, the fattest citizen in Würtzburg; the old smith of the court; an old woman; a little girl, nine or ten years old; a younger girl, her little sister; the mother of the two little aforementioned girls; Liebler's daughter; Goebel's child, the most beautiful girl in Würtzburg; a student who knew many languages; two boys from the Minster, each twelve years old; Stepper's little daughter; the woman who kept the bridge gate; an old woman; the little son of the town council bailiff; the wife of Knertz, the butcher; the infant daughter of Dr. Schultz; a little girl; Schwartz, canon at Hach. . . .

On and on it goes. Some were given special humane attention: "The little daughter of Valkenberger was privately executed and burnt." There were 28 public immolations, each with 4 to 6 victims on average, in that small city in a single year. This was a microcosm of what was happening all across Europe. No one knows how many were killed altogether—perhaps hundreds of thousands, perhaps millions. Those responsible for prosecuting, torturing, judging, burning and justifying were selfless. Just ask them.

They could not be mistaken. The confessions of witchcraft could not be based on hallucinations, say, or desperate attempts to satisfy the inquisitors and stop the torture. In such a case, explained the witch judge Pierre de Lancre (in his 1612 book, *Description of the Inconstancy of Evil Angels*), the Catholic Church would be committing a great crime by burning witches. Those who raise such possibilities are thus attacking the Church and *ipso facto* committing a mortal sin. Critics of witch-burning were punished and, in some cases, themselves burnt. The inquisitors and torturers were doing God's work. They were saving souls. They were foiling demons.

Witchcraft of course was not the only offense that merited torture and burning at the stake. Heresy was a still more serious crime, and both Catholics and Protestants punished it ruthlessly. In the sixteenth century the scholar William Tyndale had the temerity to contemplate translating the New Testament into English. But if people could actually read the Bible in their own language instead of arcane Latin, they could form their own, independent religious views. They might conceive of their own private unintermediated line to God. This was a challenge to the job security of Roman Catholic priests. When Tyndale tried to publish his translation, he was hounded and pursued all over Europe. Eventually he was captured, garroted, and then, for good measure, burned at the stake. His copies of the New Testament (which a century later became the basis of the exquisite King James translation) were then hunted down house-to-house by armed posses—Christians piously defending Christianity by preventing other Christians from knowing the words of Christ. Such a cast of mind, such a climate of absolute confidence that knowledge should be rewarded by torture and death were unlikely to help those accused of witchcraft.

Burning witches is a feature of Western civilization that has, with occasional political exceptions, declined since the sixteenth century. In the last judicial execution of witches in England a woman and her nine-year-old daughter were hanged. Their crime was raising a rain storm by taking their stockings off. In our time, witches and djinns are found as regular fare in children's entertainment, exorcism of demons is still practiced by the Roman Catholic and other churches, and the proponents of one cult still denounce as sorcery the cultic practices of another. We still use the word "pandemonium" (literally, all demons). A crazed and violent person is still said to be demonic. (Not until the eighteenth century was mental illness no longer generally ascribed to supernatural causes; even insomnia had been considered a punishment inflicted by demons.) More than half of Americans tell pollsters they "believe" in the Devil's existence, and 10 percent have communicated with him, as Martin Luther reported he did regularly. In a 1992 "spiritual warfare manual" called *Prepare for War*, Rebecca Brown informs us that abortion and sex outside of marriage "will almost always result in demonic infestation"; that meditation, yoga and martial arts are designed so unsuspecting Christians will be seduced into worshiping demons; and that "rock music didn't 'just happen,' it was a carefully masterminded plan by none other than Satan himself." Sometimes "your loved ones are demonically bound and blinded." Demonology is today still part and parcel of many earnest faiths.

And what is it that demons do? In the *Malleus*, Kramer and Sprenger reveal that "devils . . . busy themselves by interfering with the process of normal copulation and conception, by obtaining human semen, and themselves transferring it." Demonic artificial insemination in the Middle Ages goes back at least to St. Thomas Aquinas, who tells us in *On the Trinity* that "demons can transfer the semen which they have collected and inject it into the bodies of others." His contemporary, St. Bonaventura, spells it out in a little more detail: Succubi "yield to males and receive their semen; by cunning skill, the demons preserve its potency, and afterwards, with the permission of God, they become incubi and pour it out into female repositories." The products of these demon-mediated unions are also, when they grow up, visited by demons. A multigenerational transspecies sexual bond is forged. And these creatures, we recall, are well known to fly; indeed they inhabit the upper air.

There is no spaceship in these stories. But most of the central elements of the alien abduction account are present, including sexually obsessive non-humans who live in the sky, walk through walls, communicate telepathically, and perform breeding experiments on the human species. Unless *we* believe that demons really exist, how can we understand so strange a belief system, embraced by the whole Western world (including those considered the wisest among us), reinforced by personal experience in every generation, and taught by Church and State? Is there any real alternative besides a shared delusion based on common brain wiring and chemistry?

NOTES

1. "Science" means "knowledge" in Latin. A jurisdictional dispute is exposed, even if we look no further.

2. Likewise, in the same work, "The raising of storms by witches is attested by so many, that I think it needless to recite them." The theologian Meric Causabon argued—in his 1668 book, *Of Credulity and Incredulity*—that witches must exist because, after all, everyone believes in them. Anything that a large number of people believe must be true.

3. This mode of execution was adopted by the Holy Inquisition apparently to guarantee literal accord with a well-intentioned sentence of canon law (Council of Tours, 1163): "The Church abhors bloodshed."

4. In the murky territory of bounty hunters and paid informers, vile corruption is often the rule—worldwide and throughout all of human history. To take an example almost at random, in 1994, for a fee, a group of postal inspectors from Cleveland agreed to go underground and ferret out wrongdoers; they then contrived criminal cases against 32 innocent postal workers.

PART 6

RELIGION
AND ETHICS

Mme La Maréchale: *Are you not Monsieur Crudeli?*
Crudeli: *Yes, madame.*
L.M.: *Then you're the man who doesn't believe in anything.*
Crudeli: *In person, madame.*
L.M.: *Yet your moral principles are the same as those of a believer?*
Crudeli: *Why should they not be—as long as the believer is an honest man?*
L.M.: *And do you act upon your principles?*
Crudeli: *To the best of my ability.*
L.M.: *What? You don't steal? You don't kill people? You don't rob them?*
Crudeli: *Very rarely.*
L.M.: *Then what do you gain by not being a believer?*
Crudeli: *Nothing at all, madame. Is one a believer from motives of profit?*

—Denis Diderot
"Conversation with a Christian Lady" (1774)
trans. Derek Coltman

20

THE SYSTEM OF NATURE
(1770)

Paul-Henri Thiry, baron d'Holbach

Paul-Henri Thiry, baron d'Holbach (1723–1789) was born of a German aristocratic family. He settled in Paris in 1749, where he became acquainted with many of the leading philosophes *of the time, including Helvétius, d'Alembert, Condillac, and Diderot. He contributed 450 articles to the* Encyclopédie *(1751–66), mostly on scientific subjects. He also wrote several polemical works against religion, including* Le Christianisme dévoilé *(1767;* Christianity Unveiled*) and his most celebrated work,* Système de la Nature *(1770;* The System of Nature*), which shocked even his philosophical contemporaries by its open assertion of atheism and materialism. In this extract from a chapter of that work, d'Holbach maintains not only that atheism is not inextricably tied to immorality but that it actually produces a superior morality to that exhibited by the religious.*

AFTER HAVING PROVED THE EXISTENCE of atheists, let us return to the calumnies that are showered upon them by the theists. According to Abbadie,[1] "an atheist cannot be virtuous: to him virtue is only a chimera; probity no more than a vain scruple; honesty nothing but foolishness;—he knows no other law than his interest: where this sentiment prevails, conscience is only a prejudice; natural law only an illusion; right no more than an error; benevolence no longer has any

From Paul Henri Thiry, baron d'Holbach, *Système de la nature* (1770), trans. as *The System of Nature*, vol. 3 (London: R. Helder, 1821), pp. 169–76, 178–82, 185–91 (revised by S. T. Joshi).

foundation; the bonds of society are loosened; the ties of fidelity are removed; friend is ready to betray friend; the citizen to deliver up his country; the son to assassinate his father, in order to enjoy his inheritance, whenever they shall find occasion, and that authority or silence shall shield them from the arm of the secular power, which alone is to be feared. The most inviolable rights, and most sacred laws, must no longer be considered, except as dreams and visions."

Such, perhaps, would be the conduct, not of a feeling, thinking, reflecting being, susceptible of reason, but of a ferocious brute, an irrational wretch, who should not have any idea of the natural relations which subsist between beings, reciprocally necessary to each other's happiness. Can it actually be supposed that a man capable of experience, furnished with the faintest glimmerings of good sense, would lend himself to the conduct that is here ascribed to the atheist; that is to say, to a man who is sufficiently susceptible of reflection to undeceive himself by reasoning upon those prejudices which everyone strives to show him as important and sacred? Can it, I say, be supposed that any civilized society contains a citizen so completely blind as not to acknowledge his most natural duties, his dearest interests, the dangers he incurs in disturbing his fellow creatures or in following no other rule than his momentary appetites? Is not every human being who reasons in the least possible manner obliged to feel that society is advantageous to him; that he has need of assistance; that the esteem of his fellows is necessary to his own happiness; that he has everything to fear from the wrath of his associates; that the laws menace whoever shall dare to infringe them? Every man who has received a virtuous education, who has in his infancy experienced the tender cares of a parent, who has in consequence tasted the sweets of friendship, who has received kindness, who knows the worth of benevolence and equity, who feels the pleasure that the affection of our fellow creatures procures for us, who endures the inconveniences that result from their aversion and their scorn, is obliged to tremble at losing such manifest advantages, at incurring such imminent danger. Will not the hatred of others, the fear of punishment, his own contempt of himself, disturb his repose every time that, turning inwardly, he shall contemplate himself under the same perspective as does his neighbor? Is there then no remorse except for those who believe in a God? Is the idea that we are under the eye of a being of whom we have but vague notions more forcible than the thought that we are viewed by our fellow men; that we are viewed by ourselves; that we are compelled to be afraid; that we are under the cruel necessity of becoming despicable in our own eyes and blushing guiltily in thinking of our conduct and of the sentiments it must infallibly inspire?

This granted, we shall reply deliberately to this Abbadie, that an atheist is a man who understands nature and her laws, who understands his own nature, who knows what it imposes upon him. An atheist has experience, and this experience proves to him every moment that vice can injure him, that his most concealed faults, his most secret dispositions, may be detected and may display his character in open day. This experience proves to him that society is useful to his happiness, that his interest therefore demands he should attach himself to the country that protects him and enables him to enjoy in security the benefits of nature. Everything shows him that in order to be happy he must make himself beloved, that his father is for him the most certain of friends, that ingratitude would remove him from his benefactor, that justice is necessary to the maintenance of every association, and that no man, whatever may be his power, can be content with himself, when he knows he is an object of public hatred.

He who has maturely reflected upon himself, upon his own nature and upon that of his associates, upon his own needs, upon the means of procuring them, cannot prevent himself from becoming acquainted with his duties—from discovering the obligations he owes to himself, as well as those he owes to others: he accordingly has morality; he has actual motives to comply with its dictates; he is obliged to feel that these duties are necessary; and if his reason be not disturbed by blind passions or by vicious habits, he will find that virtue is the surest road to felicity. The atheist or the fatalist build all their systems upon necessity: thus, their moral speculations, founded upon the nature of things, are at least much more permanent, much more invariable, than those which only rest upon a God whose aspect changes according to the various dispositions and passions of those contemplate him. The essence of things, and the immutable laws of nature, are not subject to fluctuation; the atheist is always compelled to call whatever injures himself either vice or folly; whatever injures others, crime; whatever is advantageous to society or contributes to its permanent happiness, virtue.

It will be obvious, then, that the principles of the atheist are much less liable to be shaken than those of the enthusiast, who bases his morality upon an imaginary being, the conception of which varies all too frequently, even within his own brain. If the atheist denies the existence of a God, he cannot deny his own existence, nor that of beings similar to himself, by whom he sees himself surrounded; he cannot doubt the relations that subsist between them; he cannot question the necessity of the duties that spring out of these relations; he cannot doubt the principles of morality, which is nothing but the science of the relations of beings living together in society.

If, however, satisfied with a barren, speculative knowledge of his duties, the atheist should not apply it to his conduct; if, borne along by criminal passions or habits, abandoned to shameful vices, at the mercy of a vicious temperament, he appears to forget his moral obligations, it by no means follows that he has no principles or that his principles are false. It can only be concluded that in the intoxication of his passions, in the confusion of his reason, he does not give activity to doctrines grounded upon truth; that he forgets his trustworthy principles in order to follow the propensities that mislead him.

Nothing is, perhaps, more common among men than a very marked discrepancy between the mind and the heart; that is to say, between the temperament, the passions, the habits, the caprices, the imagination, and the judgment, assisted by reflection. Nothing is more rare than to find these things working in harmony; it is, however, only when they do, that we see speculation influence practice. The most certain virtues are those which are founded upon the temperament of men. Indeed, do we not every day behold mortals in contradiction with themselves? Does not their more sober judgment unceasingly condemn the extravagances to which their passions deliver them up? In short, does not everything prove to us hourly that men, with the very best theory, have sometimes the very worst practice; that others with the most vicious theory frequently adopt the most estimable line of conduct? In the blindest and most appalling superstitions, in those that are most contrary to reason, we meet with virtuous men, the mildness of whose character, the sensibility of whose hearts, the excellence of whose temperament lead them back to humanity and to the laws of their nature, despite their mad theories. Among the adorers of the most cruel, vindictive, jealous God are found peaceable souls, enemies to persecution, violence, and cruelty; among the disciples of a God filled with mercy and clemency, are seen barbarous and inhuman monsters. Nevertheless, both the one and the other acknowledge that their gods ought to serve them for a model. Why, then, do they not in all things conform themselves? It is because the temperament of man is always stronger than his Gods; that the wickedest Gods cannot always corrupt an honest soul, and that the sweetest Gods cannot rectify hearts carried away by crime. The human constitution will always be more powerful than Religion; present objects, momentary interests, rooted habits, public opinion, have much more efficacy than imaginary beings or unintelligible theories, which themselves depend upon this constitution.

The point in question, then, is to examine if the principles of the atheist are true, and not whether his conduct is commendable. An atheist, having an excellent theory, founded upon nature, experience, and reason, who delivers himself up to excesses, dangerous to himself, injurious to society, is, without doubt, an inconsistent man. But he is not more to be feared than a religious zealot, who, believing in a good, equitable, perfect God, does not scruple to commit the most frightful devastations in his name. An atheistical tyrant would assuredly not be more to be dreaded than a fanatical despot. A skeptical philosopher, however, is not so mischievous as an enthusiastic priest, who fans the flame of discord among his fellow citizens. Would, then, an atheist clothed with power be equally dangerous as a persecuting king, or a savage inquisitor, or a whimsical devotee, or a morose bigot? These are assuredly more numerous in the world than atheists, whose opinions or whose vices are far from being in a position to influence society, since society is too filled with prejudice to wish to pay any attention to them. . . .

Indeed, if men condescended to examine things coolly, they would find that the name of God has on this earth only served as a pretext for human passions. Ambition, imposture, and tyranny have often formed a league to avail themselves of its influence, in order to blind the people and bend them beneath the yoke. The monarch sometimes employs it to give a divine lustre to his person, the sanction of heaven to his rights, an oracular tone to his most unjust, most extravagant whims. The priest uses it to give currency to his pretensions, so that he may with impunity gratify his avarice, his pride, and his independence. The vindictive, enraged, superstitious being introduces the cause of his God so that he may give free scope to his fury, which he qualifies with zeal. In short, religion is dangerous, because it justifies and lends legitimacy and praise to the passions and crimes whose fruit it does not fail to gather: according to its ministers, everything is permitted to revenge the most high; thus the name of the Divinity is used to authorize and excuse the most injurious transgressions. The atheist, when he commits crimes, cannot, at least, pretend that it is his God who commands and approves them; this is the excuse that superstitious beings offer for their perversity, the tyrant for his persecutions, the priest for his cruelty and his sedition, the fanatic for his excesses, the penitent for his uselessness.

"It is not," says Bayle,[2] "the general opinions of the mind, but the passions, which determine us to act. Atheism is a system which will not make a good man wicked, nor will it make a wicked man good. Those," says the same author, "who embraced the sect of Epicurus did not become debauchees because they had adopted the doctrine of Epicurus; they only adopted the doctrine, then badly understood, because they were debauchees." In the same manner, a perverse man may embrace atheism, because he will flatter himself that this system will give full scope to his passions: he will nevertheless be deceived. Atheism, if well understood, is founded upon nature and upon reason, which never can, like superstition, either justify or expiate the crimes of the wicked.

From the diffusion of doctrines that make morality depend upon the existence and the will of God, and which are proposed to men for a model, there has unquestionably resulted very great inconvenience. Corrupt souls, in discovering how much each of these suppositions are erroneous or doubtful, give loose to the rein of their vices, and conclude there are not more substantive motives for acting well; they imagine that virtue, like the Gods, is only an illusion; that there is no reason for practicing it in this world. Nevertheless, it must be evident that it is not as the creatures of God that we are bound to fulfill the duties of morality; it is as men, as sensible beings living together in society and seeking to secure for ourselves a happy existence, that we should feel the moral obligation. Whether a God exists or not, our duties will remain the same; our nature, if consulted, will incontestibly prove that vice is an evil and that virtue is an actual good.

If, then, there are found atheists who have denied the distinction between good and evil, or who have dared to strike at the foundations of morality, we ought to conclude that upon this point they have reasoned badly; that they have understood neither the nature of man, nor the true source of his duties; that they have falsely imagined that ethics, as well as theology, was only an ideal science, and that once the Gods were destroyed, there no longer remained any bonds to connect mortals. Nevertheless, the slightest reflection would have incontestibly proved to them that morality is founded upon immutable relations subsisting between sensible, intelligent, sociable beings; that without virtue, no society can maintain itself; that without putting the curb on his desires, no mortal can conserve himself. Men are constrained by their nature to love virtue and to dread crime, by the same necessity that obliges them to seek happiness and fly from sorrow: this nature compels them to make a distinction between those objects which please and those objects which injure them. Ask a man, who is sufficiently irrational to deny the difference between virtue and vice, if it would be indifferent to him to be beaten, robbed, insulted, treated with ingratitude, dishonored by his wife, insulted by his children, betrayed by his friend? His answer will prove to you that whatever he may say, he discriminates the actions of mankind; that the distinction between good and evil does not depend either upon the conventions of men, nor upon the ideas which they may have of divinity, nor upon the rewards or punishments that this divinity prepares for them in another life.

On the contrary, an atheist who should reason justly would feel himself more interested than another in practicing those virtues to which he finds his well-being attached in this world. If his views do not extend themselves beyond the limits of his present existence, he must, at least, desire to see his days roll on in happiness and in peace. Every man who, during the calm of his passions, falls back upon himself, will feel that his interest invites him to his own preservation; that his happiness demands he should take the necessary means to enjoy life peaceably, free of alarms and remorse. Man owes something to man, not because he would offend a God if he was to injure his fellow creature, but because in doing him an injury he would offend a man and violate the laws of equity, in the maintenance of which every human being finds himself interested. . . .

The principles of atheism are not formed for the mass of the people, who are commonly under the tutelage of their priests; they are not calculated for those frivolous and dissipated minds who fill society with their vices and their uselessness; they will not gratify the ambitious, the intriguers, those restless beings who find their interest in making a disturbance: much less are they made for a great number of persons who, enlightened in other respects, have not sufficient courage to divorce themselves from the received prejudices.

So many causes unite to confirm man in those errors which he draws in with his mother's milk that every step that removes him from them costs him infinite pain. Those persons who are most enlightened frequently cling on some side to some universal prejudice. We feel ourselves, as it were, isolated: whenever we stand alone in our opinions, we no longer seem to speak the language of society; it requires courage to adopt a mode of thinking that is approved by so few. In those countries where human knowledge has made some progress, and where, besides, a certain freedom of thinking is enjoyed, one may easily find a great number of deists or skeptics, who, contented with having trampled underfoot the grosser prejudices of the illiterate, have not dared to go back to the source, and to bring divinity itself before the tribunal of reason. If these thinkers did not stop on the road, reflection would quickly prove to them that the God they have not the fortitude to examine is an equally injurious being, equally revolting to good sense, as any of those dogmas, mysteries, fables, and superstitious practices whose futility they have already acknowledged; they would feel, as we have already proved, that all these things are nothing more than the necessary consequences of those primitive conceptions by which men have made this divine phantom for themselves, and that in admitting this phantom, they no longer have any rational cause to reject the deductions which the imagination has drawn from it. A little attention would distinctly show them that it is precisely this phantom which is the true cause of all the evils of society; that those endless disputes, those bloody quarrels to which religion and the spirit of party every instant give birth are the inevitable effects of the importance they attach to an illusion, which is always ready to inflame their minds. In short, nothing is easier than to convince ourselves that an imaginary being, always portrayed in a terrifying aspect, must act vividly upon the imagination and sooner or later produce disputes, enthusiasm, fanaticism, and delirium.

Many persons acknowledge that the extravagances to which superstition lends activity are very real evils; many complain of the abuses of religion, but there are very few who feel that these abuses and these evils are the necessary consequences of the fundamental principles of all religion, which are founded upon the most grievous notions that one is compelled to make about deity. We daily see persons undeceived about religion, who nevertheless pretend that this religion *is necessary for the people;* that without it, they could not be controlled. But to reason thus, is it not to say that poison is beneficial to the people, that therefore it is proper to poison them in order to prevent them from abusing their power? Is it not in fact to pretend that it is advantageous to render them absurd, mad, extravagant; that they have need of hobgoblins to blind them, to make them giddy, to cause them to submit them to impostors or fanatics, who will avail themselves of their follies to disturb the universe? Again, is it indeed true that religion has had a truly useful influence over the morals of the people? It is easy to see that it subjugates them without making them better; that it produces a herd of ignorant slaves whom panic terrors keep under the yoke of tyrants and priests; that it makes fools who know no other virtue save an appalling submission to futile customs, to which they attach a much greater value than to the actual virtues and moral duties whose existence has never been made known to them. If this religion does by chance restrain a few frightened individuals, it has no effect on the greater number, who suffer themselves to be borne along by the epidemical vices with which they are infected. It is in those countries where superstition has the greatest power that we always find the least morality. Virtue is incompatible with ignorance, superstition, slavery: slaves can only be restrained by the fear of punishment; ignorant children are only for a few moments intimidated by imaginary terrors. In order to mould men, in order to have virtuous citizens, we must instruct them, show them virtue, speak rationally with them, make them understand their interests, teach them to respect themselves and to fear shame, inspire within them the idea of true *honor,* make them understand the value of virtue and the motives for following it. How can we expect these happy effects from a religion that degrades them, or from a tyranny that proposes nothing more than to subjugate and divide them, and keep them in humiliation?

The false ideas that so many persons have of the utility of religion, which they at least judge to be calculated to restrain the people, arise from the fatal prejudice that it is a *useful error,* and that truths may be dangerous. This principle has complete efficacy to perpetuate the sorrows of the earth. Whoever shall have the courage to examine these things will without hesitation acknowledge that all the miseries of the human race are to be ascribed to his errors; that of these, religious error must be the most harmful of all, from the arrogance it inspires in sovereigns, the importance that is usually attached to it, the degradation it prescribes to subjects, the frenzies it excites among the people. We shall, therefore, be obliged to conclude that the superstitious errors of man are exactly those that, for the permanent interest of mankind, demand the most complete destruction, and that it is principally to their annihilation that the efforts of a sound philosophy ought to be directed. It is not to be feared that this attempt will produce disturbances or revolutions: the more freedom shall accompany the voice of truth, the more peculiar it will appear; the more simple it shall be, the less it will influence men, who are only smitten with the marvellous; even those individuals who seek after truth most ardently have frequently an irresistible inclination that urges them on, and incessantly disposes them to reconcile error with truth.

Here is, unquestionably, the true reason why atheism, whose principles have not hitherto been sufficiently developed, appears to alarm even those persons who are the most destitute of prejudice. They find too great an interval between vulgar superstition and an absolute lack of religion; they imagine they take a wise medium in compounding with error; they therefore reject the consequences, while admitting the principle; they preserve the shadow without foreseeing that, sooner or later, it must produce the same effects and, little by little, hatch the same follies in human minds. The majority of skeptics and reformers do no more than prune a cankered tree, to whose root they dare not apply the axe; they do not perceive that this tree will in the end produce the same fruit. Theology or religion will always be a heap of combustible matter brooded in the imagination of mankind; it will always finish by causing the most terrible explosions. As long as the sacerdotal order shall have the right to infect youth, to accustom them to tremble before mere words, to alarm nations with the name of a terrible God, so long will fanaticism be master of the human mind; imposture will, at its pleasure, cause discord in the nation. The simplest delusion, perpetually fed, modified, exaggerated by the imagination of men, will by degrees become a colossus, sufficiently powerful to overturn minds and overthrow empires. Deism is a system at which the human mind cannot make a long sojourn; founded upon error, it will, sooner or later, degenerate into the most absurd, the most dangerous superstition.

NOTES

1. [Jacques Abbadie (1654?–1727), *Traité de la verité de la religion chrétienne* (1679–89).]

2. [Pierre Bayle (1647–1706), French philosopher whose *Dictionnaire historique et critique* (1697) was condemned by the church for its arguments undermining religious orthodoxy. Holbach quotes from Bayle's *Pensées diverses* (1683).]

21

THE AGE OF REASON
(1796)

Thomas Paine

Thomas Paine (1737–1809) was born in England, the son of a Quaker, but came to the United States in 1784. He immediately established himself as a leading propagandist for the American Revolution with the publication of Common Sense *(1776). Later, on a trip to Europe, he wrote two works that embroiled him in controversy:* The Rights of Man *(1791–92), in which he urged Englishmen to overthrow the monarchy, and* The Age of Reason *(1794–96), which was taken to be the work of an atheist in its scorn of religious revelation and dogma (in fact, Paine is probably to be classified as a deist). These works caused him to be socially ostracized upon his return to the United States, and he was denied burial in consecrated ground upon his death. In this extract from* The Age of Reason, *Paine criticizes religion on two fronts: many evils have been committed in religion's name, and religious morality itself is flawed and at times incoherent.*

REVELATION . . . , SO FAR AS THE term has relation between God and man, can only be applied to something which God reveals of his will to man; but though the power of the Almighty to make such a communication is necessarily admitted, because to that power all things are possible, yet, the thing so revealed (if any thing ever was revealed, and which, by the bye, it is impossible to prove) is revelation

From Thomas Paine, *The Age of Reason* (1794–96), in *The Writings of Thomas Paine,* ed. Moncure Daniel Conway, vol. 4 (New York: G. P. Putnam's Sons, 1894–96), pp. 183–88.

to the person *only to whom it is made.* His account of it to another is not revelation; and whoever puts faith in that account, puts it in the man from whom the account comes; and that man may have been deceived, or may have dreamed it; or he may be an impostor and may lie. There is no possible criterion whereby to judge of the truth of what he tells; for even the morality of it would be no proof of revelation. In all such cases, the proper answer should be, "When it is revealed to me, I will believe it to be revelation; but it is not and cannot be incumbent upon me to believe it to be revelation before; neither is it proper that I should take the word of man as the word of God, and put man in the place of God." This is the manner in which I have spoken of revelation in the former part of *The Age of Reason*; and which, whilst it reverentially admits revelation as a possible thing, because, as before said, to the Almighty all things are possible, it prevents the imposition of one man upon another, and precludes the wicked use of pretended revelation.

But though, speaking for myself, I thus admit the possibility of revelation, I totally disbelieve that the Almigity ever did communicate any thing to man, by any mode of speech, in any language, or by any kind of vision, or appearance, or by any means which our senses are capable of receiving, otherwise than by the universal display of himself in the works of the creation, and by that repugnance we feel in ourselves to bad actions, and disposition to good ones.

The most detestable wickedness, the most horrid cruelties, and the greatest miseries, that have afflicted the human race, have had their origin in this thing called revelation, or revealed religion. It has been the most dishonourable belief against the character of the divinity, the most destructive to morality, and the peace and happiness of man, that ever was propagated since man began to exist. It is better, far better, that we admitted, if it were possible, a thousand devils to roam at large, and to preach publicly the doctrine of devils, if there were any such, than that we permitted one such impostor and monster as Moses, Joshua, Samuel, and the Bible prophets, to come with the pretended word of God in his mouth, and have credit among us.

Whence arose all the horrid assassinations of whole nations of men, women, and infants, with which the Bible is filled; and the bloody persecutions, and tortures unto death and religious wars, that since that time have laid Europe in blood and ashes; whence arose they, but from this impious thing called revealed religion, and this monstrous belief that God has spoken to man? The lies of the Bible have been the cause of the one, and the lies of the Testament [of] the other.

Some Christians pretend that Christianity was not established by the sword; but of what period of time do they speak? It was impossible that twelve men could begin with the sword: they had not the power; but no sooner were the professors of Christianity sufficiently powerful to employ the sword than they did so, and the stake and faggot too; and Mahomet could not do it sooner. By the same spirit that Peter cut off the ear of the high priest's servant (if the story be true) he would cut off his head, and the head of his master, had he been able. Besides this, Christianity grounds itself originally upon the [Hebrew] Bible, and the Bible was established altogether by the sword, and that in the worst use of it—not to terrify, but to extirpate. The Jews made no converts: they butchered all. The Bible is the sire of the [New] Testament, and both are called the *word of God*. The Christians read both books; the ministers preach from both books; and this thing called Christianity is made up of both. It is then false to say that Christianity was not established by the sword.

The only sect that has not persecuted are the Quakers; and the only reason that can be given for it is, that they are rather Deists than Christians. They do not believe much about Jesus Christ, and they call the scriptures a dead letter. Had they called them by a worse name, they had been nearer the truth.

It is incumbent on every man who reverences the character of the Creator, and who wishes to lessen the catalogue of artificial miseries, and remove the cause that has sown persecutions thick among mankind, to expel all ideas of a revealed religion as a dangerous heresy, and an impious fraud. What is it that we have learned from this pretended thing called revealed religion? Nothing that is useful to man, and every thing that is dishonourable to his Maker. What is it the Bible teaches us?— rapine, cruelty, and murder. What is it the Testament teaches us?—to believe that the Almighty committed debauchery with a woman engaged to be married; and the belief of this debauchery is called faith.

As to the fragments of morality that are irregularly find thinly scattered in those books, they make no part of this pretended thing, revealed religion. They are the natural dictates of conscience, and the bonds by which society is held together, and without which it cannot exist; and are nearly the same in all religions, and in all societies. The

Testament teaches nothing new upon this subject, and where it attempts to exceed, it becomes mean and ridiculous. The doctrine of not retaliating injuries is much better expressed in Proverbs, which is a collection as well from the Gentiles as the Jews, than it is in the Testament. It is there said, (xxv. 21) *"If thine enemy be hungry, give him bread to eat; and if he be thirsty, give him water to drink:"* but when it is said, as in the Testament, *"If a man smite thee on the right cheek, turn to him the other also,"* it is assassinating the dignity of forbearance, and sinking man into a spaniel.

Loving of enemies is another dogma of feigned morality, and has besides no meaning. It is incumbent on man, as a moralist, that he does not revenge an injury; and it is equally as good in a political sense, for there is no end to retaliation; each retaliates on the other, and calls it justice: but to love in proportion to the injury, if it could be done, would be to offer a premium for a crime. Besides, the word *enemies* is too vague and general to be used in a moral maxim, which ought always to be clear and defined, like a proverb. If a man be the enemy of another from mistake and prejudice, as in the case of religious opinions, and sometimes in politics, that man is different to an enemy at heart with a criminal intention; and it is incumbent upon us, and it contributes also to our own tranquillity, that we put the best construction upon a thing that it will bear. But even this erroneous motive in him makes no motive for love on the other part; and to say that we can love voluntarily, and without a motive, is morally and physically impossible.

Morality is injured by prescribing to it duties that, in the first place, are impossible to be performed, and if they could be would be productive of evil; or, as before said, be premiums for crime. The maxim of *doing as we would be done unto* does not include this strange doctrine of loving enemies; for no man expects to be loved himself for his crime or for his enmity.

Those who preach this doctrine of loving their enemies, are in general the greatest persecutors, and they act consistently by so doing; for the doctrine is hypocritical, and it is natural that hypocrisy should act the reverse of what it preaches. For my own part, I disown the doctrine, and consider it as a feigned or fabulous morality; yet the man does not exist that can say I have persecuted him, or any man, or any set of men, either in the American Revolution, or in the French Revolution; or that I have, in any case, returned evil for evil. But it is not incumbent on man to reward a bad action with a good one, or to return good for evil; and wherever it is done, it is a voluntary act, and not a duty. It is also absurd to suppose that such doctrine can make any part of a revealed religion. We imitate the moral character of the Creator by forbearing with each other, for he forbears with all; but this doctrine would imply that he loved man, not in proportion as he was good, but as he was bad.

If we consider the nature of our condition here, we must see there is no occasion for such a thing as *revealed religion*. What is it we want to know? Does not the creation, the universe we behold, preach to us the existence of an Almighty power, that governs and regulates the whole? And is not the evidence that this creation holds out to our senses infinitely stronger than any thing we can read in a book, that any impostor might make and call the word of God? As for morality, the knowledge of it exists in every man's conscience.

22

A LETTER ON RELIGION
(1918)

H. P. Lovecraft

American writer Howard Phillips Lovecraft (1890–1937) gained celebrity as the leading writer of supernatural fiction in the twentieth century, author of such pioneering tales as "The Call of Cthulhu" (1926), "The Colour out of Space" (1927), and At the Mountains of Madness *(1931). The recent publication of his letters has revealed him to be an atheist of keen penetration. In the following letter, written to Maurice W. Moe on May 15, 1918, Lovecraft pungently refutes his correspondent's assertion that religion is morally useful regardless of its truth or falsity.*

YOUR WONDERMENT "WHAT I HAVE against religion" reminds me of your recent *Vagrant* essay—which I had the honour of perusing in manuscript some three years ago. To my mind, that essay *misses one point altogether.* Your "agnostic" has neglected to mention the very crux of all agnosticism—namely that the Judaeo-Christian mythology is NOT TRUE. I can see that in your philosophy *truth per se* has so small a place, that you can scarcely realise what it is that Galpin[1] and I are insisting upon. In your mind, MAN is the centre of everything, and his exact conformation to certain regulations of conduct HOWEVER EFFECTED, the only problem in the universe. Your world (if you will pardon my saying so) is *contracted*. All the mental vigour and erudition of the ages fail to disturb your complacent endorsement of empirical doctrines and purely pragmatical notions, because you voluntarily limit your horizon—*excluding certain facts, and certain undeniable mental tendencies of mankind*. In your eyes, man is torn between *only two* influences; the degrading instincts of the savage, and the temperate impulses of the philanthropist. To you, men are of but two classes—lovers of self and lovers of the race. To you, men have but two types of emotion—self-gratification, to be combated; and altruism, to be fostered. But you, consciously or unconsciously, are leaving out a vast and potent *tertium quid*—making an omission which cannot but interfere with the validity of your philosophical conceptions. You are forgetting a human impulse which, despite its restriction to a relatively small number of men, has all through history proved itself as real and as vital as hunger—as potent as thirst or greed. I need not say that I refer to that simplest yet most exalted attribute of our species—the acute, persistent, unquenchable craving TO KNOW. Do you realise that to many men it makes a vast and profound difference whether or not the things about them are as they appear? . . .

I recognise a distinction between dream life and real life, between appearances and actualities. I confess to an over-powering desire to know whether I am asleep or awake—whether the environment and laws which affect me are external and permanent, or the transitory products of my own brain. I admit that I am very much interested in the relation I bear to the things about me—the time relation, the space relation, and the causative relation. I desire to know approximately what my life is in terms of history—human, terrestrial, solar, and cosmical; what my magnitude may be in terms of extension,—terrestrial, solar, and cosmical; and above all, what may be my manner of linkage to the general system—in what way, through what agency, and to what extent, the obvious guiding forces of creation act upon me and govern my existence. And if there be any less obvious forces, I desire to know them and their relation to me as well. Foolish, do I hear you say? Undoubtedly! I had better be a consistent pragmatist: get drunk and confine myself to a happy, swinish, contented little world—the gutter—till some policeman's No. 13 boot intrudes upon my philosophic repose. But I *cannot*. Why? Because some well-defined human impulse prompts me to discard the relative for the absolute. You would encourage me as far as the moral stage. You would agree with me that I had better see the world as it is than to forget my woes in the flowing bowl. But because I have a certain *momentum*, and am carried a step further from the merely relative, you frown upon me and declare me to be a queer, unaccountable creature, "immersed . . . in the VICIOUS abstractions of philosophy!"

Here, then, is the beginning of my religious or philosophical thought. I have not begun talking about *morality* yet, because I have not reached that point in the argument. *Entity* precedes morality. It is a prerequisite. What am I? What is the nature of the energy about me, and how does it affect me? So far I have seen nothing which could possibly give me the notion that cosmic force is the manifestation of a mind and will like my own infinitely magnified; a potent and purposeful consciousness which deals individually and directly with the miserable denizens of a wretched little flyspeck on the back door of a microscopic universe, and which singles this putrid excrescence out as the one spot whereto to send an onlie-begotten Son, whose mission is to redeem those accursed flyspeck-inhabiting lice which we call human beings—bah!! Pardon the "bah!" I feel several "bahs!," but out of courtesy I only say one. But it is all so very childish. I cannot help taking exception to a philosophy which would force this rubbish down my throat. "What have I against religion?" That is what I have against it! . . .

Now let us view *morality*—which despite your preconceived classification and identification has nothing to do with any particular form of religion. Morality is the adjustment of matter to its environment—the natural arrangement of molecules. More especially it may be considered as dealing with organic molecules. Conventionally it is the science of reconciling the animal *homo* (more or less) *sapiens* to the forces and conditions with which he is surrounded. It is linked with religion only so far as the natural elements it deals with are deified and personified. Morality antedated the Christian religion, and has many times risen superior to co-existent religions. It has powerful support from very non-religious human impulses. Personally, I am intensely moral and intensely irreligious. My morality can be traced to two distinct sources, scientific and aesthetic. My love of truth is outraged by the flagrant disturbance of sociological relations involved in so-called wrong; whilst my aesthetic sense is outraged and disgusted with the violations of taste and harmony thereupon attendant. But to me the question presents no ground for connexion with the grovelling instinct of religion. However—you may exclude me from the argument, if you will. I *am* unduly secluded though unavoidably so. We will deal only with materials which may presumably lie within my feeble reach. Only one more touch of ego. I am *not* at all passive or indifferent in my zeal for a high morality. But I cannot consider morality the essence of religion as you seem to. In discussing religion, the whole fabric must bear examination before the uses or purposes are considered. We must investigate the cause as well as alleged effects if we are to define the relation between the two, and the reality of the former. And more, granting that the phenomenon of faith is indeed the true cause of the observed moral effects; the absolute basis of that phenomenon remains to be examined. The issue between theists and atheists is certainly not, as you seem to think, the mere question of whether religion is useful or detrimental. In your intensely pragmatical mind, this question stands paramount—to such an extent that you presented no other subject of discussion in your very clever *Vagrant* article. But the "agnostic" of your essay must have been a very utilitarian agnostic (that such "utilitarian Agnostics" do exist, I will not deny. *Vide* any issue of *The Truthseeker*![2] But are they typical?)! What the honest thinker wishes to know, has nothing to do with complex human conduct. He simply demands a scientific *explanation* of the things he sees. His only animus toward the church concerns its deliberate inculcation of demonstrable untruths in the community. This is human nature. No matter how white a lie may be—no matter how much good it may do—we are always more or less disgusted by its diffusion. The honest agnostic regards the church with respect for what it has done in the direction of virtue. He even supports it if he is magnanimous, and he certainly does nothing to impair whatever public usefulness it may possess. But in private, he would be more than a mere mortal if he were able to suppress a certain abstract resentment, or to curb the feeling of humour and so-called irreverence which inevitably arises from the contemplation of pious fraud, howsoever high-minded and benevolent.

The good effects of Christianity are neither to be denied, nor lightly esteemed, though candidly I will admit that I think them overrated. For example, the insignia of the Red Cross is practically the only religious thing about it. It is purely humanitarian and philanthropic, and has received just as much of its vitality from agnostic—or Jewish—sources, as from Christian sources. ... These nominally Christian societies usurp the lion's share of social service merely because they are on the ground first. Free and rational thought is relatively new, and rationalists find it just as practicable to support these existing Christian charities as to organise new ones which might create a division of energy and therefore decrease the efficiency of organised charity as a whole. And by the way—was not Belgium relief work largely non-religious? I may be mistaken—but all this is aside from my main argument anyway. I am not protesting against the recognition of Christianity's accomplishments. This has nothing to do with absolute bases of faith.

NOTES

1. [Alfred Galpin (1901–1983), a young colleague of Lovecraft's whose materialism influenced his own thought at this time.]

2. [*The Truth Seeker* was a magazine founded in 1872 by DeRobigne Mortimer Bennett to promote freethinking and criticism of religion.]

23
THE FAITH OF A HERETIC
(1961)

Walter Kaufmann

Walter Kaufmann (1921–1980) was born in Germany. Raised as a Lutheran, he found himself unable to accept many features of Christian doctrine and converted to Judaism at the age of eleven. Nazi attacks on Jews compelled him to leave Germany in 1939. He came to the United States and studied philosophy at Williams College and later at Harvard. By this time he had given up belief in religion. He began a long association with Princeton University in 1947. Around this time he discovered the work of Nietzsche, whose philosophy he believed to have been widely misinterpreted as a forerunner of Nazi ideology. This was the thrust of his landmark biographical study, Nietzsche: Philosopher, Psychologist, Antichrist *(1950). Kaufmann also translated many of Nietzsche's works. Among his other books are* Critique of Religion and Philosophy *(1958) and a translation of Goethe's* Faust *(1961).* The Faith of a Heretic *(1961) is his most exhaustive and personal statement on religion. In the following extract from chapter 6, "Suffering and the Bible," Kaufmann keenly analyzes several arguments that attempt to justify God's benevolence in a world full of suffering, and concludes that the popular conception of God is irremediably flawed.*

From Walter Kaufmann, *The Faith of a Heretic* (Garden City, N.Y.: Doubleday, 1961), pp. 149–52, 168–69, 170–72, 177–78, 180–81. Copyright © 1960, 1961 by Walter Kaufmann. Reprinted by permission of David Kaufmann, trustee of the Estate of Walter Kaufmann.

38

N O OTHER PROBLEM OF THEOLOGY or the philosophy of religion has excited so sustained and wide an interest as the problem of suffering. In spite of that, people keep saying, as if it were a well-known truth, that you cannot prove or disprove God's existence. This cliché is as true as the assertion that you cannot prove or disprove the existence of y. Of course, it is easy to construct a formally valid proof that y, or God, exists—or, for that matter, that they do not exist: x said that y exists; x always spoke the truth (in fact, he said: I am the truth); hence, y exists. Or: y is a z; no z exists; hence, y does not exist. But whether the existence or non-existence of y, or God, can be proved from plausible premises depends on the meaning we assign to y, or to God. And the term "God" . . . is almost, though not quite, as elastic as the symbol "y."

One's strategy in trying to defend or to attack the claim that God exists obviously depends on what is meant by "God." It may be objected that it is not so difficult to isolate what might be called the popular conception of God. *The problem of suffering is of crucial importance because it shows that the God of popular theism does not exist.*

The problem of suffering is: why is there the suffering we know? Dogmatic theology . . . has no monopoly on dealing with this problem. Let us see how a philosopher might deal with it, after repudiating dogmatic theology and endorsing the importance of the "critical, historical, and psychological study of religion." My approach will be part philosophical, part historical—only partially philosophic because the problem can be illuminated greatly by being placed in historical perspective. What matters here is not to display philosophic acumen but really to remove some of the deeply felt perplexity that surrounds this problem; and toward that end, we shall have to draw on history as well as philosophy.

There are at least three easy ways of disposing of the problem why there is suffering. If we adopt the position that everything in the universe, or at least a great deal, is due to chance, the problem is answered in effect. Indeed, as we reflect on this solution, it becomes clear that the "why" of the problem of suffering asks for a purpose; a mere cause will not do. Immediately a second solution comes to mind: if we say that the universe, far from being governed by chance, is subject to iron laws but not to any purpose, the problem of suffering is again taken care of. Thirdly, even if we assume that the world is governed by purpose, we need only add that this purpose—or, if there are several, at least one of them—is not especially intent on preventing suffering, whether it is indifferent to suffering or actually rejoices in it.

All three solutions are actually encountered in well-known religions. Although the two great native religions of China, Confucianism and Taoism, are far from dogmatic or even doctrinaire, and neither of them commands assent to any set of theories, both approximate the first solution which accepts events simply as happening, without seeking either laws or purposes behind them.

The second solution, which postulates a lawful world order but no purpose, is encountered in the two great religions which originated in India: Hinduism and Buddhism. Here an attempt is made to explain suffering: the outcaste of traditional Hinduism is held to deserve his wretched fate; it is a punishment for the wrongs he did in a previous life. We are all reborn after death in accordance with the way we behaved during our lives: we receive reward and punishment as our souls migrate from one existence to the next. The transmigration of souls proceeds in accordance with a fixed moral order, but there is no purpose behind it. The scientific world view also disposes of the problem of suffering by denying that the laws of nature are governed by any purpose.

The third solution is familiar from polytheistic religions—for example, the *Iliad* and the *Odyssey*—but present also in the Persian religion of Zarathustra (or Zoroaster), who taught that there were two gods, a god of light and goodness (Ormazd or Ahura-Mazda) and a god of darkness and evil (Ahriman). Here, and in many so-called primitive religions, too, suffering is charged to some evil purpose.

In all three cases, and for most human beings, the problem of suffering poses no difficult problem at all: one has a world picture in which suffering has its place, a world picture that takes suffering into account. To make the problem of suffering a perplexing problem, one requires very specific presuppositions, and once those are accepted the problem becomes not only puzzling but insoluble.

For atheism and polytheism there is no special problem of suffering, nor need there be for every kind of monotheism. The problem arises when monotheism is enriched with—or impoverished by—two assumptions: that God is omnipotent and that God is just. In fact, popular theism goes beyond merely asserting God's justice and claims that God is "good," that he is morally perfect, that he hates suffering, that he loves man, and that he is infinitely merciful, far transcending all human mercy, love, and perfection. Once these assumptions are granted, the problem arises: why, then, is there all the suffering we know? And as long as these assumptions are granted, this question cannot be answered. For if these assumptions were true, it would follow that there could not be all of this suffering. Conversely: since it is a fact that there is all this suffering, it is plain that at least one of these assumptions must be false. Popular theism is refuted by the existence of so much suffering. The theism preached from thousands of pulpits and credited by millions of believers is disproved by Auschwitz and a billion lesser evils.

The use of "God" as a synonym for being-itself, or for the "pure act of being," or for nature, or for scores of other things for which other terms are readily available, cannot be disproved but only questioned as pettifoggery. The assertion that God exists, if only God is taken in some such Pickwickian sense, is false, too: not false in the sense of being incorrect, but false in the sense of being misleading and to that extent deceptive.

It is widely assumed, contrary to fact, that theism necessarily involves the two assumptions which cannot be squared with the existence of so much suffering, and that therefore, *per impossibile*, they simply have to be squared with the existence of all this suffering, somehow. And a great deal of theology as well as a little of philosophy—the rationalizing kind of philosophy which seeks ingenious reasons for what is believed to begin with—has consisted in attempts to reconcile the popular image of God with the abundance of suffering.

43

. . . [One] spurious solution, which is one of the prime glories of Christian theology, claims in effect that suffering is a necessary adjunct of free will. God created man with free will, which was part of God's goodness since a creature with free will is better than one without it. (Why, in that case, he first made so many creatures without it, we are not usually told.) Man then misused his free will, disobeyed God, as God knew he would do, and ate of the fruit of the one tree in Paradise whose fruit he was not supposed to eat. This made suffering inevitable. (We are not told why.) The uncanny lack of logic in this supposed solution is generally covered up with a phrase: original sin.

How old this doctrine is is arguable. Some of the motifs are encountered in pre-Christian times, not only in Judaism but also in Greek thought. But in its familiar form it is a specifically Christian dogma. Augustine thought that he found it in Paul's Epistle to the Romans 5:12: "Therefore, as sin came into the world through one man and death through sin, and so death spread to all men—*eph ho pantes hamarton*." What was the meaning of these four Greek words? The last two clearly mean "all have sinned"; but what does *eph ho* mean? Augustine did not read Greek but Latin, and wrote Latin, too, and took it to mean "in whom" (*in quo*), while the King James Bible and the Revised Standard Version translate "in that" or "because" (*eo quod*). As George Foot Moore[1] puts it: "For . . . 'for that all have sinned,' the Latin version has "in quo omnes peccaverunt" 'in whom (*sc.* Adam) all sinned.' If the translator had rendered *eo quod*, it is possible that the Western church might have been as little afflicted with original sin as the Greeks or the Orientals."

The doctrine of original sin claims that all men sinned in Adam; but whether they did or whether it is merely a fact that all men sin does not basically affect the problem of suffering. In either case, the following questions must be pressed.

First: if God knew that man would abuse his free will and that this would entail cancer and Auschwitz, why then did he give man free will? Second—and this question, though surely obvious, scarcely ever gets asked—is there really any connection at all between ever so much suffering and free will? Isn't the introduction of free will at this point a red herring? . . .

Far from solving the problem by invoking original sin, Augustine and most of the Christian theologians who came after him merely aggravated the problem. If such suffering as is described . . . in the *New York Times'* annual pre-Christmas survey of "The Hundred Neediest Cases," and in any number of other easily accessible places, is the inevitable consequence of Adam's sin—or if this is the price God had to pay for endowing man with free will—then it makes no sense to call him omnipotent. And if he was willing to pay this price for his own greater glory, as some Christian theologians have suggested, or for the greater beauty of the cosmos, because shadows are needed to set off highlights, as some Christian philosophers have argued, what sense does it make to attribute moral perfection to him?

At this point, those who press this . . . pseudo-solution invariably begin to use words irresponsibly. Sooner or later we are told that when such attributes as omnipotence, mercy, justice, and love are ascribed to God they do not mean what they mean applied to men. John Stuart Mill's fine response to this has been cited in Chapter II. In a less rhetorical vein, it may be said that at this point the theologians and philosophers simply repeat ancient formulas in defiance of all sense. One might as well claim that God is purple with yellow dots, or circular, or every inch a woman—provided only that these terms are not used in their customary senses. These, of course, are not ancient formulas; hence, it is not likely that anybody in his right mind would seriously say such things. But the point is that when anybody has recourse to such means, argument fails. It is as if you pointed out to someone that eleven times eleven were not equal to one hundred and he said: it is, too—though of course not if you use the terms the way one usually does.

To be sure, one need not remain speechless. One can ask for the admission that, as long as we use the terms in the only way in which they have ever been given any precise meaning, God is either not omnipotent or not perfectly just, loving, and merciful. Some people, when it comes to that, retort: How do you know that we use the words right? Perhaps the way in which we ordinarily use these terms is wrong. . . .

To this, two replies are possible. The first is philosophically interesting but may not persuade many who are sincerely perplexed. When we use English, or Greek, or Hebrew words in conformity with their generally accepted meanings and fully obeying the genius and the rules of the language, it makes no sense to say that perhaps their "real" meaning is quite different. It does make sense to suggest that a particular term has an additional technical sense; but, if that is the case, one should admit that, as long as it is used in its ordinary, non-technical sense, God is, say, unjust, or cruel, or lacking in power.

The second reply interprets the question differently. What the questioner means may well be that our ordinary conceptions of love, justice, and mercy stand in need of revision; that our ideals are perverted. If so, we should presumably model ourselves on God's "justice" and "love." But this is precisely what former ages did. Children who disobeyed and adults who broke some minor law or regulation were punished in ways that strike us as inhumanly cruel. Those who do not like reading history will find examples enough in Charles Dickens and Victor Hugo.

This last point, which is surely of very great importance, can be put differently by recalling once more Job's wonderful words: "If I sin, . . . why dost thou not pardon my transgression and take away my iniquity?" *The attempt to solve the problem of suffering by postulating original sin depends on the belief that cruelty is justified when it is retributive; indeed, that morality demands retribution.* Although Job denied this, most theologians have clung to it tenaciously; and to this day the majority of Christian theologians champion the retributive function of punishment and the death penalty. At this point, some liberal Protestants who invoke [this] pseudo-solution are less consistent than more traditional theologians and ministers: they fight as unjust and unloving what they consider compatible with perfect justice and love. But, as we have seen, the traditional theologians did not solve the problem either, and their conceptions of love and justice are inhuman—especially if one considers that Job and Jonah were part of their Bible.

Indeed, Augustine and his successors aggravated the problem of suffering in yet another way, instead of approaching a solution: by accepting as true Jesus' references in the Gospels to hell and eternal torment, and by bettering the instruction. According to Augustine and many of his successors, all men deserve eternal torture, but God in his infinite mercy saves a very few. Nobody is treated worse than he deserves, but a few are treated better than they deserve, salvation being due not to merit but solely to grace. In the face of these beliefs, Augustine and legions after him assert God's perfect justice, mercy, and goodness. And to save men from eternal torment, it came to be considered just and merciful to torture heretics, or those suspected of some heresy, for a few days. . . .

46

"What," to quote Ecclesiastes, "is the conclusion of the whole matter?"[2] There is, first of all, a Biblical notion not yet mentioned—that of vicarious suffering, beautifully expressed in Isaiah 53: "He is despised and rejected by men; a man of sorrows, and acquainted with grief. . . . Surely he has borne our griefs and carried our sorrows. . . . He was wounded for our transgressions, he was bruised for our iniquities. . . . The Lord has laid on him the iniquity of us all." Christians have seen in these words a prophecy of Christ; Jews have applied the words to their own people, in an effort to give their own perennial sufferings some meaning. The search for a purpose behind suffering is not a mere matter of metaphysical speculation, nor a frivolous pastime of theologians. Man can stand superhuman suffering if only he does not lack the conviction that it serves some purpose. Even less severe pain, on the other hand, may seem unbearable, or simply not worth enduring, if it is not redeemed by any meaning.

It does not follow that the meaning must be given from above; that life and suffering must come neatly labeled; that nothing is worth while if the world is not governed by a purpose. On the contrary, the lack of any cosmic purpose may be experienced as liberating, as if a great weight had been lifted from us. Life ceases to be so oppressive: we are free to give our own lives meaning and purpose, free to redeem our suffering by making something of it. The great artist is the man who most obviously succeeds in turning his pains to advantage, in letting suffering deepen his understanding and sensibility, in growing through his pains. The same is true of some religious figures and of men like Lincoln and Freud. It is small comfort to tell the girl born without a nose: make the most of that! She may lack the strength, the talent, the vitality. But the plain fact is that not all suffering serves a purpose; that most of it remains utterly senseless; and that if there is to be any meaning to it, it is we who must give it.

The sufferer who cannot give any meaning to his suffering may inspire someone else, possibly without even knowing it, perhaps after death. But most suffering remains unredeemed by any purpose, albeit a challenge to humanity.

There is one more verse in Job that should be quoted. At the end of the first chapter, when he has lost all his possessions and then his children as well, he says: "Naked I came from my mother's womb, and naked shall I return; the Lord gave, and the Lord has taken away; blessed be the name of the Lord." Without claiming that the following remarks represent or distill "the immortal soul" of his words, one can find more meaning in them, or find them more suggestive, than meets the eye at first glance.

Job's forthright indictment of the injustice of this world is surely right. The ways of the world are weird and much more unpredictable than either scientists or theologians generally make things look. Job personifies the inscrutable, merciless, uncanny in a god who is all-powerful but not just. . . .

Those who believe in God because their experience of life and the facts of nature prove his existence must have led sheltered lives and closed their hearts to the voice of their brothers' blood. "Behold the tears of the oppressed, and they had no one to comfort them! On the side of the oppressors there was power, and there was no one to comfort them. And I thought the dead who are already dead more fortunate than the living who are still alive; but better than both is he who has not yet been, and has not seen the evil deeds done under the sun." Whether Ecclesiastes, who "saw all the oppressions that are practiced under the sun," retained any faith in God is a moot point, but Jeremiah and Job and the psalmists who speak in a similar vein did. Pagan piety rose to similar heights of despair and created tragedies.

The deepest difference between religions is not that between polytheism and monotheism. To which camp would one assign Sophocles? Even the difference between theism and atheism is not nearly so profound as that between those who feel and those who do not feel their brothers' torments. The Buddha, like the prophets and the Greek tragedians, did, though he did not believe in any deity. There is no inkling of such piety in the callous religiousness of those who note the regularities of nature, find some proof in that of the existence of a God or gods, and practice magic, rites, or pray to ensure rain, success, or speedy passage into heaven.

Natural theology is a form of heathenism, represented in the Bible by the friends of Job. The only theism worthy of our respect believes in God not because of the way the world is made but in spite of that. The only theism that is no less profound than the Buddha's atheism is that represented in the Bible by Job and Jeremiah.

Their piety is a cry in the night, born of suffering so intense that they cannot contain it and must shriek, speak, accuse, and argue with God—not about him—for there is no other human being who would understand, and the prose of dialogue could not be faithful to the poetry of anguish. In time, theologians come to wrench some useful phrases out of Latin versions of a Hebrew outcry, blind with tears, and try to win some argument about a point of dogma. Scribes, who preceded them, carved phrases out of context, too, and used them in their arguments about the law. But for all that, Jewish piety has been a ceaseless cry in the night, rarely unaware of "all the oppressions that are practiced under the sun," a faith in spite of, not a heathenish, complacent faith because.

The profound detachment of Job's words at the end of the first chapter is certainly possible for an infidel: not being wedded to the things of this world, being able to let them go—and yet not repudiating them in the first place like the great Christian ascetics and the Buddha and his followers. In the form of an anthropomorphic faith, these words express one of the most admirable attitudes possible for man: to be able to give up what life takes away, without being unable to enjoy what life gives us in the first place; to remember that we came naked from the womb and shall return naked; to accept what life gives us as if it were God's own gift, full of wonders beyond price; and to be able to part with everything. To try to fashion something from suffering, to relish our triumphs, and to endure defeats without resentment: all that is compatible with the faith of a heretic.

NOTES

1. [George Foot Moore (1851–1931), American scholar on religion. Kaufmann cites his *History of Religions* (1913–19).]

2. [Ecclesiastes 12:13: "Let us hear the conclusion of the whole matter" (KJV).]

PART 7

RELIGION
AND THE STATE

Religion is the sigh of the oppressed creature, the feeling of a heartless world, and the soul of soulless circumstances. It is the opium of the people.

—Karl Marx
"Towards a Critique of Hegel's
Philosophy of Right" (1843)

24

THELOGICO-POLITICAL TREATISE
(1670)

Benedict de Spinoza

Benedict de Spinoza (1632–1677) was born in Amsterdam, the son of a Dutch family of Jewish origin. He initially studied the Talmud, but later abandoned his Jewish practice and belief. His skepticism resulted in his excommunication from his synagogue in 1656, whereupon he became a lens grinder to support himself. Spinoza became a great proponent of rationalism, asserting that the universe is capable of being understood by the human mind, and that human beings are most happy when living according to this knowledge. Ethics *(1677) is his most celebrated work; it is written in the manner of Euclid, since Spinoza believed mathematics to be the key to understanding the universe. Although far from being an atheist, Spinoza was frequently thought to be one: he identified God with Nature and frequently advocated religious toleration and freedom of thought. His* Tractatus Theologico-Politicus *(1670;* Theologico-Political Treatise) *attacks the authority of Scripture as a revelation of the word of God and rejects its accounts of prophecies and miracles as unverifiable or erroneous. In the following extracts from the preface to this work, Spinoza condemns the influence of religious superstition in political affairs.*

MEN WOULD NEVER BE SUPERSTITIOUS, if they could govern all their circumstances by set rules, or if they were always

---

From Benedict de Spinoza, *Theologico-Political Treatise* (1670), in *The Chief Works of Benedict de Spinoza*, trans. R. H. M. Elwes, vol. 1 (London: George Bell & Sons, 1883), pp. 3–8.

favoured by fortune: but being frequently driven into straits where rules are useless, and being often kept fluctuating pitiably between hope and fear by the uncertainty of fortune's greedily coveted favours, they are consequently, for the most part, very prone to credulity. The human mind is readily swayed this way or that in times of doubt, especially when hope and fear are struggling for the mastery, though usually it is boastful, over-confident, and vain.

This as a general fact I suppose everyone knows, though few, I believe, know their own nature; no one can have lived in the world without observing that most people, when in prosperity, are so over-brimming with wisdom (however inexperienced they may be), that they take every offer of advice as a personal insult, whereas in adversity they know not where to turn, but beg and pray for counsel from every passer-by. No plan is then too futile, too absurd, or too fatuous for their adoption; the most frivolous causes will raise them to hope, or plunge them into despair—if anything happens during their fright which reminds them of some past good or ill, they think it portends a happy or unhappy issue, and therefore (though it may have proved abortive a hundred times before) style it a lucky or unlucky omen. Anything which excites their astonishment they believe to be a portent signifying the anger of the gods or of the Supreme Being, and, mistaking superstition for religion, account it impious not to avert the evil with prayer and sacrifice. Signs and wonders of this sort they conjure up perpetually, till one might think Nature as mad as themselves, they interpret her so fantastically.

Thus it is brought prominently before us, that superstition's chief victims are those persons who greedily covet temporal advantages; they it is, who (especially when they are in danger, and cannot help themselves) are wont with prayers and womanish tears to implore help from God: upbraiding Reason as blind, because she cannot show a sure path to the shadows they pursue, and rejecting human wisdom as vain; but believing the phantoms of imagination, dreams, and other childish absurdities, to be the very oracles of Heaven. As though God had turned away from the wise, and written His decrees, not in the mind of man but in the entrails of beasts, or left them to be proclaimed by the inspiration and instinct of fools, madmen, and birds. Such is the unreason to which terror can drive mankind!

Superstition, then, is engendered, preserved, and fostered by fear. If anyone desire an example, let him take Alexander, who only began superstitiously to seek guidance from seers, when he first learnt to fear fortune in the passes of Sysis (Curtius, v. 4); whereas after he had conquered Darius he consulted prophets no more, till a second time frightened by reverses. When the Scythians were provoking a battle, the Bactrians had deserted, and he himself was lying sick of his wounds, "he once more turned to superstition, the mockery of human wisdom, and bade Aristander, to whom he confided his credulity, inquire the issue of affairs with sacrificed victims." Very numerous examples of a like nature might be cited, clearly showing the fact, that only while under the dominion of fear do men fall a prey to superstition; that all the portents ever invested with the reverence of misguided religion are mere phantoms of dejected and fearful minds; and lastly, that prophets have most power among the people, and are most formidable to rulers, precisely at those times when the state is in most peril. I think this is sufficiently plain to all, and will therefore say no more on the subject.

The origin of superstition above given affords us a clear reason for the fact, that it comes to all men naturally, though some refer its rise to a dim notion of God, universal to mankind, and also tends to show, that it is no less inconsistent and variable than other mental hallucinations and emotional impulses, and further that it can only be maintained by hope, hatred, anger, and deceit; since it springs, not from reason, but solely from the more powerful phases of emotion. Furthermore, we may readily understand how difficult it is, to maintain in the same course men prone to every form of credulity. For, as the mass of mankind remains always at about the same pitch of misery, it never assents long to any one remedy, but is always best pleased by a novelty which has not yet proved illusive.

This element of inconsistency has been the cause of many terrible wars and revolutions; for, as Curtius well says (lib. iv. chap. 10): "The mob has no ruler more potent than superstition," and is easily led, on the plea of religion, at one moment to adore its kings as gods, and anon to execrate and abjure them as humanity's common bane. Immense pains have therefore been taken to counteract this evil by investing religion, whether true or false, with such pomp and ceremony, that it may rise superior to every shock, and be always observed with studious reverence by the whole people—a system which has been brought to great perfection by the Turks, for they consider even controversy impious, and so clog men's minds with dogmatic formulas, that they leave no room for sound reason, not even enough to doubt with.

But if, in despotic statecraft, the supreme and essential mystery be to hoodwink the subjects, and to mask the fear, which keeps them down, with the specious garb of religion, so that men may fight as bravely for slavery as for safety, and count it not shame but highest honour to risk their blood and their lives for the vainglory of a tyrant; yet in a free state no more mischievous expedient could be planned or attempted. Wholly repugnant to the general freedom are such devices as enthralling men's minds with prejudices, forcing their judgment, or employing any of the weapons of quasi-religious sedition; indeed, such seditions only spring up, when law enters the domain of speculative thought, and opinions are put on trial and condemned on the same footing as crimes, while those who defend and follow them are sacrificed, not to public safety, but to their opponents' hatred and cruelty. If deeds only could be made the grounds of criminal charges, and words were always allowed to pass free, such seditions would be divested of every semblance of justification, and would be separated from mere controversies by a hard and fast line.

Now, seeing that we have the rare happiness of living in a republic, where everyone's judgment is free and unshackled, where each may worship God as his conscience dictates, and where freedom is esteemed before all things dear and precious, I have believed that I should be undertaking no ungrateful or unprofitable task, in demonstrating that not only can such freedom be granted without prejudice to the public peace, but also, that without such freedom, piety cannot flourish nor the public peace be secure.

Such is the chief conclusion I seek to establish in this treatise; but, in order to reach it, I must first point out the misconceptions which, like scars of our former bondage, still disfigure our notion of religion, and must expose the false views about the civil authority which many have most impudently advocated, endeavouring to turn the mind of the people, still prone to heathen superstition, away from its legitimate rulers, and so bring us again into slavery. As to the order of my treatise I will speak presently, but first I will recount the causes which led me to write.

I have often wondered, that persons who make a boast of professing the Christian religion, namely, love, joy, peace, temperance, and charity to all men, should quarrel with such rancorous animosity, and display daily towards one another such bitter hatred, that this, rather than the virtues they claim, is the readiest criterion of their faith. Matters have long since come to such a pass, that one can only pronounce a man Christian, Turk, Jew, or Heathen, by his general appearance and attire, by his frequenting this or that place of worship, or employing the phraseology of a particular sect—as for manner of life, it is in all cases the same. Inquiry into the cause of this anomaly leads me unhesitatingly to ascribe it to the fact, that the ministries of the Church are regarded by the masses merely as dignities, her offices as posts of emolument—in short, popular religion may be summed up as respect for ecclesiastics. The spread of this misconception inflamed every worthless fellow with an intense desire to enter holy orders, and thus the love of diffusing God's religion degenerated into sordid avarice and ambition. Every church became a theatre, where orators, instead of church teachers, harangued, caring not to instruct the people, but striving to attract admiration, to bring opponents to public scorn, and to preach only novelties and paradoxes, such as would tickle the ears of their congregation. This state of things necessarily stirred up an amount of controversy, envy, and hatred, which no lapse of time could appease; so that we can scarcely wonder that of the old religion nothing survives but its outward forms (even these, in the mouth of the multitude, seem rather adulation than adoration of the Deity), and that faith has become a mere compound of credulity and prejudices—aye, prejudices too, which degrade man from rational being to beast, which completely stifle the power of judgment between true and false, which seem, in fact, carefully fostered for the purpose of extinguishing the last spark of reason! Piety, great God! and religion are become a tissue of ridiculous mysteries; men, who flatly despise reason, who reject and turn away from understanding as naturally corrupt, these, I say, these of all men, are thought, O lie most horrible! to possess light from on High. Verily, if they had but one spark of light from on High, they would not insolently rave, but would learn to worship God more wisely, and would be as marked among their fellows for mercy as they now are for malice; if they were concerned for their opponents' souls, instead of for their own reputations, they would no longer fiercely persecute, but rather be filled with pity and compassion.

Furthermore, if any Divine light were in them, it would appear from their doctrine. I grant that they are never tired of professing their wonder at the profound mysteries of Holy Writ; still I cannot discover that they teach anything but speculations of Platonists and Aristotelians, to which (in order to save their credit for Christianity) they have made Holy Writ conform; not content to rave with the Greeks themselves, they want to make the prophets rave also; showing conclusively, that never even in sleep have they caught a glimpse of Scripture's Divine nature. The very vehemence of their admiration for the mysteries plainly attests, that their belief in the Bible is a formal assent rather than a living faith: and the fact is made still more apparent by their laying down beforehand, as a foundation for the study and true interpretation of Scripture, the principle that it is in every passage true and divine. Such a doctrine should be reached only after strict scrutiny and thorough comprehension of the Sacred Books (which would teach it much better, for they stand in need of no human fictions), and not be set up on the threshold, as it were, of inquiry.

As I pondered over the facts that the light of reason is not only despised, but by many even execrated as a source of impiety, that human commentaries are accepted as divine records, and that credulity is extolled as faith; as I marked the fierce controversies of philosophers raging in Church and State, the source of bitter hatred and dissension, the ready instruments of sedition and other ills innumerable, I determined to examine the Bible afresh in a careful, impartial, and unfettered spirit, making no assumptions concerning it, and attributing to it no doctrines, which I do not find clearly therein set down. With these precautions I constructed a method of Scriptural interpretation, and thus equipped proceeded to inquire—What is prophecy? in what sense did God reveal Himself to the prophets, and why were these particular men chosen by Him? Was it on account of the sublimity of their thoughts about the Deity and nature, or was it solely on account of their piety? These questions being answered, I was easily able to conclude, that the authority of the prophets has weight only in matters of morality, and that their speculative doctrines affect us little.

25

THE SPIRIT OF RATIONALISM IN EUROPE
(1865)

W. E. H. Lecky

William Edward Hartpole Lecky (1838–1903), was born in Dublin, although his family was of Scottish ancestry. After attending Trinity College, Dublin, he began writing poetry and articles; some of his early essays—notably "The Religious Tendencies of the Age" (1859) and "The Declining Sense of the Miraculous" (1863)—anticipate his great scholarly work, History of the Rise and Influence of the Spirit of Rationalism in Europe *(1865), an immediate success that established Lecky as a leading intellectual historian of his time. He then wrote* History of European Morals *(1869) and his greatest work, the eight-volume* History of England in the Eighteenth Century *(1878–90). Lecky later entered Parliament as M.P. for Dublin University, although his secularism elicited reservations on the part of some clerical electors. In this extract, Lecky stresses the gradual intellectual shift that occurred in Europe whereby politics was secularized, so that orthodox religion became reactionary and marginalized.*

T O THOSE WHO HAVE APPRECIATED the great truth that a radical political change necessarily implies a corresponding change in the mental habits of society, the process which I have traced will furnish a decisive evidence of the declining influence of dogmatic theology. That vast department of thought and action which is comprised under the name of politics was once altogether guided by its power. It is now

---

From W. E. H. Lecky, *History of the Rise and Influence of the Spirit of Rationalism in Europe*, vol. 2 (London: Longmans, Green, 1865), pp. 126–32, 133–36.

passing from its influence rapidly, universally, and completely. The classes that are most penetrated with the spirit of special dogmas were once the chief directors of the policy of Europe. They now form a baffled and desponding minority, whose most cherished political principles have been almost universally abandoned, who are struggling faintly and ineffectually against the ever-increasing spirit of the age, and whose ideal is not in the future but in the past. It is evident that a government never can be really like a railway company, or a literary society, which only exercises an influence over secular affairs. As long as it determines the system of education that exists among its subjects, as long as it can encourage or repress the teaching of particular doctrines, as long as its foreign policy brings it into collision with governments which still make the maintenance of certain religious systems a main object of their policy, it will necessarily exercise a gigantic influence upon belief. It cannot possibly be uninfluential, and it is difficult to assign limits to the influence that it may exercise. If the men who compose it (or the public opinion that governs them) be pervaded by an intensely-realised conviction that the promulgation of a certain system of doctrine is incomparably the highest of human interests, that to assist that promulgation is the main object for which they were placed in the world, and should be the dominant motive of their lives, it will be quite impossible for these men, as politicians, to avoid interfering with theology. Men who are inspired by an absorbing passion will inevitably gratify it if they have the power. Men who sincerely desire the happiness of mankind will certainly use to the uttermost the means they possess of promoting what they feel to be beyond all comparison the greatest of human interests. If by giving a certain direction to education they could avert fearful and general physical suffering, there can be no doubt that they would avail themselves of their power. If they were quite certain that the greatest possible suffering was the consequence of deviating from a particular class of opinions, they could not possibly neglect that consideration in their laws. This is the conclusion we should naturally draw from the nature of the human mind, and it is most abundantly corroborated by experience.[1] In order to ascertain the tendencies of certain opinions, we should not confine ourselves to those exceptional intellects who, having perceived the character of their age, have spent their lives in endeavoring painfully and laboriously to wrest their opinions in conformity with them. We should rather observe the position which large bodies of men, governed by the same principles, but living under various circumstances and in different ages, naturally and almost unconsciously occupy. We have ample means of judging in the present case. We see the general tone which is adopted on political subjects by the clergy of the most various creeds, by the religious newspapers, and by the politicians who represent that section of the community which is most occupied with dogmatic theology. We see that it is a tendency distinct from and opposed to the tendencies of the age. History tells us that it was once dominant in politics, that it has been continuously and rapidly declining, and that it has declined most rapidly and most steadily in those countries in which the development of intellect has been most active. All over Europe the priesthood are now associated with a policy of toryism, of reaction, or of obstruction. All over Europe the organs that represent dogmatic interests are in permanent opposition to the progressive tendencies around them, and are rapidly sinking into contempt. In every country in which a strong political life is manifested, the secularisation of politics is the consequence. Each stage of that movement has been initiated and effected by those who are most indifferent to dogmatic theology, and each has been opposed by those who are most occupied with theology.

And as I write these words, it is impossible to forget that one of the great problems on which the thoughts of politicians are even now concentrated is the hopeless decadence of the one theocracy of modern Europe, of the great type and representative of the alliance of politics and theology. That throne on which it seemed as though the changeless Church had stamped the impress of her own perpetuity—that throne which for so many centuries of anarchy and confusion had been the Sinai of a protecting and an avenging law—that throne which was once the centre and the archetype of the political system of Europe, the successor of Imperial Rome, the inheritor of a double portion of her spirit, the one power which seemed removed above all the vicissitudes of politics, the iris above the cataract, unshaken amid so much turmoil and so much change—that throne has in our day sunk into a condition of hopeless decrepitude, and has only prolonged its existence by the confession of its impotence. Supported by the bayonets of a foreign power, and avowedly incapable of self-existence, it is no longer a living organism, its significance is but the significance of death. There was a time when the voice that issued from the Vatican shook Europe to its foundations, and sent forth the proudest armies to the deserts of Syria. There was a time when all the valour and all the chivalry of Christendom would have followed the banner of the Church in any field and against any foe. Now a few hundred French, and Belgians, and Irish are all who would respond to its appeal. Its august antiquity, the reverence that centres around its chief, the memory of the unrivalled influence it has exercised, the genius that has consecrated its past, the undoubted virtues that have been displayed by its rulers, were all unable to save the papal government from a decadence the most irretrievable and the most hopeless. Reforms were boldly initiated, but they only served to accelerate its ruin. A repressive policy was attempted, but it could not arrest the progress of its decay. For nearly a century, under every ruler and under every system of policy, it has been hopelessly, steadily, and rapidly declining. At last the influences that had so long been corroding it attained their triumph. It fell before the Revolution, and has since been unable to exist, except by the support of a foreign army. The principle of its vitality has departed.

No human pen can write its epitaph, for no imagination can adequately realise its glories. In the eyes of those who estimate the greatness of a sovereignty, not by the extent of its territory, or by the valour of its soldiers, but by the influence which it has exercised over mankind, the papal government has had no rival, and can have no successor. But though we may not fully estimate the majesty of its past, we can at least trace the causes of its decline. It fell because it neglected the great truth that a government to be successful must adapt itself to the ever-changing mental condition of society; that a policy which in one century produces the utmost prosperity, in another leads only to ruin and to disaster. It fell because it represented the union of politics and theology, and because the intellect of Europe has rendered it an anachronism by pronouncing their divorce. It fell because its constitution was essentially and radically opposed to the spirit of an age in which the secularisation of politics is the measure and the condition of all political prosperity.

The secularisation of politics is, as we have seen, the direct consequence of the declining influence of dogmatic theology. I have said that it also reacts upon and influences its cause. The creation of a strong and purely secular political feeling diffused through all classes of society, and producing an ardent patriotism, and a passionate and indomitable love of liberty, is sufficient in many respects to modify all the great departments of thought, and to contribute largely to the formation of a distinct type of intellectual character.

It is obvious, in the first place, that one important effect of a purely secular political feeling will be to weaken the intensity of sectarianism. Before its existence sectarianism was the measure by which all things and persons were contemplated. It exercised an undivided control over the minds and passions of men, absorbed all their interests, and presided over all their combinations. But when a purely political spirit is engendered, a new enthusiasm is introduced into the mind, which first divides the affections and at last replaces the passion that had formerly been supreme. Two different enthusiasms, each of which makes men regard events in a special point of view, cannot at the same time be absolute. The habits of thought that are formed by the one, will necessarily weaken or efface the habits of thought that are formed by the other. Men learn to classify their fellows by a new principle. They become in one capacity the cordial associates of those whom in another capacity they had long regarded with unmitigated dislike. They learn to repress and oppose in one capacity those whom in another capacity they regard with unbounded reverence. Conflicting feelings are thus produced which neutralise each other; and if one of the two increases, the other is proportionately diminished. Every war that unites for secular objects nations of different creeds, every measure that extends political interests to classes that had formerly been excluded from their range, has therefore a tendency to assuage the virulence of sects. . . .

But probably the most important, and certainly the most beneficial, effect of political life is to habituate men to a true method of enquiry. Government in a constitutional country is carried on by debate, all the arguments on both sides are brought forward with unrestricted freedom, and every newspaper reports in full what has been said against the principles it advocates by the ablest men in the country. Men may study the debates of Parliament under the influence of a strong party bias, they may even pay more attention to the statements of one party than to those of the other, but they never imagine that they can form an opinion by an exclusive study of what has been written on one side. The two views of every question are placed in juxtaposition, and every one who is interested in the subject examines both. When a charge is brought against any politician, men naturally turn to his reply before forming an opinion, and they feel that any other course would be not only extremely foolish, but also extremely dishonest. This is the spirit of truth as opposed to the spirit of falsehood and imposture, which in all ages and in all departments of thought has discouraged men from studying opposing systems, lamented the circulation of adverse arguments, and denounced as criminal those who listen to them. Among the higher order of intellects, the first spirit is chiefly cultivated by those philosophical studies which discipline and strengthen the mind for research. But what philosophy does for a very few, political life does, less perfectly, indeed, but still in a great degree, for the many. It diffuses abroad not only habits of acute reasoning, but also, what is far more important, habits of impartiality and intellectual fairness, which will at last be carried into all forms of discussion, and will destroy every system that refuses to accept them. Year after year, as political life extends, we find each new attempt to stifle the expression of opinion received with an increased indignation, the sympathies of the people immediately enlisted on behalf of the oppressed teacher, and the work which is the object of condemnation elevated in public esteem often to a degree that is far greater than it deserves. Year after year the conviction becomes more general, that a provisional abnegation of the opinions of the past and a resolute and unflinching impartiality are among the highest duties of the enquirer, and that he who shrinks from such a research is at least morally bound to abstain from condemning the opinions of his neighbour.

If we may generalise the experience of modern constitutional governments, it would appear that this process must pass through three phases. When political life is introduced into a nation that is strongly imbued with sectarianism, this latter spirit will at first dominate over political interests, and the whole scope and tendency of government will be directed by theology. After a time the movement I have traced in the present chapter will appear. The secular element will emerge into light. It will at length obtain an absolute ascendency, and, expelling theology successively from all its political strongholds, will thus weaken its influence over the human mind. Yet in one remarkable way the spirit of sectarianism will still survive: it will change its name and object, transmigrate into political discussion, and assume the form of an intense party-spirit. The increasing tendency, however, of political life seems to be to weaken or efface this spirit, and in the more advanced stages of free government it almost disappears. A judicial spirit is fostered which leads men both in politics and theology to eclecticism, to judge all questions exclusively on the ground of their intrinsic merits, and not at all according to their position in theological or political systems. To increase the range and intensity of political interests is to strengthen this tendency; and every extension of the suffrage thus diffuses over a wider circle a habit of thought that must eventually modify theological belief. If the suffrage should ever be granted to women, it would probably, after two or three generations, effect a complete revolution in their habits of thought, which by acting upon the first period of education would influence the whole course of opinion.

NOTE

1. This has been very clearly noticed in one of the ablest modern books in defence of the Tory theory. "At the point where Protestantism becomes vicious, where it receives the first tinge of latitudinarianism, and begins to join hands with infidelity by superseding the belief of an objective truth in religion, necessary for salvation; at that very spot it likewise assumes an aspect of hostility to the union of church and State." (Gladstone, on *Church and State*, p. 188.)

26

GOD IN THE CONSTITUTION
(1890)

Robert G. Ingersoll

In the following essay, first published in the Arena *for January 1890, Ingersoll strongly advocates the complete separation of church and state in the United States, specifically rejecting the notion—then being widely discussed in political and journalistic circles—of "recognizing" God in the constitution by means of a constitutional amendment, since such a recognition would entail bigotry, hypocrisy, and persecution, and would be contrary to the philosophical and political ideals embraced by the founders of the nation.*

"All governments derive their just powers from the consent of the governed."[1]

I N THIS COUNTRY IT IS admitted that the power to govern resides in the people themselves; that they are the only rightful source of authority. For many centuries before the formation of our Government, before the promulgation of the Declaration of Independence, the people had but little voice in the affairs of nations. The source of authority was not in this world; kings were not crowned by their subjects, and the sceptre was not held by the consent of the governed. The king sat on his throne by the will of God, and for that reason was not accountable to

---

From Robert G. Ingersoll, "God in the Constitution" (1890), in *The Works of Robert G. Ingersoll*, vol. 11 (New York: Dresden Publishing Co., 1906), pp. 121–34.

the people for the exercise of his power. He commanded, and the people obeyed. He was lord of their bodies, and his partner, the priest, was lord of their souls. The government of earth was patterned after the kingdom on high. God was a supreme autocrat in heaven, whose will was law, and the king was a supreme autocrat on earth whose will was law. The God in heaven had inferior beings to do his will, and the king on earth had certain favorites and officers to do his. These officers were accountable to him, and he was responsible to God.

The Feudal system was supposed to be in accordance with the divine plan. The people were not governed by intelligence, but by threats and promises, by rewards and punishments. No effort was made to enlighten the common people; no one thought of educating a peasant—of developing the mind of a laborer. The people were created to support thrones and altars. Their destiny was to toil and obey—to work and want. They were to be satisfied with huts and hovels, with ignorance and rags, and their children must expect no more. In the presence of the king they fell upon their knees, and before the priest they groveled in the very dust. The poor peasant divided his earnings with the state, because he imagined it protected his body; he divided his crust with the church, believing that it protected his soul. He was the prey of Throne and Altar—one deformed his body, the other his mind—and these two vultures fed upon his toil. He was taught by the king to hate the people of other nations, and by the priest to despise the believers in all other religions. He was made the enemy of all people except his own. He had no sympathy with the peasants of other lands, enslaved and plundered like himself. He was kept in ignorance, because education is the enemy of superstition, and because education is the foe of that egotism often mistaken for patriotism.

The intelligent and good man holds in his affections the good and true of every land—the boundaries of countries are not the limitations of his sympathies. Caring nothing for race, or color, he loves those who speak other languages and worship other gods. Between him and those who suffer, there is no impassable gulf. He salutes the world, and extends the hand of friendship to the human race. He does not bow before a provincial and patriotic god—one who protects his tribe or nation, and abhors the rest of mankind.

Through all the ages of superstition, each nation has insisted that it was the peculiar care of the true God, and that it alone had the true religion—that the gods of other nations were false and fraudulent, and that other religions were wicked, ignorant and absurd. In this way the seeds of hatred had been sown, and in this way have been kindled the flames of war. Men have had no sympathy with those of a different complexion, with those who knelt at other altars and expressed their thoughts in other words—and even a difference in garments placed them beyond the sympathy of others. Every peculiarity was the food of prejudice and the excuse for hatred.

The boundaries of nations were at last crossed by commerce. People became somewhat acquainted, and they found that the virtues and vices were quite evenly distributed. At last, subjects became somewhat acquainted with kings—peasants had the pleasure of gazing at princes, and it was dimly perceived that the differences were mostly in rags and names.

In 1776 our fathers endeavored to retire the gods from politics. They declared that "all governments derive their just powers from the consent of the governed." This was a contradiction of the then political ideas of the world; it was, as many believed, an act of pure blasphemy—a renunciation of the Deity. It was in fact a declaration of the independence of the earth. It was a notice to all churches and priests that thereafter mankind would govern and protect themselves. Politically it tore down every altar and denied the authority of every "sacred book," and appealed from the Providence of God to the Providence of Man.

Those who promulgated the Declaration adopted a Constitution for the great Republic.

What was the office or purpose of that Constitution?

Admitting that all power came from the people, it was necessary, first, that certain means be adopted for the purpose of ascertaining the will of the people, and second, it was proper and convenient to designate certain departments that should exercise certain powers of the Government. There must be the legislative, the judicial and the executive departments. Those who make laws should not execute them. Those who execute laws should not have the power of absolutely determining their meaning or their constitutionality. For these reasons, among others, a Constitution was adopted.

This Constitution also contained a declaration of rights. It marked out the limitations of discretion, so that in the excitement of passion, men shall not go beyond the point designated in the calm moment of reason.

When man is unprejudiced, and his passions subject to reason, it is well he should define the limits of power, so that the waves driven by the storm of passion shall not overbear the shore.

A constitution is for the government of man in this world. It is the chain the people put upon their servants, as well as upon themselves. It defines the limit of power and the limit of obedience.

It follows, then, that nothing should be in a constitution that cannot be enforced by the power of the state—that is, by the army and navy. Behind every provision of the Constitution should stand the force of the nation. Every sword, every bayonet, every cannon should be there.

Suppose, then, that we amend the Constitution and acknowledge the existence and supremacy of God—what becomes of the supremacy of the people, and how is this amendment to be enforced? A constitution does not enforce itself. It must be carried out by appropriate legislation. Will it be a crime to deny the existence of this constitutional God? Can the offender be proceeded against in the criminal courts? Can his lips be closed by the power of the state? Would not this be the inauguration of religious persecution?

And if there is to be an acknowledgment of God in the Constitution, the question naturally arises as to which God is to have this honor. Shall we select the God of the Catholics—he who has established an infallible church presided over by an infallible pope, and who is delighted with certain ceremonies and placated by prayers uttered in exceedingly common Latin? Is it the God of the Presbyterian with the Five Points of Calvinism, who is ingenious enough to harmonize necessity and responsibility, and who in some way justifies himself for damning most of his own children? Is it the God of the Puritan, the enemy of joy—of the Baptist, who is great enough to govern the universe, and small enough to allow the destiny of a soul to depend on whether the body it inhabited was immersed or sprinkled?

What God is it proposed to put in the Constitution? Is it the God of the Old Testament, who was a believer in slavery and who justified polygamy? If slavery was right then, it is right now; and if Jehovah was right then, the Mormons are right now. Are we to have the God who issued a commandment against all art—who was the enemy of investigation and of free speech? Is it the God who commanded the husband to stone his wife to death because she differed with him on the subject of religion? Are we to have a God who will re-enact the Mosaic code and punish hundreds of offences with death? What court, what tribunal of last resort, is to define this God, and who is to make known his will? In his presence, laws passed by men will be of no value. The decisions of courts will be as nothing. But who is to make known the will of this supreme God? Will there be a supreme tribunal composed of priests?

Of course all persons elected to office will either swear or affirm to support the Constitution. Men who do not believe in this God, cannot so swear or affirm. Such men will not be allowed to hold any office of trust or honor. A God in the Constitution will not interfere with the oaths or affirmations of hypocrites. Such a provision will only exclude honest and conscientious unbelievers. Intelligent people know that no one knows whether there is a God or not. The existence of such a Being is merely a matter of opinion. Men who believe in the liberty of man, who are willing to die for the honor of their country, will be excluded from taking any part in the administration of its affairs. Such a provision would place the country under the feet of priests.

To recognize a Deity in the organic law of our country would be the destruction of religious liberty. The God in the Constitution would have to be protected. There would be laws against blasphemy, laws against the publication of honest thoughts, laws against carrying books and papers in the mails in which this constitutional God should be attacked. Our land would be filled with theological spies, with religious eavesdroppers, and all the snakes and reptiles of the lowest natures, in this sunshine of religious authority, would uncoil and crawl.

It is proposed to acknowledge a God who is the lawful and rightful Governor of nations; the one who ordained the powers that be. If this God is really the Governor of nations, it is not necessary to acknowledge him in the Constitution. This would not add to his power. If he governs all nations now, he has always controlled the affairs of men. Having this control, why did he not see to it that he was recognized in the Constitution of the United States? If he had the supreme authority and neglected to put himself in the Constitution, is not this, at least, *prima facie* evidence that he did not desire to be there?

For one, I am not in favor of the God who has "ordained the powers that be." What have we to say of Russia—of Siberia? What can we say of the persecuted and enslaved? What of the kings and nobles who live on the stolen labor of others? What of the priest and cardinal and pope who wrest, even from the hand of poverty, the single coin thrice earned?

Is it possible to flatter the Infinite with a constitutional amendment? The Confederate States acknowledged God in their constitution, and yet they were overwhelmed by a people in whose organic law no reference to God is made. All the kings of the earth acknowledge the existence of God, and God is their ally; and this belief in God is used as a means to enslave and rob, to govern and degrade the people whom they call their subjects.

The Government of the United States is secular. It derives its power from the consent of man. It is a Government with which God has nothing whatever to do—and all forms and customs, inconsistent with the fundamental fact that the people are the source of authority, should be abandoned. In this country there should be no oaths—no man should be sworn to tell the truth, and in no court should there be any appeal to any supreme being. A rascal by taking the oath appears to go in partnership with God, and ignorant jurors credit the firm instead of the man. A witness should tell his story, and if he speaks falsely should be considered as guilty of perjury. Governors and Presidents should not issue religious proclamations. They should not call upon the people to thank God. It is no part of their official duty. It is outside of and beyond the horizon of their authority. There is nothing in the Constitution of the United States to justify this religious impertinence.

For many years priests have attempted to give to our Government a religious form. Zealots have succeeded in putting the legend upon our money: "In God We Trust;" and we have chaplains in the army and navy, and legislative proceedings are usually opened with prayer. All this is contrary to the genius of the Republic, contrary to the Declaration of Independence, and contrary really to the Constitution of the United States. We have taken the ground that the people can govern themselves without the assistance of any supernatural power. We have taken the position that the people are the real and only rightful source of authority. We have solemnly declared that the people must determine what is politically right and what is wrong, and that their legally expressed will is the supreme law. This leaves no room for national superstition—no room for patriotic gods or supernatural beings—and this does away with the necessity for political prayers.

The government of God has been tried. It was tried in Palestine several thousand years ago, and the God of the Jews was a monster of cruelty and ignorance, and the people governed by this God lost their nationality. Theocracy was tried through the Middle Ages. God was the Governor—the pope was his agent, and every priest and bishop and cardinal was armed with credentials from the Most High—and the result was that the noblest and best were in prisons, the greatest and grandest perished at the stake. The result was that vices were crowned with honor, and virtues whipped naked through the streets. The result was that hypocrisy swayed the sceptre of authority, while honesty languished in the dungeons of the Inquisition.

The government of God was tried in Geneva when John Calvin was his representative; and under this government of God the flames climbed around the limbs and blinded the eyes of Michael Servetus, because he dared to express an honest thought.[2] This government of God was tried in Scotland, and the seeds of theological hatred were sown, that bore, through hundreds of years, the fruit of massacre and assassination. This government of God was established in New England, and the result was that Quakers were hanged or burned—the laws of Moses re-enacted and the "witch was not suffered to live." The result was that investigation was a crime, and the expression of an honest thought a capital offence. This government of God was established in Spain, and the Jews were expelled, the Moors were driven out, Moriscoes were exterminated, and nothing left but the ignorant and bankrupt worshipers of this monster. This government of God was tried in the United States when slavery was regarded as a divine institution, when men and women were regarded as criminals because they sought for liberty by flight, and when others were regarded as criminals because they gave them food and shelter. The pulpit of that day defended the buying and selling of women and babes, and the mouths of slave-traders were filled with passages of Scripture, defending and upholding the traffic in human flesh.

We have entered upon a new epoch. This is the century of man. Every effort to really better the condition of mankind has been opposed by the worshipers of some God. The church in all ages and among all peoples has been the consistent enemy of the human race. Everywhere and at all times, it has opposed the liberty of thought and expression. It has been the sworn enemy of investigation and of intellectual development. It has denied the existence of facts, the tendency of which was to undermine its power. It has always been carrying fagots to the feet of Philosophy. It has erected the gallows for Genius. It has built the dungeon for Thinkers. And to-day the orthodox church is as much opposed as it ever was to the mental freedom of the human race.

Of course, there is a distinction made between churches and individual members. There have been millions of Christians who have been believers in liberty and in the freedom of expression—millions who have fought for the rights of man—but churches as organizations have been on the other side. It is true that churches have fought churches—that Protestants battled with the Catholics for what they were pleased to call the freedom of conscience; and it is also true that the moment these Protestants obtained the civil power, they denied this freedom of conscience to others.

Let me show you the difference between the theological and the secular spirit. Nearly three hundred years ago, one of the noblest of the human race, Giordano Bruno,[3] was burned at Rome by the Catholic Church—that is to say, by the "Triumphant Beast." This man had committed certain crimes—he had publicly stated that there were other worlds than this—other constellations than ours. He had ventured the supposition that other planets might be peopled. More than this, and worse than this, he had asserted the heliocentric theory—that the earth made its annual journey about the sun. He had also given it as his opinion that matter is eternal. For these crimes he was found unworthy to live, and about his body were piled the fagots of the Catholic Church. This man, this genius, this pioneer of the science of the nineteenth century, perished as serenely as the sun sets. The Infidels of to-day find excuses for his murderers. They take into consideration the ignorance and brutality of the times. They remember that the world was governed by a God who was then the source of all authority. This is the charity of Infidelity,—of philosophy. But the church of to-day is so heartless, is still so cold and cruel, that it can find no excuse for the murdered.

This is the difference between Theocracy and Democracy—between God and man.

If God is allowed in the Constitution, man must abdicate. There is no room for both. If the people of the great Republic become superstitious enough and ignorant enough to put God in the Constitution of the United States, the experiment of self-government will have failed, and the great and splendid declaration that "all governments derive their just powers from the consent of the governed" will have been denied, and in its place will be found this: All power comes from God; priests are his agents, and the people are their slaves.

Religion is an individual matter, and each soul should be left entirely free to form its own opinions and to judge of its accountability to a supposed supreme being. With religion, government has nothing whatever to do. Government is founded upon force, and force should never interfere with the religious opinions of men. Laws should define the rights of men and their duties toward each other, and these laws should be for the benefit of man in this world.

A nation can neither be Christian nor Infidel—a nation is incapable of having opinions upon these subjects. If a nation is Christian, will all the citizens go to heaven? If it is not, will they all be damned? Of course it is admitted that the majority of citizens composing a nation may believe or disbelieve, and they may call the nation what they please. A nation is a corporation. To repeat a familiar saying, "it has no soul." There can be no such thing as a Christian corporation. Several Christians may form a corporation, but it can hardly be said that the corporation thus formed was included in the atonement. For instance: Seven Christians form a corporation—that is to say, there are seven natural persons and one artificial—can it be said that there are eight souls to be saved?

No human being has brain enough, or knowledge enough, or experience enough, to say whether there is, or is not, a God. Into this darkness Science has not yet carried its torch. No human being has gone beyond the horizon of the natural. As to the existence of the supernatural, one man knows precisely as much, and exactly as little as another. Upon this question, chimpanzees and cardinals, apes and popes, are upon exact equality. The smallest insect discernible only by the most powerful microscope is as familiar with this subject as the greatest genius that has been produced by the human race.

Governments and laws are for the preservation of rights and the regulation of conduct. One man should not be allowed to interfere with the liberty of another. In the metaphysical world there should be no interference whatever. The same is true in the world of art. Laws cannot regulate what is or is not music, what is or what is not beautiful—and constitutions cannot definitely settle and determine the perfection of statues, the value of paintings, or the glory and subtlety of thought. In spite of laws and constitutions the brain will think. In every direction consistent with the well-being and peace of society, there should be freedom. No man should be compelled to adopt the theology of another; neither should a minority, however small, he forced to acquiesce in the opinions of a majority, however large.

If there be an infinite Being, he does not need our help—we need not waste our energies in his defence. It is enough for us to give to every other human being the liberty we claim for ourselves. There may or may not be a Supreme Ruler of the universe—but we are certain that man exists, and we believe that freedom is the condition of progress; that it is the sunshine of the mental and moral world, and that without it man will go back to the den of savagery, and will become the fit associate of wild and ferocious beasts.

We have tried the government of priests, and we know that such governments are without mercy. In the administration of theocracy, all the instruments of torture have been invented. If any man wishes to have God recognized in the Constitution of our country, let him read the history of the Inquisition, and let him remember that hundreds of millions of men, women and children have been sacrificed to placate the wrath, or win the approbation of this God.

There has been in our country a divorce of church and state. This follows as a natural sequence of the declaration that "governments derive their just powers from the consent of the governed." The priest was no longer a necessity. His presence was a contradiction of the principle on which the Republic was founded. He represented, not the authority of the people, but of some "Power from on High," and to recognize this other Power was inconsistent with free government. The founders of the Republic at that time parted company with the priests, and said to them: "You may turn your attention to the other world—we will attend to the affairs of this." Equal liberty was given to all. But the ultra theologian is not satisfied with this—he wishes to destroy the liberty of the people—he wishes a recognition of his God as the source of authority, to the end that the church may become the supreme power.

But the sun will not be turned backward. The people of the United States are intelligent. They no longer believe implicitly in supernatural religion. They are losing confidence in the miracles and marvels of the Dark Ages. They know the value of the free school. They appreciate the benefits of science. They are believers in education, in the free play of thought, and there is a suspicion that the priest, the theologian, is destined to take his place with the necromancer, the astrologer, the worker of magic, and the professor of the black art.

We have already compared the benefits of theology and science. When the theologian governed the world, it was covered with huts and hovels for the many, palaces and cathedrals for the few. To nearly all the children of men, reading and writing were unknown arts. The poor were clad in rags and skins—they devoured crusts, and gnawed bones. The day of Science dawned, and the luxuries of a century ago are the necessities of to-day. Men in the middle ranks of life have more of the conveniences and elegancies than the princes and kings of the theological times. But above and over all this, is the development of mind. There is more of value in the brain of an average man of to-day—of a master-mechanic, of a chemist, of a naturalist, of an inventor, than there was in the brain of the world four hundred years ago.

These blessings did not fall from the skies. These benefits did not drop from the outstretched hands of priests. They were not found in cathedrals or behind altars—neither were they searched for with holy candles. They were not discovered by the closed eyes of prayer, nor did they come in answer to superstitious supplication. They are the children of freedom, the gifts of reason, observation and experience—and for them all, man is indebted to man.

Let us hold fast to the sublime declaration of Lincoln. Let us insist that this, the Republic, is "A government of the people, by the people, and for the people."

NOTES

1. [Ingersoll has somewhat compressed a statement from the Declaration of Independence: "That to secure these rights [life, liberty, and the pursuit of happiness], Governments are instituted among Men, deriving their just powers from the consent of the governed . . ."]

2. [Michael Servetus (1511?–1553), French physician who wrote several works rejecting the doctrine of the Trinity and, at John Calvin's urging, was burned as a heretic by the Inquisition.]

3. [Italian philosopher Giordano Bruno (1548–1600) was burned at the stake by the Inquisition for several works embodying a kind of pantheism that orthodox religious leaders found heretical.]

27

THE LORD'S DAY ALLIANCE
(1928)

Clarence Darrow

Although Clarence Darrow (1847–1938) gained his greatest celebrity as defense lawyer in the Scopes trial of 1925, he had been a well-known figure since the 1890s, when he assisted Judge John Peter Altgeld in seeking amnesty for the defendants in the Haymarket riots in Chicago, who had been falsely branded as anarchists and revolutionaries. He also defended Nathan Leopold and Richard Loeb in the celebrated murder trial of 1924, saving them from execution. Darrow was a prolific writer on a wide variety of subjects, and he frequently spoke out against religious orthodoxy. With Wallace Rice he coedited An Agnostic's Anthology *(1929). He also spoke eloquently of his atheism in his autobiography,* The Story of My Life *(1932). In the following article, first published in* Plain Talk *(March 1928), Darrow criticizes an organization of the 1920s called the Lord's Day Alliance, which promoted legislation prohibiting a variety of activities on Sundays. The organization's writings and beliefs strikingly echo those of contemporary fundamentalists.*

AMONG THE VARIOUS SOCIETIES THAT are engaged in the business of killing pleasure, the Lord's Day Alliance of New York deserves a place of honor. If any poor mortal is caught enjoying life on Sunday its agents gleefully hie themselves to the nearest legislature and urge a law to stop the fun. Their literature and periodicals tell very plainly the kind of business they are in. This association of crape-hangers seems to

From Clarence Darrow, "The Lord's Day Alliance," *Plain Talk* 2, no. 3 (March 1928): 257–66, 267–70.

be especially interested in the State of New York, which contains about one-tenth of the population of the Union, and among them an unusually large number of foreigners and other heathen who have not been taught the proper regard for the sanctity of the Sabbath.

The activities of this Alliance in New York still leave them ample time to watch the sinners in the other states and bring to book the wicked who are bent on having pleasure on the holy Sabbath Day. In their own language, the work is "in the interests of the preservation and promotion of the Lord's Day as the American Christian Sabbath . . . to oppose all adverse measures seeking to weaken the law and to seek the passage of such measures as would tend to strengthen it." The Alliance informs us that "in the last four years it has furnished sixty-seven addresses per month, on an average. During this time over three hundred and twenty institute meetings have been held for the study of the Sabbath question. Several million pages of literature have been distributed." It "also furnishes press articles and syndicate matter for the newspapers." Imagine an institute spending so much time in the study of the Sabbath question! If they have learned anything on that subject it is not revealed in their tracts.

These Lord's Day folk seek to protect the day "in the interest of the home and the church," "to exalt Jesus Christ who is Lord of the Sabbath Day and to spread the knowledge of the will of God that His Kingdom may come and His will may be done." Though the organization is still young it points to a long list of glorious achievements. We are informed that "no adverse measure affecting the Sabbath has passed Albany during this time, although forty-two such measures have been introduced in the legislature. . . . A representative of our organization has been present on each occasion to oppose any such adverse measures." It boasts that it "opposed the opening of the State Fair in 1925 on Sunday, by vigorous protest to the members of the Commission and the Attorney General." The result was a ruling from the Attorney General sustaining the law. Of course, so long as no one could go to the fair on Sunday the people were obliged to go to church. It "has defeated annually an average of forty commercial and anti-Sunday bills in our legislature and has brought about the closing of the First and Second-Class Post-Offices on Sunday. . . . As a result, thousands are in our churches each Sunday." It has been "thanked by President Coolidge for the services rendered hundreds of thousands of government employees in the

District of Columbia and elsewhere throughout the nation." What further honor could anybody get on earth? It has "accepted the challenge and in scores of places defeated . . . commercialized amusement forces which have declared a nation-wide fight to the finish for Sunday movies and are even proposing to enlist the aid of the churches in their unholy campaign." It succeeded in "changing the date of the gigantic air carnival to which admission was charged, from Sunday, August 2, 1925, to Saturday, August 1, 1925, held at Bolling Field, Washington." No one but a parson has the right to charge for his performance on Sunday. Through its request "the War Department issued orders on November 2, 1925, covering every military post in the United States, banning Sunday public air carnivals and maneuvers." It is "now leading a country-wide movement for the enactment of a Sunday rest law for the District of Columbia. Washington needs and must have a Sunday rest law." It informs us that the "day must be kept above the Dollar, Christ above Commercialism on the Lord's Day, the person must have the right of way over the Pocketbook on our American Sunday."

Surely this is a great work and deserves the active support and sympathy of all people who are really interested in driving pleasure-seekers from golf grounds, automobile trips, baseball parks, moving-picture houses and every other form of pleasure on Sunday. It is possible that for lack of any other place to go, some of them might be compelled to park themselves in church. If America does not succeed in bringing back the ancient Puritan Sabbath with its manifold blessings, it will not be the fault of the Lord's Day Alliance.

As a part of this noble work the organization publishes various pamphlets and leaflets and scatters them broadcast through the land. As a rule, these pamphlets are the effusions of more or less obscure parsons. These preachers have special knowledge of God's plans and God's will. Their sermonettes are conflicting in their statements and utterly senseless in their assertions. The sentries of the Alliance on guard at the state capitals and in the national Congress, while these wise bodies are in session, have no doubt succeeded in coercing spineless members of legislative bodies to yield to their will and their parade of votes; and thus spread considerable gloom over the United States on the Sabbath Day.

These Lord's Day Alliance gentlemen are not only religious but scientific. For instance, they publish a pamphlet written by one Dr. A. Haegler, of Basle, Switzerland, in which he says that experiments have shown that during a day's work a laborer expends more oxygen than he can inhale. True, he catches up with a large part of this deficiency through the night time, but does not regain it all. It follows, of course, that if he keeps on working six days a week, for the same time each day, he will be out a considerable amount of oxygen, and the only way he can make it up is to take a day off on Sunday and go to church. This statement seems to be flawless to the powerful intellects who put out this literature. Any person who is in the habit of thinking might at once arrive at the conclusion that if the workman could not take in enough oxygen gas in the ordinary hours of work and sleep he might well cut down his day's work and lengthen his sleep and thus start even every morning. This ought to be better than running on a shortage of gas all through the week. Likewise, it must occur to most people that there are no two kinds of labor that consume the same amount of oxygen gas per day, and probably no two human systems that work exactly alike. Then, too, if the workman ran behind on his oxygen gas in the days when men worked from ten to sixteen hours a day he might break even at night, since working hours have been reduced to eight or less, with a Saturday half-holiday thrown in. It might even help the situation to raise the bedroom window at night. These matters, of course, do not occur to the eminent doctor who wrote the pamphlet and the scientific gentlemen who send it out. To them the silly statement proves that a man needs to take a day off on Sunday and attend church in order that he may catch up on his oxygen. To them it is perfectly plain that for catching up on oxygen the church has a great advantage over the golf links or the baseball park, or any other place where the wicked wish to go. This in spite of the fact that in crowded buildings the oxygen might be mixed with halitosis.

The exact proof that these parsons marshal for showing that the need of a Sunday rest is manifest in the nature of things is marvelous. If the need of Sunday rest was meant to be shown by natural law it seems as if this should have been clearly indicated, especially if the righteous God had determined to punish Sunday violations with death and hell. There was no reason why the Creator should have been content to leave the proof to a revelation said to have been made in a barbarous age to an unknown man, hidden in the clouds on the top of a high mountain peak. Humans would not have graven such an important message on a tablet of stone and then insisted that the tablet should be destroyed before any being except Moses had set eye upon it. Even God should not ask for faith that amounts to credulity and gross superstition.

A deity could have written the Sabbath requirements plain on the face of nature. For instance, he might have made the waves be still on the seventh day of the week; the grass might have taken a day off and rested from growing until Monday morning; the wild animals of the forest and glen might have refrained from fighting and eating and chasing and maiming and have been made to close their eyes on the Sabbath Day, and to have kept peace and tranquility. The earth might have paused in its course around the sun or stood still on its axis. It should have been as important to make this gesture in homage of the day as it was to help Joshua hold the sun in leash that a battle might be prolonged. If nature had made plain provision for the Sabbath Day it would be patent to others as well as to the medicine men who insist that the Sabbath Day was made for their profit alone.

But let us pass from the realm of science, where pastors never did especially shine, into a field where they are more likely to excel. Here it is fairly easy to see what it is all about. The Reverend McQuilkin,[1] Pastor at Orange, New Jersey, furnishes a pamphlet for The Lord's Day Alliance. Read what the Doctor says:

> God claims the Sabbath for himself in a very unique, distinctive way as a day of rest and worship. He again and again commands you to spend its hours in the conservation of our spiritual power in the exercise of public and private worship. To spend this holy day in pleasure or unnecessary secular labor is to *rob God*. We have got to be careful how we take the hours of the Sabbath for secular study or work, for God will surely bring us to judgment concerning the matter. Church attendance is a definite obligation, a debt which we owe to God.

Here is where the Alliance seems to strike pay dirt! What reason has God to claim the Sabbath for Himself, and why is God robbed if a man should work on Sunday? It can hardly be possible that the puny insects that we call men could disturb God in His Sunday rest. Is it not a little presumptuous even to parsons, to say that a debt to the church is a debt to God?

To emphasize the importance of leaving the Sabbath to the

preachers, we are warned of the fate of the sinner who profanes the Sabbath by work or play. The Lord's Day Alliance has issued a little folder on which there is the following heading in large letters: THE IMPORTANCE OF THE DEATH PENALTY. Under it is printed this timely caution: "Six days shall work be done, but on the seventh day is a Sabbath of solemn rest, holy to Jehovah; whosoever doeth any work on the Sabbath Day shall surely be put to death. Ex. 31–15." The pamphlet also states that a wealthy business man is furnishing the money for the distribution of this sheet. If this barbarous statement represents the views of the Lord's Day Alliance then what is the mental caliber of the Congressmen, members of the legislatures, judges, and the public that are influenced by their ravings? Can anyone but an idiot have any feeling but contempt for men who seek to scare children and old women with such infamous stuff?

Let us see what the Bible says on this important subject. In Exodus 19:8–12 we find not only the commandment which was delivered to Moses in reference to the Sabbath, but the reasons for such a commandment:

> Remember the Sabbath Day to keep it holy. Six days shalt thou labor and do all thy work; but the seventh day is the Sabbath of the Lord thy God. In it thou shalt do no work, thou, nor thy son, nor thy daughter, nor thy man servant nor thy maid servant nor thy cattle which is within thy gates; *for in six days the Lord made heaven and earth, the sea and all that is in them and rested the seventh day, wherefore the Lord blessed the Sabbath Day and hallowed it.*

It is plain from this commandment that the Sabbath was not instituted in obedience to any natural law or so that man might catch up on his supply of oxygen, but because the Lord in six days had performed the herculean task of creating the universe out of nothing, and took a day off to rest on the seventh. Therefore, every man must rest on the seventh, no matter whether he has been working and is tired or not. This is made even more binding in Exodus 35:2:

> Six days shall work be done; upon the seventh day there shall be to you a holy day, the Sabbath of the rest of the Lord. Whosoever doeth work therein shall be put to death.

In view of the commands of God, certainly his special agents on the earth cannot be blamed for cruelty, no matter what ferocious doctrine they may preach. In Numbers 28:9–10, in connection with various offerings that the Law required on the Sabbath, a provision is made for meat offerings and drink offerings. The meat offerings enjoin the sacrifice of lambs by fire as "a sweet savor unto the Lord," and then the Lord provides that the pastor shall further:

> Sacrifice on the Sabbath Day two lambs of first year without spot and two-tenths of a part of an ephah of fine flour for a meal-offering, mingled with oil and the drink offering thereof: this is the burnt-offering of every Sabbath, besides the continual burnt-offering and his drink offering.

It is evident that the lambs less than one year old, without spot, were to be burned because they were so young and innocent and would therefore make such a "sweet savor unto the Lord." Nothing is lacking in this smell but mint sauce. If Moses is to be obeyed on pain of hell in his command to abstain from work or play on the Sabbath why is the rest of the program any less sacred? How can the holy parsons release their congregations from the sacrifice of the two spotless lambs and the two-tenths of an ephah of fine flour mingled with oils?

In the Fifteenth Chapter of Numbers, it is related that while the children of Israel were in the wilderness they found a man gathering sticks on the Sabbath Day. The Hebrews were evidently at a loss to know what should be done with him for this most heinous offense, so they put him in "ward" to await the further orders of the Lord. It is then related, "and the Lord said unto Moses: The man shall surely be put to death; all the congregation shall stone him with stones without the camp. And all the congregation brought him without the camp and stoned him to death with stones: *as Jehovah commanded Moses.*" In spite of manifold texts like this there are persons who protest that they love this bloody, barbarous, tribal God of the Jews. The literature of the Alliance clearly indicates that its sponsors would follow this command of Jehovah at the present time if they could only have their way.

Dr. McQuilkin further tells us that the defenders of the day have often been too superficial in their contentions on behalf of this holy Sabbath; that they should soft-pedal the "thou shalt nots" and "we should thunder our 'thou shalts' into the ears of the foolish, wicked men who for the sake of pleasure or financial profit would rob their fellow men or themselves of the precious rest God had given them for the cultivation and nurture of their immortal souls. Such men," he continues, "must be identified with murderers and suicides." The common punishment for murder is death, and suicide *is* death, therefore Dr. McQuilkin, with the rest of his associates and with his God, believes in the death penalty for working or playing on the Sabbath.

How one involuntarily loves this righteous Dr. McQuilkin of Orange, New Jersey. He must be a man whose love and understanding oozes from every pore of his body. No doubt the people of Orange who are burdened with sorrow or sin bring their sore troubles and lay them on his loving breast. I am sure that little children in their grief rush to his outstretched arms for solace and relief.

The Reverend Doctor McQuilkin makes short work of the idea that you cannot make people good by law. In fact, that seems to him to be the only way to make them good. Therefore people and enterprises that commercialize Sundays by baseball games and moving pictures, who "whine about the impossibility of making people good by law, ought to go either to school or to jail." Probably the pastor would be in favor of the jail. The Reverend Doctor is very much exercised about his idea that the Sabbath should be spent in cultivating our "spiritual nature." From the gentle and kindly character of the doctor's utterances, one judges that he must spend several days a week cultivating his "spiritual nature."

The godly doctor is indeed earnest about the church-going. He says, "God will surely bring us to judgment in the matter of staying away from church, for church attendance is a definite obligation, a debt which we owe to God." The doctor has a naïve way of mixing up himself and his private business affairs with the Lord.

Could it be possible that the Reverend Doctor McQuilkin's serious case of rabies might be due to vacant pews? Such cases are related in the following extract from a very disheartening paragraph put out by the Lord's Day Alliance in a folder entitled "Let's Save Our American Christian Sabbath."

A significant part of this falling away from old American ideals has been the neglect of the churches—life among Christian people dropping to a lower plane on Sunday. The lure of pleasure and the drift to seven-day slavery within a few years have utterly changed the character of the day. The average attendance at Sunday morning services, taken for all the churches of New York State—counting large city churches as well as small country ones—has steadily dropped until it has now reached only *fifty-three* persons. This amounts to but little more than one fourth of their total enrolled membership! The old days of tithes are gone! Lack of support is making the situation more and more critical and many churches have had to be abandoned. Is the church to survive? *Are we to remain a Christian nation?*

This is indeed distressing. I can well imagine the feeling of chagrin that steals over the parson when he talks to fifty persons on a Sunday morning. Here are the few parishioners, solemn-visaged and sitting impatiently in their pews while a joyous crowd rolls by in automobiles on their road to hell. I cannot help thinking of the parson on a Sunday morning, telling the same story over and over again to his half hundred listeners.

I have seen this pastor and this congregation in the country church and the city church. What have they in common with the world today? Who are these faithful fifty? One-third of them, at least, are little boys and girls, twisting and turning and yawning and fussing in their stiff, uncomfortable clothes, in the hard church pews. Then there are the usual fat old women, wearing their Sunday finery. Their faces are dull and heavy and altogether unlovely. They no longer think of the world; they are looking straight into space at the Promised Land. They hold a hymn book or a Bible in their time-worn hands. Perhaps there are ten full grown men in church; two or three of these look consumptive; one or two are merchants who think that being at church will help them sell prunes; the rest are old and tottering. It has been long years since a new thought or even an old one has found lodgment in their atrophied brains. They are decrepit and palsied and done; so far as life and the world are concerned, they are already dead. One feels sympathetic toward the old. But why should the aged, who have lived their lives, grumble and complain about youth with its glow and ambition and hope? Why should they sit in the fading light and watch the world go by and vainly reach out their bony hands to hold it back?

Aside from the Lord's Day Alliance's way of appealing to the law to make people go to church, I can think of only two plans to fill the pews. First, to abandon a large number of the churches and give the parsons a chance to find some useful and paying job. Secondly, to get more up-to-date, human and intelligent preachers into the church pulpits.

The literature issued by the Alliance shows great concern about Sunday newspapers. These papers consume a great deal of valuable time on the Sabbath Day. They are in no way the proper literature for Sunday reading. Automobile trips, too, are an abomination on the Sabbath. One pamphlet records approval of the conduct of the "venerable" John D. Paton who even refused to use street-cars on Sunday while visiting in America. He kept his appointments by long walks, sometimes even having to run between engagements. This sounds to me strangely like work. Still it might have been necessary in order to get the proper amount of oxygen gas.

Playing golf on Sunday is a sacrilegious practice. A whole leaflet is prepared by Dr. Jefferson on golf. "No one ought to play golf on Sunday. . . . The golf player may need oxygen but he should not forget his caddie." The doctor calls our attention to the fact that men in the days of Moses were mindful of even the least of these. How our parsons do love Moses and his murderous laws! We are told that a caddie works, that it is not play to trudge after a golf ball with a bag of clubs on his back. The leaflets say that the caddie does not work on Sunday for fun but for money, and it "isn't a manly thing for the golf player to hire him to work on Sunday." We are told that "there are now over one hundred thousand caddies on the golf links every Sunday. These caddies are making a living." Of course this picture is pathetic. It is too bad that the Lord's Day Alliance cannot get these hundred thousand caddies discharged. Then possibly some of them would go to church on Sunday. They might even drop a nickel in the contribution box.

Does anyone believe that if the caddies were offered the same money for going to church that they get for hunting golf balls they would choose the church? It takes a bright boy to be a caddie.

The caddies do not inspire all the tears; we are told that chauffeurs and railroad employees are necessary to take the players to and from the golf links. This no doubt true. Still, we have seen chauffeurs sitting in automobiles outside a church where they had driven their employers to get their souls saved. On our suburban railroads there are many trains put in service on Sunday to take people to and from church, but these have not come under the ban of the Lord's Day Alliance. Its complaint is that so few trains are needed for this blessed work.

There is some logic in this folder. We are told that "if golf is allowable on Sunday, then, so is tennis, baseball, basketball, football, bowling and all other games which our generation is fond of." "You can't forbid one without forbidding the others," says the Alliance. We heartily agree with the Reverend Doctor on this particular question.

No one needs to go to ball games or movies or play golf on Sunday unless he wants to spend his time that way. I have never seen anybody who objected to the members of the Lord's Day Alliance or any others from abstaining from all kinds of work and all sorts of play and every method of enjoyment on Sunday.

Dr. Robert E. Speer of Englewood, New Jersey, is very definite and specific as to the proper way to spend Sunday and the sort of recreation man should naturally enjoy on this holy day. Dr. Speer says, "God wants the worship of the Lord's Day and he wants us to have the indispensable comforts and pleasure of it." One would think that Dr. Speer got daily messages from God. "We need the day for meditation and prayer and plans for better living." No one questions the good doctor's right to satisfy his needs in such way as seems necessary and pleasurable for him. All that I contend for is that I, too, shall decide these questions for myself.

Dr. Speer says:

> There are some things deadly in their power to spoil it (referring to the Sabbath). One is the Sunday newspapers. . . . I pass by all that may be denounced as defiling in it. . . . There is harm enough in its "wallow of secularity" . . . Look at the men who feed their minds and souls on Sunday with this food. They miss the calm and holy peace, the glowing divinity of the day.

It is just conceivable that one might read a Sunday newspaper and still have time for "the glowing divinity of the day," to glow long enough to satisfy every desire.

Dr. Speer condemns those who berate the quality of the sermons preached on Sunday and informs us that the wisest man can learn something from the poorest preacher, although he neglects to say just what. He tells us that a country preacher's sermon is superior to the country editor's writings or the country lawyer's speeches. This may be true. It is, at all events, true to Dr. Speer, and there is no reason in the world why he should not hunt up the "poorest preacher" that he can find and listen to him on every Sunday. No doubt Dr. Speer might learn something from him.

Dr. Speer disapproves of riding on railroad trains on Sunday if it can be avoided. "Certainly no one should take long railroad journeys on Sunday." He tells us, "Sunday golf, newspapers, and all that sort of thing are bad and weakening in their influence. These are particular evidence of the trend of the man who thus abandons his birthright." The doctor is more definite in his beautiful picture of just what one ought to do on the Sabbath Day. On this subject he says:

> I do not believe that anyone who grew up in a truly Christian home in which the old ideas prevailed can have any sympathy with this modern abuse of the old-fashioned observance of Sunday. There, on Sunday, the demands of the week were laid aside. The family gathered over the Bible and the Catechism. There was a quiet calm through the house. Innumerable things rendered it a marked day, as distinct from other days, and probably it ended with a rare walk with the father at the son's side and some sober talk over what is abiding and what is of eternal worth.

We could hazard a guess that the reason that the mother was not present on this joyful occasion was because she was at home washing the dishes from a big Sunday dinner that she had prepared.

It is entirely possible that Dr. Speer's picture of the ideal Sabbath is a good picture. Doubtless it is good to him. Still, hidden in my mind and recalled by Dr. Speer's alluring language, is the memory of his ideal Presbyterian Sunday. This was a day of unmitigated pain. No spirit of life or joy relieved the boredom and torture of the endless hours. The day meant misery to all the young. Even now I can feel the blank despair that overcame youth and hope as we children left our play on Saturday night and sadly watched the sun go down and the period of gloom steal across the world. Why should Dr. Speer and the other dead seek to force that sort of a Sabbath upon men and women who want to take in their oxygen gas in the baseball bleachers, or the golf links?

From Dr. Speer's picture of the ideal Sabbath I infer that he is a Presbyterian. This opinion has been confirmed by reference to *Who's Who*. I find that for long years he has been a Presbyterian preacher, not only in America, but he has carried the blessed gospel even into China that the heathen of that benighted land might not live and die without the consoling knowledge of eternal hell.

Dr. Speer's beautiful picture of the old-time Christian Sabbath describes "the family gathered over the Bible and the Catechism." I, too, sat under the ministrations of a Presbyterian preacher and was duly instructed in the Westminster Catechism. In spite of the aversion and terror that its reference inspired, I took down the book to read once more the horrible creed of the twisted and deformed minds who produced this monstrosity which has neither sense, meaning, justice nor mercy, but only malignant depravity. A devilish creed which shocks every tender sentiment of the human mind. I am inclined to think from their internal evidence that most of the sermonettes circulated by the Lord's Day Alliance had their origin in the warped minds of the Presbyterian clergy. I would hazard a bet that the tender, gentle, loving Dr. McQuilkin is a Presbyterian. I sought to confirm this belief by consulting *Who's Who*, but found that the editors had stupidly left out his name. Still I am convinced that he is a Presbyterian. . . .

When one thinks of this organization with its senseless leaflets, its stern endeavors, its blank despair, its half-shut eyes blinking at life, one is reminded of the frogs in the green scum-covered pond in the woods who sit on their haunches in the dark and croak all day. No doubt these frogs believe that the germ infested pond is a sacred pool. They are oblivious of the rolling, living ocean that lies just beyond.

Dr. Speer, like all the other members of the Lord's Day Alliance, is very sure that one of the chief occupations of Sunday should be attending church. But what church, pray? We are informed that any preacher is better to listen to and read from than any editor, lawyer or other person. Most of us have heard all sorts of preachers. We have listened to some whose churches could only be filled if the Lord's Day Alliance should succeed and make it an offense punishable by death not to go to church. We have heard preachers who had something to say and could say it well. There is as much difference in the views and ability of preachers as in other men. Would Dr. Speer think that we should go to hear the Fundamentalists or the Unitarians? Should we listen to the Holy Rollers or the Modernists?

There are few men outside of the Lord's Day Alliance who would care to listen to their favorite preacher for a *full day* and there are few preachers who would undertake to talk for a whole day. What, then, must one do for the rest of the time? One simply cannot sleep *all* day on Sunday.

In all this literature we are constantly urged to preserve our "American Sabbath." Is there any special holiness that lurks around an "American Sabbath"? Are not European Christians as competent to determine the right way to employ their time on Sundays as American Christians? The Lord's Day folk say that reading the Sunday newspapers, playing golf, riding in automobiles, and witnessing baseball games and movies is "un-American." This compound word has been used to cover a multitude of sins. What it means nobody knows. It is bunkum meant to serve every cause, good and bad alike. By what license does the Lord's Day Alliance call its caricature of Sunday an "American Sabbath"? On what grounds does it urge it as against the European Sabbath? Is this nightmare which the Lord's Day Alliance is so anxious to force upon the United States a product of America? Everyone knows that Sunday, with the rest of the Christian religion, came to us from Europe. The weird ideas of the Lord's Day Alliance are European. When and how it came to us is worth finding out.

Jesus and His disciples did not believe in the Jewish Sabbath. They neither abstained from work nor play. St. Paul, specially, condemned the setting apart of days and said to his disciples, "Ye observe days and months and times and years. I am afraid of ye lest I have bestowed upon ye labor in vain."

The early fathers did not approve of any such day as the Lord's Day Alliance insists shall be fastened upon America. St. Jerome and his group attended church services on Sunday, but otherwise pursued their usual occupations. St. Augustine calls Sunday a festal day and says that the Fourth Commandment is in no literal sense binding upon Christianity. Even Luther and Calvin enjoined no such a day upon the Christians as these moderns wish to fasten upon America that the churches may be filled. The righteous John Knox "played bowls" on Sunday, and in his voluminous preaching used no effort to make Sunday a day of gloom wherein people should abstain from work and play. It was not until 1595 that an English preacher of Suffolk first insisted that the Jewish Sabbath should be maintained. The controversy over this question lasted for a hundred years and resulted in a law proscribing every kind of Sunday recreation, even "vainly and profanely walking for pleasure." England soon reacted against this blue Sabbath and permitted trading, open theatres and frivolity in the afternoon and evening. Under the leadership of the Church of England the Sabbath no longer was a day of gloom and despair.

The real American Sabbath was born in Scotland after the death of John Knox. It fits the stern hills, the bleak moors and the unfriendly climate of this northern land. It was born of fear and gloom and it lives by fear and gloom. Early in the Seventeenth Century, Scotland adopted this stern theory of the Jewish Sabbath and applied it ruthlessly. The Westminster Confession was adopted by the General Assembly of the Kirk of Scotland in 1647 and has remained the formal standard of faith to the present day. Ordinary recreations were disallowed. Books and music were forbidden except such as were recognized as religious in a narrow sense. No recreation but whiskey-drinking remained. This Presbyterian Sabbath of Scotland was brought to New England by the early settlers of America and is, in fact, a Scotch Sabbath—not an American Sabbath.

Even in spite of the natural gloom and cold of Scotland, Sunday strictness has been greatly modified there in the last fifty years. It is not the present Scotch Sabbath that these modern Puritans insist on forcing upon America. It is the old, ferocious, Scotch Sabbath of the Westminster Confession. It was brought from a land of gloom into a land of sunshine, and the Lord's Day Alliance prefers the gloom and hardness of this outworn, out-lived Scotch Sabbath to the sunshine and joy that comes with a fertile soil, a mild climate and natural human emotions.

It is almost unbelievable that a handful of men without reason or humanity should be able to force their cruel dogmas upon the people. Not one in twenty of the residents of the United States believes in the Sabbath of the Lord's Day Alliance. Our cities, villages, and even country districts, protest against the bigotry and intolerance of The Lord's Day Alliance and their kind. Still, in spite of this, by appeal to obsolete statutes, religious prejudice, crass ignorance and unfathomable fanaticism, they carry on their mighty campaign of gloom.

After long years of effort, with the lazy, cowardly public that does not want to be disturbed, the Legislature of New York, in the face of the opposition of the Lord's Day Alliance, managed to pass a law providing that incorporated cities and towns should have the right to legalize baseball games and moving picture shows on Sunday after two o'clock in the afternoon and charge an admission fee for seeing the entertainment. Why after two o'clock? The answer is perfectly plain: It is possible that someone might be forced into church in the morning if there was nowhere else to go. Were the hours after two o'clock any less sacred in the laws of Moses and the prophets than the hours before two o'clock? Or was the Legislature induced to pass this law simply to give the minister a privilege that it grants to no one else?

Ours is a cosmopolitan country, made up of all sorts of people with various creeds. There should be room enough to allow each person to spend Sunday and every other day according to his own pleasure and his own profit. In spite of the Lord's Day Alliance and all other alliances, it is too late in the history of the world to bring back the Mosaic Sabbath. Regardless of their best endeavors it will probably never again be a crime punishable by death to work or play on what they are pleased to call the Lord's Day. Those ministers who have something to say that appeals to men and women will be able to make themselves heard without a law compelling people to go to church. If the Lord's Day Alliance can provide something equally attractive to compete with the Sunday newspapers, golf, baseball games, movies and the open air, they will get the trade. If they cannot provide such entertainment, then in spite of all their endeavors the churches will be vacant. It is time that those who believe in tolerance, and in freedom, should make themselves heard in no uncertain way. It is time that men should determine to defend their right to attend to their own affairs and live their own lives, regardless of the bigots who in all ages have menaced the welfare of the world and the liberty of man.

NOTE

1. [Robert Crawford McQuilkin (1886–?), American theologian.]

28

MONOTHEISM AND ITS DISCONTENTS
(1992)

Gore Vidal

Gore Vidal (b. 1925) published his first novel at the age of nineteen, and has since gone on to write an array of books that has made him one of the leading American novelists and essayists of his generation. A number of his novels deal with religion, including Messiah *(1954), a futuristic satire about a new Messiah manufactured on Madison Avenue;* Julian *(1964), a sympathetic portrayal of the Roman emperor who attempted to halt the spread of Christianity;* Creation *(1981), an atheistic parable with the Greek philosopher Democritus as its protagonist; and the pungent religious satire* Live from Golgotha *(1992). Vidal's many essays and reviews have been gathered in several volumes, most notably the omnibus* United States: Essays 1952–1992 *(1993). In the following essay, first published in the* Nation *for July 13, 1992, Vidal urges "an all-out war" on the supporters of monotheistic religions, who are striving to restrict the principles of freedom upon which the United States was founded.*

T HE WORD "RADICAL" DERIVES FROM the Latin word for root. Therefore, if you want to get to the root of *anything* you must be radical. It is no accident that the word has now been totally demonized by our masters, and no one in politics dares even to use the word favorably, much less track any problem to its root. But then a ruling class that has been able to demonize the word "liberal" is a master at controlling—indeed stifling—any criticism of itself. "Liberal" comes from the Latin *liberalis*, which means pertaining to a free man. In politics, to be liberal is to want to extend democracy through change and reform. One can see why that word had to be erased from our political lexicon.

Meanwhile, the word "isolationist" has been revived to describe those who would like to put an end to the national security state that replaced our Republic a half-century ago while extending the American military empire far beyond our capacity to pay for it. The word was trotted out in the presidential election of 1992 to describe one Pat Buchanan, who was causing great distress to the managers of our national security state by saying that America must abandon the empire if we are ever to repair the mess at home. Also, as a neo-isolationist, Buchanan must be made to seem an anti-Semite. This is not hard to do. Buchanan is a classic Archie Bunker type, seething with irrational prejudices and resentments, whose origin I'll get to presently.

The country is now dividing, as it did a half-century ago, between those who think that America comes first versus those who favor empire and the continued exertion of force everywhere in the name of democracy, something not much on display here at home. In any case, as the whole world is, more or less, a single economic unit in which the United States is an ever smaller component, there are no isolationists today. But the word games go on and the deliberate reversals of meaning are always a sign that our corporate masters are worried that the people are beginning to question their arrangements. Many things are now coming into focus. The *New York Times* promptly dismissed Buchanan as a minor irritant, which was true, but it ignored his potentially major constituency—those who now believe that it was a mistake to have wasted, since 1950, most of the government's revenues on war.

Another candidate, Jerry Brown, alarmed the *Times* even more than Buchanan did. There was the possibility that he could be elected. More important, he might actually change our politics in the sense of who pays for whom. In a sudden frenzy, the *Times* compared him to Péron—our Jerry?—a dangerous demagogue whose "sharp-edged anger . . . resonates among a variety of Americans." Plainly, the ownership of the country is frightened that the current hatred of politicians, in general, may soon be translated into a hatred of that corporate few who control the many through Opinion, as manufactured by the *Times*, among others.

Now to the root of the matter. The great unmentionable evil at the center of our culture is monotheism. From a barbaric Bronze Age text known as the Old Testament, three antihuman religions have evolved—Judaism, Christianity and Islam. These are sky-god religions. They are, literally, patriarchal—God is the omnipotent father—hence the loathing of women for 2,000 years in those countries afflicted by the sky-god and his earthly male delegates. The sky-god is a jealous god, of course. He requires total obedience from everyone on earth, as he is in place not just for one tribe but for all creation. Those who would reject him must be converted or killed for their own good. Ultimately, totalitarianism is the only sort of politics that can truly serve the sky-god's purpose. Any movement of a liberal nature endangers his authority and that of his delegates on earth. One God, one King, one Pope, one master in the factory, one father-leader in the family at home.

The founders of the United States were not enthusiasts of the sky-god. Many, like Jefferson, rejected him altogether and placed man at the center of the world. The young Lincoln wrote a pamphlet *against* Christianity, which friends persuaded him to burn. Needless to say, word got around about both Jefferson and Lincoln and each had to cover his tracks. Jefferson said that he was a deist, which could mean anything or nothing, while Lincoln, hand on heart and tongue in cheek, said he could not support for office anyone who "scoffed" at religion.

From the beginning, sky-godders have always exerted great pressure in our secular republic. Also, evangelical Christian groups have traditionally drawn strength from the suppressed. African slaves were allowed to organize heavenly sky-god churches, as a surrogate for earthly freedom. White churches were organized in order to make certain that the rights of property were respected and that the numerous religious taboos in the New and Old Testaments would be enforced, if necessary, by civil law. The ideal to which John Adams subscribed—that we would be a nation of laws, not of men—was quickly subverted when the churches forced upon everyone, through supposedly neutral and just laws, their innumerable taboos on sex, alcohol, gambling. We are now indeed a nation of laws, mostly bad and certainly antihuman.

Roman Catholic migrations in the last century further reinforced the Puritan sky-god. The Church has also put itself on a collision course with the Bill of Rights when it asserts, as it always has, that "error has no rights." The last correspondence between John Adams and Thomas Jefferson expressed their alarm that the Jesuits were to be allowed into the United States. Although the Jews were sky-god folk, they followed Book One, not Book Two, so they have no mission to convert others; rather the reverse. Also, as they have been systematically demonized by the Christian sky-godders, they tended to be liberal and so turned not to their temple but to the ACLU. Unfortunately, the recent discovery that the sky-god, in his capacity as realtor, had given them, in perpetuity, some parcels of unattractive land called Judea and Samaria has, to my mind, unhinged many of them. I hope this is temporary.

In the First Amendment to the Constitution the Founders made it clear that this was not to be a sky-god nation with a national religion like that of England, from whom we had just separated. It is curious how little understood this amendment is—yes, everyone has a right to worship any god he chooses but he does *not* have the right to impose his beliefs on others who do not happen to share in his superstitions and taboos. This separation was absolute in our original Republic. But the sky-godders do not give up easily. During the Civil War, they actually got the phrase "In God We Trust" onto the currency, in direct violation of the First Amendment, while "Under God" was added to the Oath of Allegiance under Eisenhower.

Although many of the Christian evangelists feel it necessary to convert everyone on earth to their primitive religion, they have been prevented—so far—from forcing others to worship as they do, but they *have* forced—most tyrannically and wickedly—their superstitions and hatreds upon all of us through the civil law and through general prohibitions. So it is upon that account that I now favor an all-out war on the monotheists.

Let us dwell upon the evils they have wrought. The hatred of blacks comes straight from their Bad Book. As descendants of Ham (according to Redneck divines), blacks are forever accursed, while Saint Paul tells the slaves to obey their masters. Racism is in the marrow of the bone of the true believer. For him, black is forever inferior to white and deserves whatever ill fortune may come his way. The fact that some monotheists can behave charitably means, often, that their prejudice is at so deep a level that they are not aware it is there at all. In the end, this makes any radical change of attitude impossible. Meanwhile, welfare has been the price the sky-godders were willing to pay to exclude blacks from their earthly political system. So we must live—presumably forever—with a highly enervating race war, set in train by the One God and his many hatreds.

Patriarchal rage at the thought of Woman ever usurping Man's place at the helm, in either home or workplace, is almost as strong now as it ever was, while the ongoing psychopathic hatred of same-sexuality has made the United States the laughingstock of the civilized world. After all, in most of the First World, monotheism is weak. Where it is weak or nonexistent, private sexual behavior has nothing at all to do with those not involved, much less with the law. At least when the Emperor Justinian, a sky-god man, decided to outlaw sodomy, he had to come up with a good *practical* reason, which he did. It is well known, Justinian declared, that buggery is a principal cause of earthquakes, and so must be prohibited. But our sky-godders, always eager to hate, still quote Leviticus, as if that loony text had anything useful to say about anything except, perhaps, the inadvisability of eating shellfish in the Jerusalem area.

We are now, slowly, becoming alarmed at the state of the planet. For a century, we have been breeding like a virus under optimum conditions, and now the virus has begun to attack its host, the earth. The lower atmosphere is filled with dust, we have just been told from our satellites in space. Climate changes; earth and water are poisoned. Sensible people grow alarmed; sky-godders are serene, even smug. The planet is just a staging area for heaven. Why bother to clean it up? Did not the sky-god tell his slaves to "be fruitful and multiply, and replenish the earth, and subdue it, and have dominion . . . over every living thing that moveth upon the earth." Well, we did just like you told us, massa. We've used everything up. We're ready for heaven now. Or maybe Mars will do.

Ordinarily, as a descendant of the eighteenth-century Enlightenment, which shaped our Republic, I would say live and let live and I would try not to "scoff"—to use Lincoln's verb—at the monotheists. But I am not allowed to ignore them. They won't let me. They are too busy. They have a divine mission to take away our rights as private citizens. We are forbidden abortion here, gambling there, same-sex almost everywhere, drugs, alcohol in a dry county. Our prisons are the most terrible and the most crowded in the First World. Our death-row executions are a source of deep disgust in civilized countries, where more and more we are regarded as a primitive, uneducated and dangerous people. Although we are not allowed, under law, to kill ourselves or to take drugs that the good folk think might be bad for us, we are allowed to buy a handgun and shoot as many people as we can get away with.

Of course, as poor Arthur (There Is This Pendulum) Schlesinger Jr. would say, these things come in cycles. Every twenty years liberal gives way to conservative, and back again. But I suggest that what is wrong now is not cyclic but systemic. And our system, like any system, is obeying the second law of thermodynamics. Everything is running down; and we are well advanced along the cold, dusty road to entropy. I don't think much of anything can be done to halt this progress under our present political-economic system. We lost poor Arthur's pendulum in 1950 when our original Constitution was secretly replaced with the apparatus of that national security state, which still wastes most of our tax money on war or war-related matters. Hence deteriorating schools, and so on.

Another of our agreed-upon fantasies is that we do not have a class system in the United States. The Few who control the Many through Opinion have simply made themselves invisible. They have convinced us that we are a classless society in which anyone can make it. Ninety percent of the stories in the pop press are about winners of lotteries or poor boys and girls who, despite adenoidal complaints, become overnight millionaire singers. So there is still hope, the press tells the folks, for the 99 percent who will never achieve wealth no matter how hard they work. We are also warned at birth that it is not polite to hurt people's feelings by criticizing their religion, even if that religion may be damaging everyone through the infiltration of our common laws.

Happily, the few cannot disguise the bad times through which we are all going. Word is spreading that America is now falling behind in the civilization sweepstakes. So isn't it time to discuss what we all really think and feel about our social and economic arrangements?

Although we may not discuss race other than to say that Jesus wants each and every one of us for a sunbeam, history is nothing more than the bloody record of the migration of tribes. When the white race broke out of Europe five hundred years ago, it did many astounding things all over the globe. Inspired by a raging sky-god, the whites were able to pretend that their conquests were in order to bring the One God to everyone, particularly those with older and subtler religions. Now the tribes are on the move again. Professor Pendulum is having a nervous breakdown because so many different tribes are now being drawn to this sweet land of liberty and, thus far, there is no indication that any of the new arrivals intends ever to read *The Age of Jackson*. I think the taking in of everyone can probably be overdone. There may not be enough jobs for very many more immigrants, though what prosperity we have ever enjoyed in the past was usually based on slave or near-slave labor.

On the other hand, I think Asians and Hispanics are a plus cultur-ally, and their presence tends to refocus, somewhat, the relentless white versus black war. Where I *am* as one with friend Pendulum is that the newcomers must grasp certain principles as expressed in the Declara-tion of Independence and the Bill of Rights. Otherwise, we shall become a racially divided totalitarian state enjoying a Brazilian economy.

To revert to the unmentionable, religion. It should be noted that religion seemed to be losing its hold in the United States in the second quarter of this century. From the Scopes trial in 1925 to the repeal of Prohibition in 1933, the sky-godders were confined pretty much to the backwoods. Then television was invented and the electronic pulpit was soon occupied by a horde of Elmer Gantrys, who took advantage of the tax exemption for religion. Thus, out of greed, a religious revival has been set in motion and the results are predictably poisonous to the body politic.

It is usual, on the rare occasions when essential problems are addressed, to exhort everyone to be kinder, gentler. To bring us together, O Lord, in our common humanity. Well, we have heard these exhorta-tions for a couple of hundred years and we are further apart than ever. So instead of coming together in order that the many might be one, I say let us separate so that each will know where he stands. From the *one*, *many*, and each of us free of the sky-god as secular lawgiver. I preach, to put it bluntly, confrontation.

Whether Brown and Buchanan knew it or not, they were revealing two basic, opposing political movements. Buchanan speaks for the party of God—the sky-god with his terrible hatred of women, blacks, gays, drugs, abortion, contraception, gambling—you name it, he hates it. Buchanan is a worthy peddler of hate. He is also in harmony not only with the prejudices and superstitions of a good part of the popu-lation but, to give him his due, he is a reactionary in the good sense—reacting against the empire in favor of the old Republic, which he mis-takenly thinks was Christian.

Brown speaks for the party of man—feminists can find another noun if they like. Thomas Paine, when asked *his* religion, said he sub-scribed only to the religion of humanity. There now seems to be a polarizing of the country of a sort that has never happened before. The potential fault line has always been there, but whenever a politician got too close to the facts of our case, the famed genius of the system would eliminate him in favor of that mean which is truly golden for the own-ership, and no one else. The party of man would like to re-establish a representative government firmly based upon the Bill of Rights. The party of God will have none of this. It wants to establish, through legal prohibitions and enforced taboos, a sky-god totalitarian state. The United States ultimately as prison, with mandatory blood, urine and lie-detector tests and with the sky-godders as the cops, answerable only to God.

For once, it's all out there, perfectly visible, perfectly plain for those who can see. For the first time in 140 years, we now have the outline of two parties. Each knows the nature of its opposite, and those who are wise will not try to accommodate or compromise the two but will let them, at last, confront each other.

Jefferson's famous tree of liberty is all that we have ever really had. Now, for want of nurture—the blood of tyrants and of patriots—it is dying before our eyes. Of course, the sky-god never liked it. But some of us did—and some of us do. So, perhaps, through facing who and what we are, we may achieve a nation not under God but under man—or should I say our common humanity?

PART 8

RELIGION
AND SOCIETY

I do not believe that Christianity holds anything more of importance for the world. It is finished, played out. The only trouble lies in how to get rid of the body before it begins to smell too much.

—John Beevers
World without Faith (1935)

29

THE CHRISTIAN CHURCH AND WOMAN
(1885)

Elizabeth Cady Stanton

Elizabeth Cady Stanton (1815–1902) espoused numerous social and political causes in her long life, including temperance and abolition, but has gained especial renown for her pioneering work in promoting women's rights. With Lucretia Mott, she organized the first conference on women's rights in 1848. She met Susan B. Anthony in 1851, and for the next half-century they were in the forefront of the women's movement. They established the National Woman Suffrage Association in 1869, and Stanton was for many years its president. Among her voluminous writings are the multi-volume History of Woman Suffrage *(1881–86), coedited with Anthony, and the highly controversial* The Woman's Bible *(1895–98), in which Stanton and others wrote commentaries on various books of the Bible from a woman's point of view. (Many scholars refused to participate in the project for fear of criticizing the Bible.) Stanton saw religion is a significant barrier to the establishment of women's legal, political, and social equality with men. In the following essay, taken from her pamphlet,* Bible and Church Degrade Woman *(1885), Stanton, although making a distinction between the teachings of Christ and later developments in Christianity, asserts bluntly that "the Church has done more to degrade woman than all other adverse influences put together" and that the church remains an obstacle to women's search for equality with men.*

From Elizabeth Cady Stanton, "The Christian Church and Woman," in *Bible and Church Degrade Woman* (Chicago: H. L. Green, [1885]), pp. 11–20.

THE GRAND IDEAS OF CONFUCIUS, Zoroaster, Buddha, Mohammed, Jesus, have been slowly transforming the world from the reign of brute force to moral power, and science has been as slowly emancipating mankind from their fears of the unknown; but the Christian Church has steadily used its influence against progress, science, the education of the masses and freedom for woman. It is often asserted that woman owes all the advantages of the position she occupies to-day to Christianity, but the facts of history show that the Christian Church has done nothing specifically for woman's elevation. In the general march of civilization she has necessarily reaped the advantage of man's higher development; but we must not claim for Christianity all that has been achieved by science, discovery and invention.

If we admit that the truth it has taught, as an offset to its many errors, has been one of the factors in civilization, we shall concede all that can be fairly claimed. The prolonged slavery of woman is the darkest page in human history; and she has touched the depths of misery since in Bethlehem the Magi gathered round the child in the manger, who was hailed as the Savior of mankind. But the life and teachings of Jesus, all pointing to the complete equality of the human family, were too far in advance of his age to mould its public opinion. We must distinguish between the teachings attributed to Jesus and those of the Christian Church. One represents the ideal the race is destined to attain; the other, the popular sentiment of its time.

Had Jesus lived in Russia in the nineteenth century, he would have been exiled as a Nihilist for his protests against tyranny and his sympathy with the suffering masses. He would have been driven from Germany as a socialist, from France as a communist, and imprisoned as a blasphemer in England and America, had he taught in London and New York the radical ideas he proclaimed in Palestine.

I speak of the Christian Church, Catholic and Protestant, of the priesthood, the bulls of its popes, the decrees of its councils, the articles and resolutions of its general assemblies, presbyteries, synods, conferences, which, all summed up, compose the canon law, which has held Christendom during what are called the Dark Ages until now under its paralyzing influence, moulding civil law and social customs and plunging woman into absolute slavery.

The worst features of the canon law reveal themselves to-day in woman's condition as clearly as they did fifteen hundred years ago. The clergy in their pulpits teach the same doctrines in regard to her from the same texts, and echo the same old platitudes and false ideas promulgated for centuries by ecclesiastical councils. According to Church teaching, woman was an after-thought in the creation, the author of sin, being at once in collusion with Satan. Her sex was made a crime; marriage a condition of slavery, owing obedience; maternity a curse; and the true position of all womankind one of inferiority and subjection to all men; and the same ideas are echoed in our pulpits to-day.

England and America are the two nations in which the Christian religion is dominant; yet, by their ethics taught in the pulpit, the ideal woman is comparatively more degraded than in pagan nations. I say comparatively, for, because of the various steps of progress in education, science, invention and art, woman is now more fully the equal of man in these countries than in any other nation or period of the world. And yet the old ideas taught by the Church in the Dark Ages of her inferiority and depravity are still maintained; and, just in proportion as women are the equals of the men by their side, the more keenly they feel every invidious distinction based on sex. To those not conversant with the history of the Christian Church and the growth of the canon law, it may seem a startling assertion; but it is, nevertheless, true that the Church has done more to degrade woman than all other adverse influences put together. And it has done this by playing the religious emotions (the strongest feelings of her nature) to her own complete subjugation. The same religious conscience that carried the widows to the funeral pyre of their husbands now holds some women in the Turkish seraglios, others in polygamy under the Mormon theocracy, and others in the Christian churches, in which, while rich women help to build and support them, they may not speak or vote or enjoy any of the honors conferred on men, and all alike are taught that their degradation is of divine ordination, and thus their natural feelings of self-respect are held in abeyance to what they are taught to believe is God's will. Out of the doctrine of original sin grew the crimes and miseries of asceticism, celibacy, and witchcraft, woman becoming the helpless victim of all the delusions generated in the brain of man.

Having decided that she was the author of sin and the medium through whom the devil would effect the downfall of the Church, godly men logically inferred that the greater the distance from themselves and all womankind, the nearer they were to God and heaven. With this idea, they fought against all woman's influence, both good and evil. At one period, they crucified all natural affections for mother, sister, wife and daughter, and continued a series of persecutions that blackened the centuries with the most horrible crimes.

This more than any other one influence was the cause of that general halt in civilization, that retrogressive movement of the Dark Ages, for which no historian has satisfactorily accounted. At no period of the world was the equilibrium of the masculine and feminine elements of humanity so disturbed. The result was moral chaos—just what would occur in the material world, if it were possible to destroy the equilibrium of the positive and negative electricity or of the centripetal and centrifugal force.

For the supposed crimes of heresy and witchcraft hundreds of women endured such persecutions and tortures that the most stolid historians are said to have wept in recording them; and no one can read them to-day but with a bleeding heart. And, as the Christian Church grew stronger, woman's fate grew more helpless. Even the Reformation and Protestantism brought no relief, the clergy being all along their most bitter persecutors, the inventors of the most infernal tortures. Hundreds and hundreds of fair young girls, innocent as the angels in heaven, hundreds and hundreds of old women, weary and trembling with the burdens of life, were hunted down by emissaries of the Church, dragged into the courts, with the ablest judges and lawyers of England, Scotland and America on the bench, and tried for crimes that never existed but in the wild, fanatical imaginations of religious devotees. Women were accused of consorting with devils and perpetuating their diabolical propensities. Hundreds of these children of hypothetical origin were drowned, burned and tortured in the presence of their mothers, to add to their death agonies. These things were not done by savages or pagans; they were done by the Christian Church. Neither were they confined to the Dark Ages, but permitted by law in England far into the eighteenth century. The clergy everywhere sustained witchcraft as Bible doctrine, until the spirit of rationalism laughed the whole thing to scorn, and science gave mankind a more cheerful view of life.

So large a place as the nature and position of woman occupied in the councils of the Church that the Rev. Charles Kingsley facetiously remarked that the Christian Church was swamped by hysteria from the third to the sixteenth century. Speaking of witchcraft, Lecky says the

Reformation was the signal for a fresh outburst of the superstition in England; and there, as elsewhere, its decline was represented by the clergy as the direct consequence and the exact measure of the progress of religious skepticism. In Scotland, where the reformed ministers exercised greater influence than in any other country, and where the witch trials fell almost entirely into their hands, the persecution was proportionately atrocious. Preobably the ablest defender of the belief was Glanvil, a clergyman of the English Establishment; and one of the most influential was Baxter, the greatest of the Puritans.[1] It spread with Puritanism into the New World, and the executions in Massachusetts form one of the darkest pages in American history. The greatest religious leader of the last century, John Wesley, was among the latest of its supporters. He said giving up witchcraft was giving up the Bible. Skepticism on the subject of witches first arose among those who were least governed by the Church, advanced with the decline of the influence of the clergy, and was commonly branded by them as a phase of infidelity.

One remarkable fact stands out in the history of witchcraft; and that is, its victims were chiefly women. Scarce one wizard to a hundred witches was ever burned or tortured.

Although the ignorance and crimes of the race have ever fallen most heavily on woman, yet in the general progress of civilization she has had some share. As man became more enlightened, she of necessity enjoyed the results; but to no form of popular religion has woman ever been indebted for one pulsation of liberty. Obedience and subjection have been the lessons taught her by all alike.

Lecky, in his *History of Rationalism* and his *European Morals*, gives facts sufficient to convince any woman of common sense that the greatest obstacle in the way of the freedom and elevation of her sex has been, and is, the teaching of the Church in regard to her rights and duties. Women have ever been the chief victims in the persecutions of the Church amid all its awful tragedies, and on them have fallen the heaviest penalties of the canon law.

But the canon law did not confine itself to social relations; it laid its hand with withering touch on the civil law, and blighted many personal and property rights accorded woman under the Roman Code.

Speaking of the Roman Code before the introduction of Christianity (Gaius), Maine[2] says: "The jurisconsults had evidently at this time assumed the equality of the sexes as a principle to the code of equity. The situation of the Roman woman, whether married or single, became one of great personal and property independence, but Christianity tended somewhat from the very first to narrow this remarkable liberty. The prevailing state of religious sentiment may explain why modern jurisprudence has adopted these rules concerning the position of woman, which belong peculiarly to an imperfect civilization. No society which preserves any tincture of Christian institutions is likely to restore to married women the personal liberty conferred on them by middle Roman law. Canon law has deeply injured civilization."

Rev. Charles Kingsley[3] says: "Whoever wishes to gain insight into that great institution, Canon Law, can do so most effectively by studying Common Law in regard to woman. There will never be a good world for woman until the last remnant of Canon Law is civilized off the face of the earth. Meanwhile, all the most pure and high-minded women in England and Europe have been brought up under the shadow of the Canon Law, and have accepted it, with the usual divine self-sacrifice, as their destiny by law of God and nature, and consider their own womanhood outraged, when it, their tyrant, is meddled with." Women accept their position under the shadow of the canon law for the best of reasons—they know nothing about it. And, if they should undertake to explore it, they would waste their lives in the effort.

This is one of the peculiarities of woman's position; she knows nothing of the laws, either canon or civil, under which she lives; and such churchmen as the Rev. Morgan Dix[4] are determined she never shall. Nero was thought the chief of tyrants because he made laws and hung them up so high the people could not read them.

As the result of the canon law, what is woman's position in the State and the Church to-day? We have woman disenfranchised, with no voice in the government under which she lives, denied until recently the right to enter colleges or professions, laboring at half-price in the world of work; a code of morals that makes man's glory woman's shame; a civil code that makes her in marriage a nonentity, her person, her children, her earnings the property of her husband. In adjusting this institution of marriage, woman has never yet in the history of the world had one word to say. The relation has been absolutely established and perpetuated without her consent. We have thus far had the man marriage. He has made all the laws concerning it to suit his own convenience and love of power. He has tried every possible form of it, and is as yet satisfied with none of his experiments. If an inhabitant of some other planet could suddenly light in one of our law libraries, and read over our civil and criminal codes, he would be at a loss to know what kind of beings women are, so anomalous is the position we hold, with some rights partially recognized in one place and wholly obliterated in another. In the criminal code, we find no feminine pronouns. All criminals are designated as "he," "his," "him." We might suppose our fathers thought women were too pure and angelic ever to commit crimes, if we did not find in the law reports, cases in which women had been imprisoned and hung as "he," "his," "him." And yet, when it comes to privileges we are excluded, because the laws and constitutions do not contain the feminine pronouns "she," "hers," "her." We are a kind of half human, half animal being, like those wonderful questioning sphinxes we see in the Old World.

And we present very much the same appearance in the Church. Go into any little country town, and the chief excitement among the women is found in fairs, donation parties, festivals, church building and decorating. The women are the chief, untiring, pertinacious beggars for the church. They compose the vast majority of the congregation. Rich women give large sums to clear church debts, to educate young men for the ministry, and to endow theological seminaries. Poorer women decorate the temples for Christmas and Easter, make surplices and gowns, embroider table covers for the altar, and slippers for the rector; and all alike think they are serving God in sustaining the church and the priesthood.

In return, the whole tone of Church teaching in regard to woman is, to the last degree, contemptuous and degrading.

Perchance the very man educated by some sewing society of women will ascend the pulpit, and take his text in 1 Corinthians xiv. 34, 35: "Let your women keep silence in the churches; for it is not permitted unto them to speak; but they are commanded to be under obedience, as also saith the law. And if they will learn anything, let them ask their husbands at home, for it is a shame for women to speak in the church." Ephesians v. 23: "Wives, submit yourselves unto your own husbands, as unto the Lord. For the husband is the head of the wife, even as Christ is the head of the Church." 1 Timothy ii. 11, 12, 13: "Let the women learn in silence with all subjection. But I suffer not a woman to teach nor to usurp authority over the man. . . . For Adam was first formed, then Eve." 1 Corinthians xi, 8, 9: "For the man is not of the woman, but the woman of the man. Neither was the man created for the woman but the woman for the man."

In all the great cathedrals in England and in some here in New York, boys from ten to fifteen chant the hymns of praise that woman's lips may not profane, while they, oblivious to these insults to their sex, swell the listening crowd, and worship the very God who they are told made them slaves, and cursed them with sufferings that time can never mitigate.

While in England, I visited the birthplace of Dean Stanley.[5] The old homestead was occupied by a curate and his two daughters. They escorted us all over the place—in the school where poor children were taught, in the old church where the dean had long preached. "Do you see that table cover in the altar?" said one of the daughters. "Sister and I worked that." "Did you spread it on the table?" said I. "Oh, no," said she; "no woman is allowed to enter this enclosure." "Why?" said I. "Oh! it is too sacred." "But," said I, "men go there; and it is said that women are purer, more delicate, refined, and naturally religious than they are." "Yes, but women are not allowed." "Shall I explain the reason to you?" I replied. "Yes," she said, with a look of surprise. "Well," said I, "it is because the Church believes that woman brought sin into the world, that she was the cause of man's fall from holiness, that she was cursed of God, and has ever since been in collusion with the devil. Hence, the Church has considered her unfit to sing in the choir or enter the Holy of Holies." She looked very thoughtful, and said, "I never supposed these old customs had such significance." "Yes," I replied, "every old custom, every fashion, every point of etiquette, is based on some principle, and women ignorantly submit to many degrading customs, because they do not understand their origin."

These indignities have their root in the doctrine of original sin, gradually developed in the canon law—a doctrine never taught in the primitive Christian Church. In spite of the life, character and teachings of Jesus, ever proclaiming the essential equality and oneness of the whole human family, the priesthood, claiming apostolic descent, so interprets Christianity as to make it the basis of all religious and political disqualifications for women, sustaining the rights of man alone.

The offices woman held during the apostolic age she has been gradually deprived of through ecclesiastical enactments. Although, during the first four hundred years of the Christian Church, women were the chosen companions of Jesus and his followers, doing their utmost to spread the new faith, as preachers, elders, deacons, officiating in all the sacraments, yet these facts are carefully excluded from all the English translations of the Scriptures; while woman's depravity, inferiority and subordination are dwelt upon wherever the text will admit of it. Under all the changes in advancing civilization for the last fifteen hundred years, this one idea of woman has been steadily promulgated; and to-day, in the full blaze of the sunlight of the late years of the nineteenth century, it is echoed in the pulpit by nearly every sect and in the halls of legislation by political leaders.

Whatever oppressions man has suffered, they have invariably fallen more heavily on woman. Whatever new liberties advancing civilization has brought to man, ever the smallest measure has been accorded to woman, as a result of church teaching. The effect of this is seen in every department of life.

There is nothing so cheap as womanhood in the commerce of the world. You can scarcely take up a paper that does not herald some outrage on woman, from the dignified matron on her way to church to the girl of fourteen gathering wild flowers on her way to school. I hold men in high places responsible for the actions of the lower orders. The sentiments and opinions expressed by clergymen and legislators mould the morals of the highway. So long as the Church and the State, in their creeds and codes, make woman an outcast, she will be the sport of the multitudes. Whatever can be done to dignify her in the eyes of man will be a shield and helmet for her protection. If the same respect the masses are educated to feel for cathedrals, altars, symbols and sacraments was extended to the mothers of the race, as it should be, all these distracting problems, in which their interests are involved, would be speedily settled. You cannot go so low down in the scale of being as to find men who would enter our churches to desecrate the altars or toss about the emblem of the sacrament, because they have been educated with a holy reverence for these things. But where are any lessons of reverence for woman taught to the multitude?

And yet is she not, as the mother of the race, more exalted than sacraments, symbols, altars, and vast cathedral domes? Are not the eternal principles of justice engraven on her heart more sacred than canons, creeds and codes written on parchment by Jesuits, bishops, cardinals and popes? Yet where shall we look for lessons of honor and respect to her?

Do our sons in the law schools rise from their studies of the invidious statutes and opinions of jurists in regard to women with a higher respect for their mothers? By no means. Every line of the old common law of England on which the American system of jurisprudence is based, touching the interests of woman, is, in a measure, responsible for the wrongs she suffers to-day.

Do our sons in their theological seminaries rise from their studies of the Bible, and the popular commentaries on the passages of Scripture concerning woman's creation and position in the scale of being, with an added respect for their mothers? By no means. They come ofttimes fresh from the perusal of what they suppose to be God's will and law, fresh from communion with the unseen, perhaps with the dew of inspiration on their lips, to preach anew the subjection of one-half the race to the other.

A very striking fact, showing the outrages women patiently endure through the perversion of their religious sentiments by crafty priests, is seen in the treatment of the Hindu widow, the civil law in her case, as in so many others, being practically annulled by theological dogmas.

"The most liberal of the Hindu schools of jurisprudence,"[6] says Maine, "that prevailing in Bengal proper, gives a childless widow the enjoyment of her husband's property under certain restrictive conditions during her life;" and in this it agrees with many bodies of unwritten local custom. If there are male children, they succeed at once; but if there are none the widow comes in for her life before the collateral relatives. At the present moment, marriages among the upper classes of Hindus being very commonly infertile, a considerable portion of the soil of the wealthiest Indian provinces is in the hands of childless widows as tenants for life. But it was exactly in Bengal proper that the English, on entering India, found the suttee, or widow-burning, not merely an occasional, but a constant and almost universal practice with the wealthier classes; and, as a rule, it was only the childless widow, and never the widow with minor children, who burnt herself on her husband's funeral pyre. There is no question that there was the closest connection between the law and the religious custom; and the widow was made to sacrifice herself, in order that her tenancy for life might be gotten rid of. The anxiety of her family that the rite should be performed, which seemed so striking to the first English observers of the practice, was in fact explained by the coarsest motives; but the Brahmins who exhorted her to the sacrifice were undoubtedly influenced by a purely professional dislike to her enjoyment of property. The ancient rule of the civil law, which made her a tenant for life, could not be gotten rid of; but it was combated by the modern institution, which made it her duty to devote herself to a frightful death. The reasoning on this subject, current even in comparatively ancient times, is thus given in the Mitakshava: "The wealth of a regenerate man is designed for religious uses; and a woman's succession to such property is unfit, because she is not competent to the performance of religious rites." Thus the liberal provisions of the civil law were disposed of by burning the widow, and she was made willing for the sacrifice by a cultivated sense of religious duty. What is true in this case is true of women in all ages. They have been trained by their religion to sacrifice themselves, body and soul, for the men of their families and to build up the churches. We do not burn the bodies of women to-day; but we humiliate them in a thousand ways, and chiefly by our theologies. So long as the pulpits teach woman's inferiority and subjection, she can never command that honor and respect of the ignorant classes needed for her safety and protection. There is nothing more pathetic in all history than the hopeless resignation of woman to the outrages she has been taught to believe are ordained of God.

NOTES

1. [Joseph Glanvill (1636–1680), British religious philosopher who in *Saducismus Triumphatus* (1681) defended belief in witchcraft. Richard Baxter (1615–1691), British Puritan and author of *The Saints' Everlasting Rest* (1650).]

2. [Sir Henry Maine (1822–1888), British legal historian and author of *Ancient Law* (1861), from which Stanton here quotes.]

3. [Charles Kingsley (1819–1875), Anglican divine, novelist (*Westward Ho!*, 1855), and proponent of "muscular Christianity."]

4. [Morgan Dix (1827–1908), American theologian (Episcopal), rector of Trinity parish in New York City (1862-1908), and prolific writer on religious subjects. Stanton probably refers to his *Lectures on the Calling of a Christian Woman* (1883).]

5. [Arthur Penrhyn Stanley (1815–1881), Anglican divine, Dean of Westminster (1864–81), and one of the most influential clergymen of his time.]

6. *Early History of Institutions*, Lecture XI., on the Property of Married Women.

30

THE PRIEST
AND THE CHILD
(1895?)

J. M. Robertson

John Mackinnon Robertson (1856–1933) was one of the leading free-thinkers and essayists of his day. A largely self-educated Scotsman, he began working for the Edinburgh Evening News *in 1878, where his articles on religion came to the attention of Charles Bradlaugh, who hired him for his* National Reformer. *Robertson edited that paper for two years following Bradlaugh's death in 1891. He was a member of Parliament from 1906 to 1918. A prolific author, Robertson wrote highly regarded works of literary criticism (*Essays toward a Critical Method, *1889;* Modern Humanists, *1891;* An Introduction to the Study of Shakespeare Canon, *1924), politics (*The Evolution of States, *1912), and numerous works attacking religious orthodoxy (*The Dynamics of Religion, *1897;* Christianity and Mythology, *1900) as well as the landmark* History of Freethought in the Nineteenth Century *(1929). In the following pamphlet, issued in the 1890s, Robertson uses a controversy between the Anglican Church and the Nonconformists (Protestant sects outside the Church of England) as a springboard for asserting the perniciousness of religious indoctrination in public schools. Robertson maintains that such a practice is intended merely to make converts for the religious sects, and also argues that religious morality (as represented in the Ten Commandments) is a relic of "ancient barbarism."*

From J. M. Robertson, *The Priest and the Child* (Bradford, UK: Truth Seeker Co., [1895?]), pp. 2–8.

TWO MIXED RELIGIOUS FACTIONS IN England are fighting afresh, with all the old bitterness, the old battle over the teaching of religion in the public schools. Both sides declare that some such teaching is absolutely necessary for the moral training of children. Anglican and Catholic, Baptist and Wesleyan, Independent and Unitarian, all assure us that without Bible teaching of some sort children cannot be made good citizens. But at the same time the Catholic also teaches that the others are heretics living in sin, while each of the other sects believes that all the rest are in "darkness" and "error" on some point. All stand for "religion," but no two sects can agree as to what religion is. All alike claim to stand on the same "divine revelation," but no two tell the same story of what the revelation reveals. All assert that the Christian religion is a doctrine of peace and brotherly love; but not for one day can they work or teach together in harmony. And these futile wranglers are the men who in a body claim to be listened to as infallible judges of the proper means of bringing up children.

Let us not do them injustice. They can combine for certain purposes. We see them at it. On one side are ranged the English Church and the Roman Catholics—old enemies leagued together against other enemies. On the other side are grouped the Baptists, Methodists, Congregationalists, Unitarians and the rest, all opposed to each other, but all opposed more bitterly to the Church of England and to the Church of Rome, which stands behind and begins to overshadow it. They all say that Christ died for all men, and that children must be told so; but the dissenters cannot endure that the telling should be done in the formulas of the Church of England; and the Church of England cannot endure that it should be done in any other way. That is the formal gist of the dispute. It follows that devout dissenters do not believe the Church catechism makes children good citizens, and that devout Churchmen do not believe that they can be made so by any other catechism. Some of us believe that both sides easily prove their point so far, but the rulers of the Church of Rome professedly believe the same thing, and still their organisation supports the policy of the Church of England. Why? It is not difficult to hit the answer, but it is as well to work it out in full.

Over twenty years ago the same two coalitions, fighting on the same point, came to what was called a compromise, as to what religious instruction should be given in the schools. A compromise is usually understood to be an arrangement of a dispute in which both sides give up something. But it would be hard to say what was given up in this case by the Nonconformists. They secured that the Bible should be read, and that certain general religious teaching should be given in the schools, which is all that, as a body, they could possibly ask for, and a great deal more than they could ask for without belying their own principles. No sect among them could consent to let special doctrines of any other sect be taught in the public schools. The utmost that they could collectively ask for was exactly what they got. All the "compromising" was done by the Church of England, the purpose of whose existence is to impose its special system on as many English people as possible, but who in this matter was treated merely as one sect among others. If that arrangement were to hold good, the Church of England, as a national church, had no logical footing left. If she is only a sect like another, her title is a farce and her endowment is a fraud. Naturally her leaders, seeing a growing disestablishment movement on the other side, have decided to meet the enemy outside the gates. Claiming to represent a national church, they naturally strive to dominate the national schools, since the other sects insist on having a footing there. The fight for the schools is part of the fight for establishment and endowment. And it is for these things, first and last, that all churches fight, the dissenting as well as the established. For it is a law of religious history, a simple and obvious law, though people contrive to talk a great deal on the subject without once putting it plainly—that *churches fight, not as creed-holders but as corporations, for their corporate interests.* The creed is the pretext, the ground of division, and at the start it may very well have been set up without any thought of money interest; but once the church is built on the creed, it is a corporation like another, a sort of priests' trade union, standing for the interests of the profession. That is why:

Firstly—All the sects alike want to have some of the main Christian doctrines taught in the schools.

Secondly—The Church of England wants to have her own special system imposed on the schools; and

Thirdly—The dissenters cannot endure that she should.

Simple self-interest explains all. It is very plain that, in consistency, Nonconformists have no business to ask for the teaching of religion in the schools at all. They protest that it is wrong to give public money to spread the religious doctrine of any church. Then it must be wrong to give public money for the teaching of any religion in the schools. State endowment is State endowment in either case. If it be a good thing to give State money for the teaching of certain "essentials" of Christian doctrine in the schools, it must be a good thing to endow the teaching of the same essentials by a church. Why do not the Nonconformists propose that? Do they hold that the "essentials" of Christianity are only for children, and the unessentials for adults? They are really too absurd. They tell us that what was taught in the schools under the "compromise" was sufficient to make children good Christians and good citizens. Then why do they run separate churches for the grown-up? If the "compromise" was so satisfactory in the schools, why do they not carry it out in their churches? If it is in their eyes right and necessary that they should maintain their separate churches with their special doctrines, how can it be sufficient to give children only the minimum doctrine remaining when all the special doctrines are left out? They give the lie to their own reasoning, and we must seek for a more rational explanation of their conduct than they offer. The rational explanation has been given above in brief, and may thus be put in full:

> The claims of dissenters are in reality the trade-union claims of the dissenting clergy, whose more devout followers back them up. Clergy and flock alike act in the spirit of self-interested corporations. They feel that if children are not trained to accept Christian doctrines before they can reason for themselves, the chances are ten to one that they will not join *any* church in later life. The dissenting clergy therefore insist that the MAIN Christian doctrines shall be taught in the schools, leaving the churches to compete among themselves for the adherence of the taught when they have left school.

This fact cannot be put too boldly. *The churches are fighting for adherents, for clients, for sources of revenue.* None of them dares to trust to the process of persuading grown men and women. Naturally they declare that they fear to run the risk of letting children grow up without any religious training; and doubtless many members of all churches persuade themselves that there would be a great danger in that. But it is easy to show that they are here humbugging themselves. As has been said above, they all believe, if they are sincere in their professions, that the *grown-up* adherents of other churches are in spiritual danger, because of being in spiritual error. Each believes that all the other churches lead men astray. Then we come back to the old absurdity: either the children taught under the compromise are in temporal and eternal danger, from the point of view of all the sects alike, or they are safe, and it is the sects, with their separate churches and warring creeds, who are gratuitously multiplying error. Either way, the sects are in a complete muddle. We must seek a common sense explanation. When men go on maintaining a nonsensical position, it is because they have some interest in maintaining it. In this case the interest is clear enough. We may agree that it is twofold. First there is the natural interest of opinion—the ordinary wish that our opinion should prevail. We all feel that it would be a sad thing if our opinions should die out. But when it comes to Nonconformists claiming that the State should pay to have some of their opinions taught in the public schools—as many of their opinions as other churches will permit to be taught—then it is clear that the bias of mere opinion is backed up by the more powerful bias of corporate interest. The Nonconformist clergy are thinking of their own incomes, and further of the future revenue of their union. It is with the teaching of religion in the schools as with the opening of museums on Sundays. The clergy in general oppose the Sunday opening of museums, mainly because it encourages people to stay away from church. Of course they put another face on the matter, saying they are concerned for the Sunday rest of the workers or the showing of proper respect for the First Cause—anything but their own interests, their own power, their own pocket; but practical men know what to think of such pleas as these, when put forward by an obviously interested body of men. Some clergymen may be individually sincere, but the corporate body certainly acts for its own interests. So it is with the schools. The clergy all round want religion taught in the public schools in order to breed church-goers; and the Nonconformist clergy, feeling the need even more than the clergy of the establishment, trample under foot their own professed principles in the effort to further their pecuniary ends. When the clergy of the establishment seek to lay *their* hands on the whole system, the Nonconformists are naturally wroth. But the Church is only seeking consistently what the Nonconformists seek inconsistently. It is a quarrel of priests for the possession of one of the sources of priestly power; and the Anglican priesthood are acting openly on their professional principles. It is the Nonconformists who pretend to oppose "sacerdotalism," while seeking to carry their own sacerdotalism as far as it conceivably could ever be carried.

II.

This brings us to the other side of the matter. On the one side stand the churches, fighting first and last for their own interests. On the other side stand the interests of education, the real interests of the children and of the nation—a very different thing. The clergy, it will be observed, never raise any question about education in the proper sense of the term; in the mass, they never trouble themselves on that score. Though nominally an educated class, they seem to have no ideal of education, no concern that children should have any other education than a "religious" one. Now, it is about time that the education question should be considered from the point of view of education, rather than from the point of view of church interests. We want to have the children of the nation educated, and by that we mean that we want them *fitted to live wisely and well*, so far as early training can fit them. Clearly, the essentials of such training are of two main sorts: the children must have certain knowledge, and they must have certain habits. They must have habits of cleanliness, kindliness, truthfulness, honesty and diligence. They ought also to have as much knowledge of a useful kind as can be given them in the time (far too short at present) during which the State keeps them at school. How far then does the present policy of the priesthoods tend to promote these great educational ends? Strictly speaking, hardly at all. On the side of knowledge, the mass of our children are very poorly educated indeed, but the priesthoods make no effort to have them better taught. The priest as a rule would rather have a child badly educated with religion than well educated without. For generations, the Church of England resisted all attempts to educate the children of the poor; then at length, when the pressure had become too strong, her clergy set up their own system of schools, in order to breed adherents for the Church of England. They avow, and the Nonconformists now in effect seem to say the same thing, that in their opinion religious teaching is of far more importance than any other. And they do not merely put this with regard to the "eternal welfare" of the child: they do not merely say that the child's Creator will burn it eternally in brimstone if it grows up and dies without hearing of certain "revelations" once made by him: they say that the religious training they give is the only training by which a child can be made moral.

Is this true? Is it true that the teaching given by priests tends to give children the habits of cleanliness, kindliness, truthfulness, honesty and diligence, which constitute goodness of character in young and old? They have been giving religious instruction for many ages. Has it worked well? Has it promoted peace on earth, kindness and justice between persons, truth in speech, and honesty in trade? Has it tended to empty the jails? Has it restrained vice? Has it made men and nations wise? With the priesthoods themselves forever at strife; with the leading nations of the world casting chronic curses at each other's heads; with millions of civilized men constantly ready for war to the death; with religious hypocrisy and commercial deceit confessedly abounding on all hands; with crime still on the increase and misery never done, what man who thinks for himself can for a moment believe that the claim of the priesthoods is true?

If we do but ask how they set about educating the consciences and forming the habits of children, we can see almost at a glance that they work on false lines. We want to make children rationally good: we want so to train them that they shall knowingly go right. To this end the priest begins by telling them what he calls The Ten Commandments— that they should "worship the Lord their God;" that they should worship no other God; that they should not make unto themselves graven images; that they should do no work on the Sabbath day; that they should honor their parents (as if the parents could not be trusted to see to that at home); that they should not commit murder; that they should not commit adultery; that they should not steal; that they should not covet their neighbour's wife, or his ox, or his ass, or his man-servant, or his maid-servant; and that they should not bear "false witness" against him. Is it possible to imagine a more preposterous set of formulas by way of giving children moral ideas? They cannot realise one in five of the commands laid on them. They have no conception of what "the Lord their God" means. They have no idea whatever of what is meant by worshipping "other Gods." The ancient veto on graven images is wholly outside their life. They are incapable of murder and adultery, and of coveting their neighbour's wife. They never dream of coveting anybody's ox; and as for manservants and maidservants, they have merely had their heads addled by a fraudulent word which should have been "slave," and which has no meaning whatever in a generation in which no priest dreams of preaching against a firm that takes an employee from another by offering him higher wages. In the whole string of these ten maxims of ancient barbarism, there is only one which comes home to the minds of children—the phrase "Thou shalt not steal." And it will be observed that this is not accompanied by the no less necessary command, "Thou shalt not lie." That, it would seem, was not considered a necessary injunction by the authorities who composed the Bible.

I shall be told, of course, that the modern priest, or the clerically trained teacher, "explains" the maxims of the ancient Hebrews in such a way as to bring them home to the minds of the young. Is this really so? And if it be, why should he need to go about the business in that strangely circuitous manner? The wrong doing of children, such as it is, never consists of worshipping "false Gods," or in bowing down to graven images, or in murder or adultery, or in coveting wives, or slaves, or oxen. It consists in little acts of selfishness, unkindness to one another, thoughtless cruelty to helpless things, petty pilfering, confused lying, animal uncleanliness. An the main way to train the child out of most of these things is to show him that they are actions which, when done to himself, he feels to be unjust or wrong. To do as he would be done by is for him the beginning of moral wisdom: the spontaneous wish to be good, to be kind and helpful, in so far as it is not innate, is to be developed by the habit of reciprocity. Beyond this, he should be taught, not to love his country better than others—he is only too prone by nature to glory in his own country and to feel animosity towards others—but to feel goodwill towards all mankind, to hate no nation, to rise above the passion for war, to realise that war is but organised barbarism, to care above all things for the well-being, physical and mental, of his fellow-creatures. Will any priest venture to say that priesthoods have ever promoted morality in this sense? Will any reasonable man venture to say that it can be best promoted by the use of the Bible as a manual for the young? Are children ever to be made kind and refined, scrupulous and civilized, lovers of peace and of mankind, by reading the narratives of the massacres and murders, the crimes and the insanities, which fill the pages of the Old Testament, or the medley of contradictory precepts and incoherent reasonings which fill the New? Is a child best to be made cleanly in body and mind by putting in his hands a book where he shall read the obscene tale of Lot and his daughters, and the description of the prophets who ate filth? Is he best to be made considerate and trustworthy by teaching him that he is to do right only because "God" commands it, and will eternally torture him if he does wrong?

We here come to the citadel of the priest's position. This, when fairly driven to a corner, is his standing ground. He will not allow that we can make children or adults rationally moral by showing them that morality consists in doing as we would be done by. Occasionally, it is true, he claims that we owe that very doctrine to his religion—that it was his Deity who first laid down the "Golden Rule." This claim every educated man knows to be utterly false, and as absurd as it is false. Every student of human development knows that the Golden Rule is the A B C of moral reasoning; that it is known to the lowest savages; that it is partly realised by all animals which live in association; that the difficulty is not the recognition of the principle but the application of it in the thousand-and-one minutiæ and complexities of conduct. But supposing the Christian claim were true, supposing the Golden Rule *had* first been been framed by a Jewish teacher nineteen hundred years ago, it would be none the less clear that the priestly method of education is vicious. The very stress laid on the Golden Rule shows that it is felt to be a good rule in itself—a rule by which men may walk aright. Then it should suffice just to teach that rule, and to show its applications. But this the priest will never consent to do. He is not content to see the child so brought up as to be able to walk aright; he insists on keeping the child's mind in religious tutelage, so that the adult can be counted on to go to church and pay pew-rent and other levies. Accordingly we are assured that mere moral training is of no avail (despite the boasting about the Golden Rule) without "sanctions;" nay, that it is sinful even to teach that men *can* be made moral by the use of their own intelligence; that the child must be taught to "lay his sins on his Savior," and to look for the reward of well-doing, not in the satisfaction of having done well, but in a state of future beatitude, in the avoidance of a state of physical torture which is shared through all eternity by all men of all ages who have not believed the priest's account of things.

And these assertions, be it observed, are *disbelieved by many of the clergy themselves, and by multitudes of those who support them in politics.*

It is doubtful whether more than one in three of the clergy now believe in the doctrines of hell and heaven, of salvation by blood, of miracles, of the answering of prayer, or of eternal life. Yet they are all prepared to go on teaching all these things, with all the fables of the Hebrew Bible into the bargain, to the children in the public schools. The fanatical clergy want to teach it all; the unbelieving clergy dare not oppose the fanatics; one great political party is ready to give the Anglican clergy what they ask, in return for their political support; and the other great political party is mostly ready to give the Nonconformist clergy what *they* ask, in return for *their* political support. All round, the real educational interests, moral and intellectual, are treated as secondary or entirely unimportant: everything turns on the conflicting interests of the priests. The children get almost no real moral training; they are not made nearly as good citizens as they might be; their time is wasted over a farrago of ancient legends, often obscene and generally absurd; and their minds are burdened with false ideas, which many of them can only painfully unlearn in later years, but which many more of them never get free of. They have been morally dwarfed and intellectually crippled in order that priests should more easily get their stipends.

To put the issue in the clearest possible way, I will set down this challenge:—Give me, or rather give a good trained teacher, of rationalist opinions, a schoolful of children within a certain age, taken indiscriminately from one district; and give a priest, or a priest-trained teacher, an equal schoolful of children taken in the same way. Let them have the same strength of staff and the same facilities, but let the first be free to train the children morally on the rational lines I have above indicated, without any religious matter whatever, while the second trains his on sacerdotal lines, with Bible and Catechism for moral manuals, and the Ten Commandments for moral code. For the rest, let the prescribed subjects of non-religious education be the same for the two schools. Then I should confidently undertake that after four or five years the general level of moral character and of general intelligence would be, to the judgment of any impartial educationist, considerably higher in the first school than in the second.

This is, of course, only an allegation; but I have said quite enough to show how reasonable it is. We may reasonably promise good results from reasonable methods; and we know sadly well that we have bad results from the present bad methods. The bad methods are doubtless often modified by judicious teachers, but nothing can hinder that moral education on the lines prescribed by the priesthoods should be miserably incomplete and partly perverse and pernicious.

I believe that the majority of the English people are now capable of realising the bearing of these facts, and of acting on the knowledge. Every man or woman who reads this paper has met with religiously-trained people who are unscrupulous or untrustworthy in matters of conduct. Then every reader knows that the claim of the priests in matters of education is false. Every practical person, again, can realise that priesthoods are at bottom only clerical trade-unions, fighting for their pecuniary interests and their social status. And every reasoning Englishman, finally, can understand that when the Church of Rome supports the policy of the Church of England it is because the Church of Rome counts on securing the whole gain in the end. And she well may; for the most zealous section of the Church of England is every year leaning more and more strongly towards Rome and ritual.

Against the final triumph of Rome in this matter there is only one sure line of resistance, and that is by way of absolutely excluding religious teaching from the public schools.

For the final tendency of all priesthoods is to strengthen and organise priestly power; and the policy of English Nonconformists is only an attempt to maintain a system of free competition in priestcraft, yet with certain State assistance for all sects alike.

That system is bound to collapse, and it deserves to do so. It is even worse in practice than in principle.

31

RELIGION AND SEX
(1919)

Chapman Cohen

Chapman Cohen (1868–1954) was a leading British freethinker of his time. He lectured widely throughout England for the National Secular Society, whose president he later became. He edited the Freethinker *from 1915 to 1951. He wrote numerous works criticizing religion, specifically Christianity; among them are* Christianity and Slavery *(1918),* Woman and Christianity: The Subjection and Exploitation of a Sex *(1919),* Theism or Atheism: The Great Alternative *(1921), the five-volume* Essays in Freethinking *(1923–39), and* God and the Universe *(1931). He wrote of his life in* Almost an Autobiography: The Confessions of a Freethinker *(1940). In the following extract from* Religion and Sex *(1919), Cohen studies religion from a psychological and anthropological perspective, attributing the continued belief in religion to the prevalence of primitive modes of thought and behavior, specifically in regard to sexual repression.*

THE STUDY OF RELIGION FALLS naturally and easily into two parts. The first is a question of origin. Under what conditions did the hypothesis that supernatural beings control the life of man come into existence? We know that in civilised times religious beliefs are in the nature of an inheritance. A member of any civilised society finds them here when he is born, he grows up with them, generally accepting them without question, or effecting certain modifications in the form in

---

From Chapman Cohen, *Religion and Sex: Studies in the Pathology of Religious Development* (London: T. N. Foulis, 1919), pp. 269–78.

which he continues to hold them. If we treat religion as a hypothesis, advanced as other hypotheses are advanced, to account for a certain class of facts, then we can safely say that religion is one of the earliest in the history of human thought. And its antiquity and universality preclude us from seeking an explanation of its origin in the mental life of civilised humanity. Whether the religious hypothesis can or cannot be justified by an appeal to civilised intelligence, it is plain it did not begin there. Its beginnings are earlier than any existing civilisation; and in its most general form may be said to be as old as mankind itself. Consequently, if any satisfactory explanation of the origin of the religious idea is to be found, it must be sought amid the very earliest conditions of human society.

Now whatever the differences of opinion concerning matters of detail, there is substantial agreement amongst European anthropologists upon one important point. They all agree that the conception of supernatural, or "spiritual," beings owes its beginning to the ignorance of primitive man concerning both his own nature and the nature of the world around him. The beginnings of human experience suggest questions that can only be satisfactorily answered by the accumulated experience of many generations. These questions do not materially differ from those that face men to-day. The why and wherefore of things are always with us; life propounds the same problem to all; it is the replies alone that vary, and the nature of these replies is determined by the knowledge at our disposal. The difference is not in nature but in man. The answers given by primitive man to these eternal questions are a complete inversion of those of his better informed descendants. The conception of natural force, of mechanical necessity, is as yet unborn, and the primitive thinker everywhere assumes the operation of personal beings as responsible for all that occurs. This is not so much the product of careful and elaborate philosophising, it is closer akin to the *naive* thinking of a child concerning a thunderstorm. Primitive thought accepts the universal operation of living and intelligent forces as an unquestionable fact. Modern thought tends more and more surely in the direction of regarding the universe as a complex of self-adjusting, non-conscious forces. Primitive thought assumes a supernatural agency as the cause of disease, and seeks, logically, to placate it by prayer or coerce it by magic. Modern thought turns to test-tube and microscope, searches for the malignant germ, and manufactures an antitoxin. The history of human thought is, as Huxley said, a record of the substitution of mechanical for vitalistic processes. The beginning of religion is found in connection with the latter. A genuine science commences with the emergence of the former.

With this aspect of the matter I have not, however, been specially concerned. It has been left on one side in order to concentrate attention upon another and a more neglected aspect of the subject—that of the conditions that have served to perpetuate the religious idea. Grant, what cannot be well denied in the face of modern investigation, that ideas of the supernatural began in primitive delusion. How comes it that this idea has not by now disappeared from civilised society? What are the causes that have given it such a lengthy lease of life? Experience has shown that all really verifiable knowledge counts as an asset of naturalism, and is so far opposed to supernaturalism. Moreover, the history of science has been such that one feels justified in the assumption that, given time and industry, there are no phenomena that are not susceptible to a naturalistic explanation. Why, then, has not supernaturalism died out? Even the religious idea cannot persist without evidence of some kind being offered in its behalf. This evidence may be to a better instructed mind inconclusive or irrelevant, but evidence of some sort there must have been all along, and must still be. Granted that the religious idea began with primitive mankind, granted also that it was based on a mistaken interpretation of natural phenomena, these reasons are quite insufficient to explain why thousands of generations later that idea is still with us. "Our fathers have told us" offers to the average mind a strong appeal, but surely the children will require some further proof than this. What kind of evidence is it that throughout the ages religious people have accepted as conclusive? A study of primitive psychology shows clearly enough how the religious idea vitalised the facts. What we next have to discern is the class of facts that have kept the religious idea alive.

The foregoing pages constitute an attempt to answer this question. The need for some such investigation was clearly shown by the publication of the late Professor William James's *Varieties of Religious Experience* and its reception by the religious press of the country as an epoch-marking work. As a mere collection of documents, the work is interesting enough. But its critical value is extremely small. How religious visionaries have felt, or what have been their experiences, can only furnish the mere data of an enquiry, and *their explanation of the cause of their experiences is a part of the data.* This, apparently, Professor James overlooked; and it will be noted by critical readers of his book that it proceeds on the assumption that the statements of religious visionaries are to be taken, not only as true concerning their subjective experiences at a given time, but also as approximately true as to the causes of their mental states. This, of course, by no means follows. A scientific enquiry cannot separate mental conditions from the subject's interpretation of their causation. Whether this interpretation is genuine or not must be decided finally by an appeal to what is known of the laws of mental life, under both normal and abnormal conditions. If these are adequate to explain the "Varieties of Religious Experience," there is no need whatever to assume the operation of a supernatural agency. Nor does calling this agency "transcendent" or "supermundane" make any substantial difference. For, in this connection, these are only names that serve to disguise a visitant of a highly undesirable character.

The evidence on behalf of a naturalistic explanation of religious phenomena has been purposely stated in a suggestive rather than in an exhaustive manner. The main lines of evidence are threefold. First, there is the indisputable fact that in the lower stages of culture all mental and bodily diseases are universally attributed to spiritual agency. This explanation holds the field; it is the only one possible at the time, and it is not replaced until a comparatively late stage of human history. But of special importance is the fact that a belief does not die out suddenly. It is only destroyed very slowly, and even after the facts upon which the belief was originally based have been otherwise interpreted, the attitude of mind engendered by the long reign of a belief remains. It has by that time become part of the intellectual environment. Theories of a quasi-philosophic or quasi-scientific character are elaborated, and give to the original belief something of a rational air. Even to-day the extent to which superstitious practices still gather round the subject of disease is known only to the curious in such matters. Not that the original reason is given for the practice. In nearly every case a different one is invented. To take only a single example. We still find saffron tea largely used in cases of measles. All medical men are aware that it possesses not the slightest curative value. Students of folklore are aware that it has its origin in the theory of sympathetic cures. Its redeeming feature is that it is harmless; so we find it still in common use, and the recovery of a child from measles is often enough attributed to the potency of the concoction. So with the relation of disease to the persistence of the belief in the supernatural. The conclusion that disease—whether bodily or mental—is due to the agency of spirits is one that follows from the existence of the religious idea; but in turn the observed facts react and strengthen the religious belief. Every case of disease becomes to the primitive mind an unanswerable proof in favour of the original hypothesis. The disease is there, and the only explanation possible is in terms of the animistic idea. And all the time the religious idea is becoming more deeply embedded in the social consciousness, more firmly established as a social fact.

The next line of evidence is that furnished by what I have called the culture of the supernatural. By some means or other—probably by accident in the first instance—it is discovered that certain herbs and vegetable drugs have a peculiar effect on one's mental state. Those who use them see or hear things other people do not normally hear or see. Abstention from food and other bodily privations produce similar results. What is the inevitable conclusion? The only one possible under the existing conditions is that communication has been set up with an invisible world from which one is shut off under normal conditions. From this to the next step is obvious and easy. If a drug, or a fast, brings one into communication with the supernatural world, one has only to repeat the conditions in order to repeat the experience. And repeated they are in all religions, with, at most, those modifications induced by changed times and circumstances. This is why fasting and other forms of "fleshly mortification" play so large a part in the history of religion. The savage medicine man, the Hindu fakir, the medieval saint, all create their ecstasies by the simple plan of disturbing the normal operations of the nervous system. It is not, of course, implied that this is done with a full consciousness of all that is involved in the practice. The derangement is to them the condition of the supernatural manifestation, not the physiological and psychological cause of the experience.

The third main line of evidence is connected with the phenomena of sexuality. It has been shown that in early stages of culture man everywhere connects the phenomena of the sexual life with the activity of supernatural forces. Following the lines of investigation indicated by Mr. Sidney Hartland,[1] we saw reason to believe that the primitive conception of procreation is not that afterwards prevalent, but that of assuming the birth of a child to be due to the direct action of spiritual beings on the mother. Proofs of this are found in existing beliefs among primitive peoples, in the magical practices so widely current to obtain children, and in numerous other customs connected with childbirth. The phenomenon of puberty in the male and of menstruation in the female gives a terrifying reality to this belief. But still more important is the fact that a great deal of assumed religious feeling is found on analysis to be little more than masked sexuality. The connection between eroticism and piety has been noted over and over again by medical observers in the cases that have been brought professionally under their notice. And it is hardly less marked in a large number of instances that are usually classed as normal. Thus great religious teachers have often emphasised the value of a celibate life as a means of furthering religious devotion, and nearly all have treated it with marked respect. The reason given for this is that marriage involves a greater absorption in material or worldly cares, while celibacy leaves one free to full devotion to the spiritual. But the bottom reason for it is that sexual and domestic feelings, lacking their proper outlet in marriage and family life, run with greater force in the outlet provided by religion. So it happens that we find unmarried men and women, devoted to the religious life, expressing themselves towards Jesus or the Virgin in language which, separated from its religious associations, leaves no doubt as to its origin in unsatisfied sexual feeling. In these cases we are dealing with a perversion of one of the deepest of human instincts. And it is one of the commonest of observations in psychology that when a feeling is denied outlet through its proper channel it finds vent in some other direction, and is to that extent masked or disguised.

Allied to the fact of perversion is that of misinterpretation. In the chapter on *Conversion* we have seen how largely this occurs at the period of adolescence. The significant features of adolescence are a development of the sexual nature and an awakening of a consciousness of race kinship. Connected with these, and flowing from them, is a more or less rapid development of what are called the altruistic feelings, the individual becoming less self-centred and more concerned for the well-being of others. From an evolutionary point it is easy to read the fundamental meaning of these transformations, although in the course of social development they have become overlaid with a number of secondary characteristics. Still, in a completely rationalized social life, with adequate knowledge concerning the nature of adolescence, every care would be taken to direct these developing energies into purely social channels. Adolescence is the great formative period; it is then that imitation and suggestion play their most important parts, and it is then that the foundations may be laid of a really good and useful citizenship. If we fail then, we fail completely.

In a society where supernaturalism still exerts considerable power another, and a more disastrous, policy is pursued. Every endeavour is made by religious organisations to exploit adolescence in their own interest. Thousands of priests, often, no doubt, with the best of motives, are engaged in impressing upon the youthful mind an entirely erroneous notion of the character and the direction of the feelings experienced. The sense of restlessness, consequent upon a period of great physiological disturbance, is utilised to create an unhealthy "conviction of sin," or the need of "getting right with God." Social duties and obligations are made incidental rather than fundamental. Activities that should be consciously directed to a social end are diverted into religious channels, and one consequence of this, as we have seen, is a large crop of nervous disorders that might be avoided were a healthier outlet provided. In this the modern priest is acting precisely as his savage forerunner acted. As the savage medicine man associates sexual phenomena with the activity of the tribal ghosts, so the modern priest often associates the psychological conditions that accompany adolescence with a supernatural influence. The distinction between the two is a purely verbal one. In neither case is there a recognition of the nature of the processes actually at work; in both cases the phenomena are used to emphasise the reality and activity of the supernatural. In both cases the social feelings are disguised by the religious interpretation given, with the result that instead of adolescence being, as it should be, the period of a conscious entry into the larger social life, it only too often marks the beginning of a lifelong servitude to retrogressive forces.

NOTE

1. [Edwin Sidney Hartland (1848–1927), British anthropologist and folklorist. Cohen refers to the two-volume treatise, *Primitive Paternity: The Myth of Supernatural Birth in Relation to the History of the Family* (1909–10).]

FURTHER READING

A. BIBLIOGRAPHIES AND ENCYCLOPEDIAS

Stein, Gordon, ed. *The Encyclopedia of Unbelief*. 2 vols. Amherst, N.Y.: Prometheus Books, 1985.

Stein, Gordon. *God Pro and Con: A Bibliography of Atheism*. New York: Garland, 1990.

B. ANTHOLOGIES

Atheism in Britain. 5 vols. Bristol, UK: Thoemmes, 1996.

Darrow, Clarence, and Wallace Rice, ed. *Infidels and Heretics: An Agnostic's Anthology*. Boston: Stratford Co., 1929.

Gaylor, Annie, ed. *Women Without Superstition: "No Gods—No Masters": The Collected Writings of Women Freethinkers of the Nineteenth and Twentieth Centuries*. Madison, Wis.: Freedom from Religion Foundation, 1997.

Haught, James A. *2000 Years of Disbelief: Famous People with the Courage to Doubt*. Amherst, N.Y.: Prometheus Books, 1996.

Stein, Gordon, ed. *An Anthology of Atheism and Rationalism*. Amherst, N.Y.: Prometheus Books, 1980.

———. *A Second Anthology of Atheism and Rationalism*. Amherst, N.Y.: Prometheus Books, 1987.

Whitehead, Fred, and Verle Myhrer, ed. *Freethought on the American Frontier*. Amherst, N.Y.: Prometheus Books, 1992.

C. GENERAL WORKS

Angeles, Peter A., ed. *Critiques of God: Making the Case Against Belief in God.* Amherst, N.Y.: Prometheus Books, 1997.

Brichto, Sidney, and Richard Harries, ed. *Two Cheers for Secularism.* Northamptonshire, UK: Pilkington Press, 1998.

Clements, Tad S. *Science versus Religion.* Amherst, N.Y.: Prometheus Books, 1990.

Ericson, Edward L. *The Humanist Way: An Introduction to Ethical Humanist Religion.* New York: Continuum, 1988.

Gillooly, Robert J. *All About Adam and Eve: How We Came to Believe in Gods, Demons, Miracles, and Magical Rites.* Amherst, N.Y.: Prometheus Books, 1998.

Hadden, Jeffrey K., and Anson Shupe, ed. *Secularization and Fundamentalism Reconsidered.* New York: Paragon House, 1989.

Hitchcock, James. *What Is Secular Humanism?* Ann Arbor, Mich.: Servant Books, 1982.

Katz, Bernard. *The Ways of an Atheist.* Amherst, N.Y.: Prometheus Books, 1999.

Kennedy, Ludovic. *All in the Mind: A Farewell to God.* London: Hodder & Stoughton, 1999.

Kurtz, Paul M. *In Defense of Secular Humanism.* Amherst, N.Y.: Prometheus Books, 1983.

———. *The Transcendental Temptation: A Critique of Religion and the Paranormal.* Amherst, N.Y.: Prometheus Books, 1986.

Lacroix, Jean. *The Meaning of Modern Atheism.* Trans. Garret Barden. New York: Macmillan, 1966.

Le Poidevin, Robin. *Arguing for Atheism: An Introduction to the Philosophy of Religion.* London: Routledge, 1996.

Luijpen, William A. *Phenomenology and Atheism.* Trans. Walter van de Putte. Pittsburgh: Duquesne University Press, 1964.

Luijpen, William A., and Henry J. Koren. *Religion and Atheism.* Pittsburgh: University of Pittsburgh Press, 1971.

Martin, Michael. *Atheism: A Philosophical Justification.* Philadelphia: Temple University Press, 1990.

Marty, Martin E. *Varieties of Unbelief.* New York: Holt, Rinehart & Winston, 1964.

More, Paul Elmer. *The Sceptical Approach to Religion.* Princeton: Princeton University Press, 1934.

Nielsen, Kai. *Naturalism Without Foundations.* Amherst, N.Y.: Prometheus Books, 1996.

———. *Philosophy and Atheism: In Defense of Atheism.* Amherst, N.Y.: Prometheus Books, 1985.

O'Hair, Madalyn Murray. *The Atheist World.* Austin, Tex.: American Atheist Press, 1991.

Penelhum, Terence. *God and Skepticism: A Study in Skepticism and Fideism.* Dordrecht, Germany: D. Reidel, 1983.

Phillips, D. Z., ed. *Can Religion Be Explained Away?* Basingstoke, UK: Macmillan Press, 1996.

Robinson, Richard. *An Atheist's Values.* Oxford: Clarendon Press, 1964.

Russell, Bertrand. *Russell on God and Religion.* Ed. Al Seckel. Amherst, N.Y.: Prometheus Books, 1986.

Smart, J. J. C., and J. J. Haldane. *Atheism and Theism.* Oxford: Basil Blackwell, 1996.

Smith, George H. *Atheism: The Case Against God.* Amherst, N.Y.: Prometheus Books, 1979.

Szczesny, Gerhard. *The Future of Unbelief.* Trans. Edward B. Garside. New York: George Braziller, 1961.

Vahanian, Gabriel. *The Death of God: The Culture of Our Post-Christian Era.* New York: George Braziller, 1961.

D. HISTORICAL STUDIES

Allen, Don Cameron. *Doubt's Boundless Sea: Skepticism and Faith in the Renaissance.* Baltimore: Johns Hopkins University Press, 1964.

Berman, David. *A History of Atheism in Britain: From Hobbes to Russell.* London: Croom Helm, 1988.

Buckley, George T. *Atheism in the English Renaissance.* Chicago: University of Chicago Press, 1932.

Buckley, Michael J. *At the Origins of Modern Atheism.* New Haven: Yale University Press, 1987.

Budd, Susan. *Varieties of Unbelief: Atheists and Agnostics in English Society, 1850-1900.* London: Heinemann, 1977.

Bury, J. B. *A History of Freedom of Thought.* New York: Henry Holt, 1913.

Champion, J. A. I. *The Pillars of Priestcraft Shaken: The Church of England and Its Enemies, 1660-1730.* Cambridge: Cambridge University Press, 1992.

Davis, R. W., and R. J. Helmstadter, ed. *Religion and Irreligion in Victorian Society: Essays in Honor of R. K. Webb.* London: Routledge, 1992.

Drachmann, Andreas Bjorn. *Atheism in Pagan Antiquity.* London: Gyldendal, 1922.

Gauna, Max. *Upwellings: First Expressions of Unbelief in the Printed Literature of the French Renaissance.* Rutherford, N.J.: Fairleigh Dickinson University Press, 1992.

Gay, Peter. *A Godless Jew: Freud, Atheism, and the Making of Psychoanalysis.* New Haven: Yale University Press, 1987.

Hunter, Michael, and David Wootton, ed. *Atheism from the Reformation to the Enlightenment.* Oxford: Clarendon Press, 1992.

Kors, Alan Charles. *Atheism in France, 1650–1729.* Princeton: Princeton University Press, 1990.

Mullen, Shirley A. *Organized Freethought: The Religion of Unbelief in Victorian England.* New York: Garland, 1987.

Popkin, Richard H., and Arjo Vanderjagt, ed. *Scepticism and Irreligion in the Seventeenth and Eighteenth Centuries.* Leiden: E. J. Brill, 1993.

Pospielovsky, Dimitry. *A History of Marxist-Leninist Atheism and Soviet Antireligious Policies.* New York: St. Martin's Press, 1987.

Royle, Edward. *Radicals, Secularists, and Republicans: Popular Freethought in Britain, 1866-1915.* Manchester, UK: Manchester University Press, 1980.

Strousma, Sarah. *Freethinkers of Medieval Islam.* Leiden: E. J. Brill, 1999.

Thrower, James. *The Alternative Tradition: Religion and the Rejection of Religion in the Ancient World.* The Hague: Mouton, 1980.

Thrower, James. *A Short History of Western Atheism.* Amherst, N.Y.: Prometheus Books, 2000.

Turner, James. *Without God, Without Creed: The Origins of Unbelief in America.* Baltimore: Johns Hopkins University Press, 1985.